W.W.W.I.:
WHAT'S WRONG WITH ISLAM?

(A new idea on how to win the war)

Damian B. Malek

ATHENA PRESS
LONDON

ISBN 10-digit: 1 84401 865 2
ISBN 13-digit: 978 1 84401 865 9

First Published 2007 by
ATHENA PRESS
Queen's House, 2 Holly Road
Twickenham TW1 4EG
United Kingdom

Printed for Athena Press

W.W.W.I.:
WHAT'S WRONG WITH ISLAM?

(A new idea on how to win the war)

Contents

The History of Islam

The nation known as Saudi Arabia was the birthplace of the collection of stories, superstition, moralities, rituals and the philosophical system known as Islam. Although many nations are named after the people who have the political and military power in the area (such as Mongolia, the Czech Republic, etc.) only Bolivia (named after Simon Bolivar) shares the distinction with Saudi Arabia ('Arabia of the Sauds' in Arabic) of being named after the person who organized an armed group to impose his leadership in a region. This person was Abdul Aziz al Saud, who in 1932 conquered the area of present-day Saudi Arabia. After thirty years of warfare and military campaigns against the other tribal kingdoms, the present state boundaries were established and recognized by Jordan, Iraq, Kuwait and Yemen. The Saud family retains absolute power today over the same area and has grown and prospered, numbering some 4,000 male members (women are not counted) and ruling over a nation of more than 27,000,000 Arabs. In the exercise of their power they have acquired some of the largest and most expensive yachts, mansions, jet airplanes and bank accounts on the planet, the public flaunting of which is apparently their collective greatest source of pleasure, seconded only by the exercise of international political power and influence. Considering that the present King Abduhlah and his generation were the first of his family to travel abroad, learn English or any other foreign language, one could expect that they would act as nouveau riche on the world stage. The previous generation was kept mostly occupied with camel herds, goatherds and hoarding gold.

The present rulers' ignorance of world affairs and modern technology was such that they gave the charge to an ex-younger schoolmate, son of their trusted royal doctor, to act as the middleman in all Saudi dealings with the world at large; Adnan Khashoggi, known in the Western media as an arms merchant after his involvement in the Iran Contra affair with Ronald Reagan. For decades

Adnan Khashoggi, a Syrian who had business interests in the USA, was the sole conduit for arms, computer systems and any technological equipment sold to Saudi Arabia, for which he received commissions in the hundreds of millions of dollars, making himself the self-proclaimed world's richest man. Vis à vis, the US presidential administrations regarded him as the foremost expert in the Arab world to which they had access. Adnan's advice was sought on every Middle East peace plan or Arab initiative studied by every administration from Nixon to Reagan, at which time he fell from grace, when as a result of following his advice, Secretary of Defense Robert McFarlane, Head of the CIA William Casey, National Security Advisor Admiral Poindexter, and others were imprisoned by the US Justice Department. Ronald Reagan himself would have been indicted but Colonel Oliver North was made into the public scapegoat, supposedly having engineered the illegal arming of the Nicaraguan contras and the exchange of weapons for the release of American hostages in Iran from his basement office in the White House.

Adnan Khashoggi became a marked man in the US government as a result of having caused this debacle (as he even caused the *New York Times* newspaper to publish a letter embarrassing Vice-President Bush) and when the opportunity arose in the ensuing Bush administration to get even with Khashoggi as a result of his involvement in the Ferdinand and Imelda Marcos' plundering of the Philippines's national coffers, he was indicted by the US Justice Department. Then Saudi ambassador to the US, Prince Bandar Bin Sultan, was heard to remark in Washington DC circles that Khashoggi was finished, thus forcing the younger generation of the Saud family to step forward into the limelight and become the public face of the kingdom, a job which they have carried on ever since, usually wearing traditional garb and headdress, outfits that Khashoggi shunned in preference of suit and tie.

The older generation, King Fahd – now deceased – and his brothers, now King Abduhlah, Prince Salman, etc., prefer to avoid any contact with a possibly hostile media, playing their role as directors of the Arabs' affairs from the background. When on his annual four-month vacation in 2003, King Fahd brought his new yacht to the

Costa del Sol in Spain (then the largest, most expensive yacht ever conceived by mankind, to join his other two yachts, which in their day held the same status) the king was wheeled onto the yacht for the first time (at eighty-one he seldom stood up any more) to go for a test cruise in the bay and to try out the super-secure satellite communication telephone. He placed the test call to US President George Bush. 'Hello, young Bush. Is my new phone working? Can you hear me alright?'

The fact that the US president is used as a test operator by the Saudi king only highlights the importance in world affairs acquired by the Saud family in the few decades since a new Rolls Royce in which to storm through the desert encompassed the apex of the previous king's wish list. During King Fahd's visit to the USA in Reagan's time, he was asked by the US president to intercede in an Arab-Israeli peace settlement – a difficult proposition considering that maps produced in Saudi Arabia show the landmass of Israel as empty sea, a geographical error that perhaps Reagan hoped to correct. This request was refused by King Fahd, based on his person not having been treated with the respect due to the Official Keeper of the Holy Mosques and Head of Islam, a religion with more than one billion followers.

Although Reagan did receive him upon his arrival, he had not gone to meet the king at the airport as he deplaned. This insult was compounded by the fact that, although Reagan attended to the king for a couple of days, he then had the audacity to go off on a trip to California, leaving the king in DC with minor officials, and did not see him off at the airport as was his duty in the presence of the head of a religion so much larger than Reagan's.

Also, at this time the trade balance was in heavy favor of the kingdom, as, thanks to the oil sales, the Sauds had saved enough US dollars to buy one-third of all the real estate in the US. This dangerous overhang of US dollars was absorbed by the following administration of George Bush Senior, as he required all the countries that had exported their Mercedes, Gameboys and petroleum (Germany, Japan, and Saudi Arabia) into the US – in exchange for green paper with George Washington's image on it (or even worse, a mere entry into a bank ledger) – to give up their claim to this trade deficit by paying for the costs of the first US-led war on Iraq. The Sauds' fortune declined. Perhaps they had been a bit naive in their eagerness to enjoy the fruits of this capitalist system recently introduced to them.

But surely the US supports the Saud family's hold on power in Saudi Arabia? Although as the Keepers of the Holy Mosques, their lifestyle while enjoying their vacations in their Costa del Sol compound in Spain (a palace resembling the White House, two dozen large mansions, two mosques and several apartment buildings) is rumored not to be as holy as befits such a position (the drinking of alcohol, the orgies where young virgins are flown in from the Philippines and elsewhere on their private jets, the €8 million-per-day expenditures on a very flamboyant lifestyle), the world is far better off with the Sauds in charge than with more radical Islamists (such as Osama Bin Laden or other followers of the Wahabi sect of Islam, originated in Saudi Arabia and growing in popularity). And so they are once again accumulating a humongous trade surplus as the price of the barrel of oil has gone through the roof, but the costs of production remain the same. In spite of the reduced price at which the Sauds sell their nation's oil to the US (an official pact by which the US maintains armed forces in the region to fight for Saud interests if need be), the family is once again storing a frighteningly large amount of US dollars. But surely they know better now than to try to spend them in the USA, and so must go about the world, quietly trying to find those who will accept these dollars in trade for material things that they can actually use. And so the great game goes on.

About 1,380 years ago, in year 1 of the Hijra (the Arab calendar is completely different to the Gregorian calendar as it is also based on lunar rather than solar observations. Therefore the year is shorter, 354 days, the reason why many Arabs cannot tell you how old they are according to the Western calendar. For example, an eighty-year-old Arab is actually seventy-seven years old in Christian years), a man named Muhammad Al Mustafa was forced to flee the desert city of Makkah (Mecca) by the local population, which included his relatives. They thought he was an obnoxious madman who had to be gone or dead. They were tired of his constant preaching about the One God, Allah. They followed the pagan creed, which had been popular for thousands of years. Their gods were many, did not care for human well-being, were not all-powerful, and filled their time toying with humans for their amusement or following some natural laws. There was no heaven or hell. Once you were dead that was final or, at least, unknown. The pagans did what they felt like, did not hold human life to be sacrosanct, appealed to their favorite gods for help when needed, even practiced human sacrifice. The most popular sects were devoted to sex (Isis), where the worshippers participated in orgies and exchanged sex partners; or to drinking alcohol, dancing to music, and sex (Dionysus, Bacchus, etc.). Some temples were attended by prostitutes who worked for free, donating their income to the upkeep of the temple and the maintenance of the priests. How times have changed. What prostitute would donate her earnings to a temple these days? Other cults involved mass ingesting of hallucinogenic substances.

Muhammad, on the other hand, had come under the influence of the Jewish books, the Torah and the Talmud, and was aghast at the backwardness of the Arab peoples around him. At this time, Christianity had become the official religion of the remains of the Roman Empire, the Visigoth kingdoms and the Eastern Roman or Byzantine Empire, and the One God was the uniting factor in the armies of these now divided lands. In the year 313, the Roman Emperor Constantine had issued the Edict of Milan (although then the calendar was different) that decriminalized Christianity and protected Christians from persecution. This change in Roman law allowed the Christian community to include the body of writings of famous Christian followers as an official addition to the Old Testament (the books of the Jewish tradition), to be known as the New Testament, and the joint collection as the Holy Bible. This codification had in the ensuing 280 years become the dominant and official state religion in the civilized northern Mediterranean shore, decisively eclipsing paganism, although the Jews retained their own religion, and the southern shore (Africa) remained in the grip of pagan or primitive religions.

Thus Muhammad was faced with an expanding philosophical system of thought that purported to be an advancement in the human condition. The Jews had their One God. The Christians had their One God. But Muhammad's Arab neighbors followed hundreds of gods and demigods. The problem with many gods was that frequently some group came along and said, 'This is our god, and he is better than your god, and now you are going to be our slaves.' When the One God came into an area, everyone had to be slaves to the group that brought Him in, thus avoiding the problem of other groups appearing later with better gods, since by definition the other gods didn't exist. This One God was not like the old gods. He was all-powerful, could do anything. He was all-knowing, you couldn't fool him. But he was also all-good. He wouldn't do you any harm. All the bad things that happened to his followers were the fault of his arch-nemesis, Satan (or Iblis in Muhammad's newly invented religion), a creature created by the One God but who turned on mankind because they weren't worshipping the One God well enough. In the Old Testament, the One God did a lot of harm to people: the destruction of Sodom and Gomorrah, the near-extinction of mankind with Noah's flood, and many other death and maiming incidents too numerous to mention. In fact, the One God was one of the biggest causes of death and misery among his imperfect worshippers. But in the New Testament, the One God was all-good. And although he was omnipotent (could do anything), he now could no longer do any harm to humans. He also came equipped with a paradise, where his good worshippers would go to upon dying, and He had a relatively new invention that had been the main claim to fame of its inventor, known as Jesus Christ: a burning hell. It was like an oven, where the bad worshippers or non-worshippers would be stuffed into upon dying and therein suffer the pain of being cooked and burned. This idea was expanded on by later Christian followers into a gigantic cavern in the bowels of the earth where the sinners would be burned for eternity, similar to the Egyptian Underworld and the Greek Hades, but with the addition of fire. Muhammad expanded upon this idea by inventing the constant regrowth of the sinner's skin to be burned off over and over again, for eternity. He also graphically described the Arab worshippers' paradise. It was not to be the standing around in white robes with halos shining around their heads, singing holy songs as in the Christian paradise. No, the Arabs would have underground streams of cool water to drink from, set in a garden brimming with dates, pomegranates and other desert fruits, but the main attraction was the copulating with many women, any way you wanted to, and they would all never have known any other man so they could not complain that you weren't doing a good job, since they didn't have a point of comparison.

This One God had it all. The old gods, you could mess with them a little bit, but the new One God, you'd better not mess with him at all. If you messed up he would make your skin burn and regrow, to be burned off again. If you did what his friends, who got to speak with him here on earth, told you to do (like Muhammad), you would get all the cool water, fresh fruit and fine ladies you could want. It was an easy choice for a hard life.

But Muhammad's religion did not convince the Makkah elite. He fled to the town of Al Madinah with a small group of followers, where he continued his enterprise of increasing his following. Soon after, Muhammad performed his first miracle. A richly loaded caravan of pack animals was crossing the desert on its way to Makkah, escorted by 1,000 warriors and camel drivers. These were some of the very inhabitants of Makkah who had forced Muhammad to flee for his life. Muhammad set up an ambush and fell upon the caravan with his 300 poorly armed followers. What they lacked in armor and weapons his followers more than made up for in their suicidal zeal. They overcame the 1,000 caravaners, the survivors fleeing for their lives, and appropriated the animals and goods, thus becoming instantly wealthy. Outnumbered three to one Muhammad and his Muslims had won the ambush. This was his first miracle. He became famous and respected and his following in Madinah increased to the point where he became in charge of the town.

The suicidal zeal and fighting fervor displayed by his outnumbered followers was due in part to Muhammad having successfully convinced them of the existence of his paradise. Although he had no proof of any kind of the existence of any of these things that he claimed existed in a world invisible to his followers, once they were convinced, equally no one could provide any proof to them that these things did not exist. To prevent this, however, Muhammad indoctrinated his followers into killing anyone who spoke to them against the invisible things he had told them were true. Since his invisible world was so vaporous that his believers could not stand up to even a few seconds of a rational conversation debunking this unprovable world, by convincing his believers to kill those who tried to persuade them of the folly of their beliefs, he was able to hold onto his following. This, of course was the same rationale used by the Roman Catholic Church, where a prominent bishop actually calculated that 534 angels could dance on the point of a pin, even though no one could see the angels.

These hardcore fanatics have always been the backbone of Islam; similar are the Iraqi execution squads that were placed behind their own lines to shoot any of their own soldiers who attempted to desert the battle. The fanatics held the less convinced believers in line. Knowing that there are determined killers ready to strike you if you dare express any doubts about following the party line has always been a tremendous incentive to suppress dissent or even critical thought, as the communist and fascist parties found out. This was also the basis of the *fatwa* or death sentence pronounced by an Islamic religious leader. A person who speaks out against Muhammad's religion can find a fatwa issued against him by any *imam* (a self-appointed priest approved by the local community).

Muhammad's followers' kamikaze attitude also derived from the harshness of the world in which they lived, and still live in to this day. In a world with abundant rivers and springs, lush plants, many animals, flowers, fruits, etc., life can be worth living. However, in a desert environment, where existence is a constant struggle to find drinking water or some scrub for the goatherds, where sun exposure can kill you in a few hours, human existence is not worth much. That is why the Arabs are easily willing to throw away their lives. Muhammad only had to promise them cool underground water. That is also why, whereas most of the world, especially the white race, worship the sun (with beach vacations, sun-tanning parlors, etc. Most near-death experience survivors report approaching a blinding white light; darkness personifies evil in Christian culture and light is the source of good. Not so for the Arabs), the Arabs worship the moon. They follow the lunar calendar, their symbol is the crescent moon, the fasting during the holy month of Ramadan ends when the moon is sighted in the Middle East. The sun here is the source of death, not of life, as in the more temperate climates.

Muhammad also found that other people were ridiculing his followers as they performed their ritual worship. So he ordered that only confirmed believers were to be allowed into the *mosques* (places of worship). If you are a white person and try to enter a mosque, you will find that you will soon be questioned about whether you have converted to Islam. You may not go to Saudi Arabia – unless you are conceded a business visa – unless you display your certificate of conversion to Islam, issued by your local imam. With the following simple but highly effective precepts, Muhammad was able to create a religion which is today the world's fastest growing and has the most numerous followers.

1) Convince the follower that if he dies fighting for Islam he will go straight to paradise where he will have water, fruit, and sex with many women.

2) Convince the follower that he must immediately kill anyone who tries to talk to him about the possibility that anything that Muhammad stated is false or mistaken, before he blasphemes.

3) Use these hardcore believers to keep the less convinced in the right path under the threat of being killed.

4) Muhammad also practiced instant conversions. Whenever his followers seized a non-believer, he would be held by the hair with a knife or sword at his throat. He would be asked to recite, 'There is no God but Allah and Muhammad is his prophet.' If he submitted, he would be spared (often made a slave). If he refused he would be slain. Thus Muhammad rapidly acquired more converts.

5) By prohibiting the presence of non-believers in the places of worship (or the entire nation of Saudi Arabia), Muhammad assured that his followers would not be contaminated by any ideas that could so easily replace his indoctrination.

In a desert world where life is harsh and unpleasant and not worth much, surplus people, goats or other animals cannot survive long. When a Bedouin brought his goatherd to a water well and the situation was bad, in that there was little water and the nearest source of water was far enough away to ensure death to any thirsty creature trying to reach it, a life-and-death problem presented itself if another group with their animal herd also appeared at the same well. If there was not enough water for both groups then it was certain that some must die. The Arabs had the choice of killing the animals equally among both flocks that were surplus to the amount of water available, or one of the groups could kill the other herders and take over their flock. This behavior pattern has been part of Arab life for thousands of years and is part of their character, and is reflected in their religion, Islam. A Christian attitude is only suitable to settled farmers. If you are farming a plot of land you will see your neighbor farmers almost every day as they are farming their nearby plots of land. You must therefore deal with them in a Christian way in order to maintain the peace that allows your community to prosper. However, a Christian would not survive but a few weeks in a desert environment. The appropriate religion for herders in those areas was Islam.

Muhammad was aware of the power shown by the One God religion and he frequently stated that his fellow Arabs need not choose between converting to Christianity or Judaism, that Muhammad had found the true religion for the Arabs. Islam found a fertile ground not only because of Muhammad's excellent marketing tricks, but also because it was appropriate for the climatic conditions and the general psychological makeup of the people there. Islam appealed (and still does) to the racial pride of the Arab race. The whole point of Islam is that it admits the existence of the Jewish prophets and Jesus Christ, but that Muhammad came afterwards and he also was a prophet of the One God, and that his teachings were more advanced and closer to the intentions of the One God, as they were revealed 650 years after Christ.

The rules applying to women were not invented by Muhammad. In the area, the custom was that a man could have as many wives as he could get. Muhammad restricted this number to four. In that world men were dangerous. When a man would meet other men, the chances of a deadly fight or a robbery ensuing were high. It was dangerous for men to go outside. Women were a valuable commodity and had no chance outside. A woman alone would immediately be seized and taken. Therefore, Muhammad only codified the existing customs that prohibited women from going outside unless accompanied by their husband, father or brother. Also, women were prohibited from speaking to a man who had not been introduced to them by their family. The power of a woman was that, if allowed to talk to strange men, within a few minutes she could convince that man to do anything that she told him to. She could immediately organize that man into plotting to kill her husband, for example. To take away this power, women had to be segregated. Throughout the rest of the planet, women were similarly treated until the 1900s. Women only gained the right to vote, etc., in the Western world when handguns that were easy to load and shoot became generally available. In a world of swords and brute strength, women were generally second-class citizens.

This dangerous environment is still very much actual in Arab countries. In nearly all Arab countries, religious police roam the cities searching for couples whom they stop to ascertain if they are indeed woman and husband, father or brother. If they are not, they can be taken to jail and fined. In Yemen, for example, the men attend the city's markets wearing not only their traditional curved dagger, but also assault rifles and hand grenades, in case there is a dispute over the price of merchandise or a fight breaks out. One of Islam's laws is well known to Westerners: an eye for an eye, a tooth for a tooth, etc. Lesser known is that if a man kills your wife, his punishment shall be that you may then kill his wife. See how he likes that! (Holy Qur'an, Sura 2:178)

After Muhammad's first miracle he became even more famous in Makkah. The people decided they'd had enough of him and formed a great army numbering some 3,000 warriors (including one of Muhammad's uncles) and marched on Al Madinah, bringing along many of their women, who also wanted a piece of Muhammad. (They were probably angry at Muhammad for having stolen all the household goods and jewelry they had been waiting for in the caravan.) Muhammad rounded up the warriors of Al Madinah and had them take defensive positions near the town. His soldiers totaled about 1,000 men, plus about 300 Arab Hypocrites.

The Hypocrites in those days (and for the 1,000 years prior) were followers of the Greek philosopher Hippocrates, the father of modern medicine. Physicians today are still required to swear the

Hippocratic oath before beginning their careers, although the oath itself was written hundreds of years after Hippocrates's death by unknown authors. Hypocrites lived in communities throughout the Mediterranean, had regular meetings to practice their hypocrisy, and were a tight-knit group, working together and defending each other. Hippocrates taught that a human could learn from experimentation and observation, that faith was tantamount to superstitious ignorance. He practiced the dissection of human cadavers to learn and teach anatomy to his pupils, a practice which caused him much trouble with the Athenian authorities.

To be a Hypocrite in those days was not shameful; rather, they were respected by the populations among whom they practiced their hypocrisy. Only much later did calling someone a hypocrite become an insult (probably because of the gospels in which Christ insults the Hypocrites). Although the qualities that constituted being a Hypocrite did not change, the world came to view them in a negative way as the world changed. In a world where aforementioned groups frequently appeared with better gods to convince the locals to obey the new god (and those who brought him), the locals had a choice: to fight and maybe die, or accept the slavery imposed upon them by the invading god. The Hypocrites chose a third path. They, together as a group, would pretend that the new god was great. The Hypocrites agreed with the warriors who brought the new god and did their best to fool the invaders into believing they had been converted to the new faith in this new invisible world, that the Hypocrites were now brothers and fellow worshippers along with the invaders of the new god or gods, as long as they were allowed to keep their weapons.

This attitude was respected by the populations that were not practicing hypocrisy. As the world changed and the One God took over in a definitive way, the Hypocrite came to be seen as: 1) someone who thinks he is better than you but keeps it hidden; 2) someone who agrees with you or compliments you, whereas in reality thinks you are a fool; or, 3) someone who lies to you in order to manipulate you. And that's exactly what they were then and exactly what they are now. The difference is the world respected them then, but since the domination of the One God, being a Hypocrite is now seen as having a lack of faith in something that the Hypocrite should believe in.

There is a bit of a Hypocrite in all of us. Try the following: accuse anyone of being a hypocrite. They will almost always instinctively deny it vehemently. That is part of the makeup of a hypocrite. If a hypocrite is going to be effective at convincing his would-be oppressors that he is on their side, then he must deny being a hypocrite if accused.

All this was known to Muhammad and his followers. So when the Makkah army and their women appeared at Al Madinah, the Hypocrite army notified Muhammad that they wished him and his luck with the battle, but that they had decided to take a defensive position inside the town walls. Muhammad was now outnumbered, 3,000 warriors to 1,000 of his followers. The battle began and Muhammad's troops initially held their position, but the day was bloody, with the Makkah army almost overrunning them, and Muhammad himself was badly wounded. As night fell and the warriors took rest, the Makkah women took to the battlefield and performed atrocities with their daggers on the dead and wounded of Muhammad's followers. As the sun rose there were many dead on both sides. As the Makkah army saw that Muhammad and his remaining followers still stood on high ground with impenetrable hills at their back, they decided the cost of taking Al Madinah that day would be too high, abandoned the battlefield and went back to Makkah. This was Muhammad's second miracle. He now became truly famous. Again outnumbered three to one, Muhammad had led his followers to victory. He made some warning to his followers not to trust the Hypocrites in the future and that if they ever pulled that stunt again, to fall upon them and slay them. But they didn't take action against the Hypocrites. After all, they still numbered 300, were armed, and Muhammad's followers had suffered heavy losses. And everyone knew they were hypocrites.

Muhammad eventually conquered Makkah and showed mercy on his previous adversaries, including his uncle who had fought against him. His followers increased in number and he led a large group of some 25,000 to the frontier with Syria as a show of force against what he feared might be a possible invasion from the Byzantine (Eastern Roman) Empire. But the empire was weak and was far more concerned in defending itself from the constant invasions of Bulgar and

Slav tribes. The entire North African and Middle Eastern region, once a thriving part of the mighty Roman Empire, now lay unattended, unprotected, as the Roman legions were fighting in their homeland and being conquered by successive hordes of barbarian invaders. Muhammad decided to expand his religion by leading his followers into military campaigns throughout the Arabian Peninsula, then Syria. His followers were hard men, prepared to survive in extreme conditions, accustomed to constant fighting, their bodies hardened by herding, many never knowing life inside a house. Muhammad made certain his conquered peoples were made into allies by offering them the choice of swearing that 'there is no God but Allah and Muhammad is His prophet', or having their throats cut. The same saying is used today in the conversion ritual in all mosques by all imams.

Eventually Muhammad commanded an army of 50,000 Arabs, but even so he relished being in the front line, striking at the unconquered peoples with his sword, making the blood flow with his own hand, but while organizing a campaign to invade Syria he fell ill from a fever and headache and soon expired. He was buried in a simple grave, attended only by six men who were his family and friends. Centuries later the tradition developed that Muhammad had ascended into the heavens, like Jesus Christ – and also from Jerusalem – but that Muhammad did it while he was alive and sleeping in his bed at his house in Makkah. Muhammad traveled to Jerusalem, ascended to paradise and returned to his home in Makkah the same night. Bara Bing! Just a small example of Arab pragmatism. After all, Muhammad could not be any less than Jesus Christ, could he? (The famous Dome of the Rock was built in Jerusalem to commemorate this miraculous ascension into heaven.) His generals decided they had a good thing going and continued the invasions of neighboring peoples until they brought the One God to all the Middle East, Persia and North Africa.

In Europe, the Germanic conquering armies also brought the One God to all the lands under their dominion, using similar tactics. The German One God was somewhat different to Muhammad's God. He wanted the subjugated peoples to obey the Germanic people as their masters, represent Jesus Christ as a chestnut-haired Germanic type (even though he was a Semitic Jew), bring evergreen trees into their houses at the start of winter and decorate these trees (perhaps as a symbol of the evergreen surviving the winter) and eat lots of food and be merry (perhaps to fatten up a bit to survive the winter and the cold). Although Christ's birth was probably in what we now call the month of May, God wanted the birthday to be celebrated on the same date as the ancient pagan festival at the beginning of winter. But most of all, He wanted the subjugated peoples to suffer, and suffer quietly. After all, Christ had suffered on the cross for them. Being humble, poor, obedient, meek and long-suffering were the ideal qualities for the followers of the One God.

Even the English word *god* originates from this time, for the Germanic tribes that conquered Europe were the Gods: the Astrogods, the Visigods, and just the plain Gods. The German word today for God and Goth is *Gott*, which could change over time and distance into God or Goth, and *Godo* in the Iberian Peninsula. But there were also the Vandals. They were a Germanic tribe that brought us the verb 'vandalize', as they took joy from destroying, defacing, and vandalizing public works, works of art, and things the subjugated peoples considered useful. There were also more ancient Germanic tribes, called the Barbars (*Barbarians* in English), who gave us that word as well as the associated behavior. Eventually the two cultures, expanding through conquest, Muhammad's Allah and the Gods' God, clashed in the Iberian Peninsula, today Spain and Portugal.

In the languages of the Iberian Peninsula, the ruling class were called *hidalgo*, *fidalgo* (*hijo* or *filho del Godo*, meaning 'son of the God'), as they were the descendants of the invading Gods. They were not well liked. As in the rest of conquered Europe, they had brought what is known historically as the Dark Ages, a time of suffering when all the ancient knowledge was lost. Aqueducts that once provided water to thriving cities crumbled due to the lack of engineering skills to repair them, the Roman roads became overgrown, damaged and unusable, and commerce between the now filthy, disease-plagued cities dwindled. Life spans were shorter due to plagues. Untreated infections became fatal due to forgotten Hippocratic knowledge. The earth became flat and the sun began to rotate around the earth, just like the moon and the rest of the astral bodies, by official edict of the followers of Jesus Christ. The ruin and misery brought onto the population of Europe was due to the fact that the Gods were an ignorant, barbaric (Barbar) people. The only thing they were any good at was striking people with their swords and battleaxes, and counting how many angels could dance on the head of a pin.

Muhammad's Allah was different. He allowed the conquered peoples some freedom of thought. There was no formal hierarchy in the church of Muhammad. Any man could become an imam (priest) if the congregation agreed to it. All imams were equal. Some became more important due to having larger congregations but there was no head imam, unlike the bishops, cardinals and pope. The rituals were very simple and easy to remember for a simple people. To go to Muhammad's paradise, one had to die fighting for Muhammad, or if not, then, 1) to pray several times every day (five times has been standardized) facing Makkah; 2) give charity to the poor; 3) fast during the holy month of Ramadan (abstain from taking any liquid or food from sunrise to sunset, unpleasant but easy for the desert Arabs to do) thus reminding one of the unimportance of creature comforts; 4) attend the communal prayer meetings every Friday; and 5) perform the pilgrimage to Makkah at least once in a lifetime, if health and money allow.

Makkah was the center of the cult because there existed an ancient site of pilgrimage, very popular with the desert Arabs, where for countless generations they would travel to in order to perform rituals of adoration, the most prominent being the throwing of small stones at a black building containing a meteorite that had fallen to the earth before some ancient tribe of goatherds, who, astounded at the sight, founded a religion based on the flaming rock and the consequent explosion that had frightened them so. Tradition says that the devil threw this flaming rock at the earth. Since it was the only proof of myriad invisible worlds and gods, it had become the most popular religion, and still is today.

Islamic tradition now also says that the *Ka'ba* (the small black building housing the meteorite) was built by Abraham, the father of the Jewish and Arab races. Ismael, Abraham's first-born son of his Egyptian servant, was cast out from Abraham's house with his mother when Sara, Abraham's legal wife, bore him a son in her very old age, Isaac. Ismael became the patriarch of the Arab race and Isaac of the Jewish race. The Ka'ba was built by Abraham and Ismael to house the meteorite (Holy Bible, Genesis 15, 16, 18, 20, 21:8–19; 25:12–17; Holy Qur'an, Sura 2:125–127). The Bible says (Genesis 16:11–12) that the descendants of Ismael shall be a fierce race, raising their hand against every man and all shall fight against them… probably as a result of being thrown out of his father's house as a child and being forced to almost die of thirst wandering the desert, and being a bastard without inheritance.

Abraham was not always called so, his original name being Abram. He changed his name when he founded a religion (the progenitor of the Jewish, Christian and Islamic traditions), the main features of which were the existence of the Father of the Gods (the one original and most powerful god) and the prohibition of human sacrifice. In those days the most popular religion in his area required human sacrifice to the god Malek. Abraham became famous because he sacrificed a ram rather than his son to his god.

The region he lived in was the crossroads of commerce between India, North Africa and Europe, as the boats arriving from India were unloaded in the Arabian Peninsula or in Iraq, to have their goods continue their journey by caravan, and likewise the North African caravans crossed that land bridge (Sinai, Israel, Lebanon) on their way to and from Europe. This area was where travelers with different cultures, ideas, sciences and religions met and communicated with each other. The Indian culture had long before developed a religion, Hinduism, in which the first god, the creator of the other gods, is called Brama; his priests are today called *Brahmin*. Abraham is the English version of the name Ibrahim (English didn't exist then. Just as 'Gotts' was changed to 'Goths', so 'Ibrahim' is now called 'Abraham', but in the actual languages of the regions no one knows why the English anglicize the names). It is striking, the coincidences in the religions: Ibrahim, the priest of the God creator of the lesser gods; Brahmin, the priests of the Hindu religion with the same concept of the god creator. Could it be that in his wanderings, Ibrahim heard of the Hindu religion from the myriad Indian merchants that surely accompanied their goods on caravans and converted to the idea, eventually assuming the somewhat distorted title of priest? Brama, the father of the gods; Abram, the founder of the Jewish, Christian and Islamic religions based upon the same concept...

The victorious Arab armies had secured dominance of the coastal area of North Africa, having conquered Egypt, Libya, Tunisia and Algeria in their quest to bring the local peoples the opportunity to worship Allah and pay tribute to Allah's messengers, the Arab army. There lived in those times – and still today in western Algeria and Morocco – the descendants of Germanic tribes that had crossed the Straits of Gibraltar and settled in those regions and the Canary Islands many thousands of years before. Called the Tuaregs or the Berbers (the more numerous tribe who still retain their original name *Barbar* in German, *Barbarian* in English, *Barbaro* in Spanish, *BerBer* after a few thousand years living among the local population), these tribes distinguish themselves from the anterior population by frequently having light-colored hair and blue or green eyes, as befits their close kinship to the Gods who had also conquered Europe.

Conquering was in their blood because they were taller and stronger than most other peoples, and the Germanic tribes have frequently swept through Europe, lastly in 1914 and again in 1939. Hopefully this 7,000-year-old tradition will have seen the last attempt by the Gods and the Barbarians to subjugate the European population. The BerBers were the dominant force in parts of Morocco and Algeria and the Arab army found it tough fighting against them. Inspired by Islamic zeal, the Arabs persevered and after a fifty-year war finally vanquished the local populations, and then dominated the entire North Africa. Their first taste of fighting against the European God tribes did not deter the Arabs from soon beginning incursions into Spain, an easy seven-mile boat crossing away. Soon the Arab army became mostly composed of BerBer warriors, now converted to Islam, and when the combined armies began to take territory in southern Spain they found that the local population aided them by fighting against the Hidalgos (sons of the Gods). For example, when the Muslim army took Sevilla, the most important city in southern Spain, the bishop of Sevilla and his followers fought on the side of Islam that day against the ruling Hidalgos (sons of the Gods) and their army. Eventually the relatives of the Gods, the BerBers, became dominant in the Iberian Peninsula and their warriors outnumbered the Arab fighters in the Islamic armies, but the BerBers remained profoundly Islamicized and still are today. Islam dominated at times more than 80% of the Iberian Peninsula, even attempting invasions of France by penetrating the Pyrenees mountain range deep into France – invasions that came to an end when the Frankish king, Charles Martel (Charles the Hammer) dealt the large Islamic army a lethal blow and sent them fleeing back into Spain.

However, in the east, Europe came under the attack of Islam as well. After the Islamic armies there succeeded in conquering the Persian Empire in AD 637, they fought numerous, almost continuous wars among themselves and with the local peoples, faced the invasions of the European Crusaders, and were eventually conquered by the Mongol hordes who soon converted to Islam. Soon arose the Ottoman Turks out of the mixture of Arabs, whites and Mongols, who became the dominant force in the area encompassing the old Eastern Roman Empire as well as the Eastern Arabic Empire. The European-Arabic-Mongol mixtures of the peoples from Turkey to Iran, to Afghanistan and northward into the new independent ex-Soviet republics have produced many distinct racial types. From the Cossacks to the Turks, to the Afghans, to the Pakistanis (mixed with the Dravidians of Indian genetics), the differences are marked. However, peoples that are not mostly white in all that wide region are currently and have been for many centuries under the dominion of Islam, whereas the mostly white people are under the influence of Christianity.

In AD 1453, Constantinople finally fell to the Islamic invaders under Ottoman Turk emperor Mehmed and Islam once again attacked Europe. The European crusaders had attacked and conquered the holy lands on several previous expeditions but had eventually been forced to flee by the local populations. Never had European armies actually been capable of entering the desert regions of the Arabian Peninsula, where Islam was born, and Makkah, its holy city, was never under any threat. Islam continued to expand into Europe but was eventually stopped by the Slavic armies in Yugoslavia. There the Turkish Arabish peoples settled for many centuries in their conquered lands, remaining Islamic to this day in Albania,

Bosnia, the Yugoslav province of Kosovo, and although the peoples mixed their blood in that region through intermarriage, the descendants of Islamic peoples retain their religion and customs to this day. For example, in the nation of Albania a noticeable portion of adult males are non-productive. These men remain inside their house for up to seven years consecutively, seldom venturing outside even to gather firewood. Local custom is that if a man is killed by another in a fight or a dispute, then all the males in that clan are fair game to be killed by any males from the victim's clan. However, as long as the hunted men remain inside their house, the offended clan members will not invade their homes to kill them. However, if the hunted men venture outside then they are fair game.

Islam has also expanded by sea. When the first European ships sailed around Africa to India, they found that the trade from India to Arabia and Persia was dominated by the Arab dhows. Sinbad the sailor had long ago established trading posts in faraway islands such as Indonesia, today the most populous Islamic nation, and Brunei, where the sultan of Brunei lives in magnificent splendor befitting his status as one of the world's richest persons. Southern Thailand, Malaysia, Singapore and southern Philippines also have large Islamic populations. Arab immigration from their homelands has also introduced sizable Islamic populations into Denmark, Holland, Germany, France, the UK, and Spain, amounting to as much as 3 to 8% of the populations of those countries. The French government, for one, does all it can to avoid problems with its Muslim residents, fearing attacks and suicide bombings.

Integration, even of the younger generation, even those born in Europe who seldom visit their homelands, is not complete. The July 2005 bombings of the metro stations and buses in London were carried out by native English citizens who were motivated by feelings of revenge against their fellow citizens. To commit suicide and kill indiscriminately one must be motivated by, 1) faith that one will be admitted to paradise for eternity; 2) hate towards the government and people who will be victims because of some evil they have committed against Islam, the Arab people or the suicide bomber himself; 3) racial and religious pride, in that one believes that one is showing his race or beliefs in a good light to the public and will be honored by

Muslims (at least the similarly radical) and will be at least admired for one's courage by the enemy; and 4) the sensation that one is striking an effective blow in the war between Islam and the West, launched by Al Qaeda, that will help achieve the goals of the terrorist network.

The September 11 attacks in the USA were a clash of cultures and ideals. The manipulating, wheeling-dealing, market society was attacked by the pure-thinking believers in life after death. The message was to the masses concerned only with acquiring material goods, and raising their status among their fellows; advancing themselves in this life, frequently resorting to dishonest actions. What about death? What about eternity? Have you thought about the truly important experience that you will be subjected to after you die? What is the value of this short, temporary existence when you are taking the path to Hell where your skin will be burned off, only to grow again to be burned anew, and so on forever? Is that not more important than achieving material advantages for fifty years or so?

In a way, the suicide terrorists see themselves as saving the West from its greed and wrongdoing. They have no hope of destroying the West, only of convincing the peoples that Islam is the moral path that they should follow, or at least teaching the West to respect Islam and leave the Muslim populations free from Western influences. The vast majority of Arabs, whether in their homelands or residing in Europe, were overjoyed by the 9/11 attacks. Not necessarily because they hope to convert the US population to Islam, but because of wanting to bloody the nose of the world colossus that supported Israel in that nation's oppression of their fellow Muslims, the Palestinians. And also, because of racial pride: in feeling uplifted in the pride of a race that dares to launch such an audacious attack at the heart of a mighty superpower. The fall of the World Trade Center towers was like a vent for the dislike that nearly all Arabs feel towards the USA. Why do they feel this dislike? Because of: 1) the US support to Israel; 2) the impression the US gives of being a manipulator that orders the international politics in their zone; 3) the Arab empire was once the most powerful in the Western world and they still hope to be raised from their current status.

So the September 11 attack represented the slap with a glove prior to a duel, in which the Muslims hope to be triumphant, or at least gain a measure of respect. Even though few Muslims may actively support terrorist attacks, the West should not take lightly those who follow the rituals of Islam, either in daily prayer, attendance of the Friday prayer meeting, or in wearing traditional dress. Witness the several daily suicide attacks taking place in Iraq during 2004, 2005, and 2006. Only tight Israeli security prevents a greater number of suicide attacks there. A percentage of the habitual readers of the Holy Qur'an are convinced that suicide attack is in their and Islam's best interests. The Western politicians are frequently seen in the mass media broadcasting the tranquillizing message that Muslims are like Christians who wear funny clothes. They state that to read a holy book and believe in the One God is good for everyone and that Muslims therefore must be good. But Allah is quite different to the Gods' God. Whereas God wants his followers to suffer quietly and be obedient and meek, Allah wants his followers to attack those meek obedient peoples and make them their subordinates, a quite effective attitude that is likely to give satisfactory results, all things being equal. Islam is today the fastest growing religion on earth. Its most wealthy officials control astonishingly large amounts of currency, with which they can, and often do, influence world events. They also control most of the planet's supply of petroleum, a vital commodity in today's world. Behind the scenes these leaders' machinations have far more influence on world events than the Vatican or all of the fragmented Protestant leaderships. They outrank the Vatican by far in, 1) number of followers; 2) dedication of followers; 3) currency available; and 4) political influence. And what Christian these days would be willing to die for his religion, much less perform a suicide bombing?

Western leaders seek to give the public the message that Muslims are good people in the Christian sense. That the basic messages of the Qur'an are the same as Christ's message. That the two religions are basically about people living together in peace. But have any of these Western leaders actually read the Qur'an? Converted to Islam? Attended prayer meetings every Friday? The frightening thing is that if you have read this far into the book, you now probably know more about Islam than any president or prime minister in the Western world.

The Torah

The Torah is the basis of the Jewish religion, as well as Christianity and Islam. The Orthodox Jews (the ones wearing the black hat and clothes and beard with long hair), especially, take its writings literally and seek to carry out its commandments. Although hard to acquire outside of Jewish circles, you may find that you already own one. It is word for word (with a few exceptions) contained in every Holy Bible because it is also known as the five books of Moses: Genesis, Exodus, Leviticus, Numbers, Deuteronomy. However the Roman Catholic version has been quite distorted, eliminating (among other things) the continuous prolonged harangue on the part of the holy authors exhorting the Jews to exterminate the innocent dwellers who before them occupied the Jews' promised land and eliminate them by killing every man, woman and child. Then wait for a few days until the survivors come out of their hiding places, and then finish off the job of killing every man, woman and child. Do not be tempted to keep the women as they may some day lead the Jews into worshipping their false gods. Kill all the women as well. Kill all the children as they some day may try to avenge their dead parents. God admonished the Jews that if they did not kill every man, woman and child who lived in the area, God would do to the Jews what He was going to do to the peoples of those lands. Only the animal stock are to be allowed to survive.

And why must the Jews kill every man, woman and child occupying the promised land? Why, in order to take over their houses, domestic animals, fields, and their gold and silver and other goods. The Jews shall live in houses full of good things that they did not fill, possess hewn cisterns that they did not hew, vineyards and olive groves that they did not plant. The King James version of the Bible is quite accurate when compared to the Torah. Read it for yourself.

The Jews tried to exterminate the peoples whose property they wished to steal but after a few years of fighting and exterminating

(Book of Joshua) they grew tired and became settled (Book of Judges), first committing the mistake of letting some women live, and mating with them, eventually degenerating into living alongside the peoples the Jews had attacked but had been unable to overcome. That's when bad things started to happen to them, as other kingdoms came and attacked the Jews, at times conquering them, even taking them into captivity. As the Jews were unable to carry out God's grand plan for them, of killing with their swords every man, woman and child in their way, eventually God's threat to the Jews – that He would do to them what He had ordered them to do to the unaware peoples who happened to be living in their promised land – came to pass, as the Jews themselves suffered genocide. First at the hands of the Roman army, who forced the survivors to flee from Israel all the way to southern Russia and anywhere they could get to by ship, and more recently at the hands of Hitler's Gods (Germanic tribes) in their hiding places in Europe. Thus the threat of God has come to pass. Of course, the Jews didn't call God 'God'. They called Him Jehovah, Yahweh.

In Genesis, the book of creation, we immediately read the reasons for the success of the Jewish, Christian and Islamic religions. Although the author thought that Yahweh separated the waters of the sea from the waters of the heavens with a membrane (this is how the original book, the Torah, reads – probably the line of the horizon over the sea as both the ocean and the sky are blue), with taps that Yahweh opened to let the rain fall, the main reasons why the peoples of the world have come to adopt this book as the basis for their lives, and why still today it forms some of the life structures most followed by humanity, are immediately apparent. We shall come to them later, to give the reader a chance to think about what is the main impact of the first few paragraphs of Genesis on the reader's life.

In the Torah the separation of the waters is a membrane. In many translated Bibles this has been intentionally falsified as a firmament or an expanse that separated the waters, one of the many blatant attempts by later church authorities to make the original writings more palatable to an audience perhaps a bit more advanced in knowledge than the herder priests who wrote the Old Testament. Another main difference between the Torah and all the versions of the Bible is that the Bible says that Moses parted the Red Sea and the water then crashed onto the Egyptian army when they tried to cross. The Torah says that Moses found a way through not the Red Sea but the Sea of Reeds, and that Pharaoh's chariots were not able to follow the Israelis. The Sea of Reeds seems to refer to a huge swamp (probably in the Nile delta region) which the Israelis, fleeing on foot, were able to find a way through, whereas the going was too difficult for the Egyptian army, composed of war chariots and cavalry. Not much of a miracle there.

To understand why the religion of Moses has had such an impact on humanity and had become the basis for three of the most followed religions on the planet earth (Judaism, Christianity, Islam), one must read the Torah, the Bible and the Qur'an. Millions and millions of people make a vow or at least state their intention to live their lives by the rules of one of these books, yet they never bother to read the book. They are too busy watching television or reading mystery novels. From a careful reading of the Torah, or an accurate translation of the Torah such as the King James version of the Bible, anyone can see that there are many gods mentioned, and not despised or negated, throughout the books of Moses. The god Astarot is mentioned several times, the god Baal (of which there were many, one for each town or city named Baal: Baal Peor, Baal-gad, Baal-tamar, and Baal Zebub who later came to symbolize Satan), and the god Malek, that required human sacrifice (apparently the first-born male child, which was the custom Abraham/Ibrahim broke with by founding a more humane, kind religion). At no time does the Torah state that these other gods are false, only that Yahweh is the god of the Jews and the Jews must worship only Him, for Yahweh is a *jealous* god who will not suffer his chosen people to worship other peoples' gods. The only introduction to the thought that there is only one god comes in the last book, Deuteronomy (4:7), when the author writes, 'What other great nation has a god so close at hand as is the Lord our God whenever we call upon him?' or (4:33–35), 'Has any people heard the voice of a god speaking out of a fire, as you have, and survived? Or has any god ventured to go and take for himself one nation from the midst of another… as the Lord your God did for you in Egypt…? You have been shown to know that the Lord alone is

God; there is none beside him.' Later on, God declares himself as the only God in a poem, (32:4), '...A faithful God, never false, true and upright is he.' 32:17, 'They sacrificed to demons, no-gods, gods they had never known.' 32:37, '...Where are their gods? ... Let them rise up to your help... See, then, that I am He; There is no God beside Me.'

This whole section, along with many of the continuous exhortations to commit genocide upon the innocent tribes whom the Jewish people wish to rob has been distorted by the compilers of the Holy Bible, mostly the Roman Catholic Church. By deliberately eliminating the plural and the article 'a', the compilers sought to make it appear as if the One God was a fact already accepted by the original authors. However some clues to the actual beliefs of the Jews have survived the Holy Bible's mistranslations, such as verse 4:34, 'Has *any* god ventured...' No wonder the Jews are the cleverest race on earth (according to standard English IQ tests). They can read the Torah, compare it to the Bible, and see how easy it is to fool the white race.

There are many other patent absurdities in these ancient tales. The numbers given for the populations of the early tribes are ridiculous. The armies raised sometimes vary between 300 or 600 warriors to 120,000. The Roman legion comprised a body of some 5,000 soldiers and seldom more than fifteen legions (75,000 soldiers) fought in any great battle in times when the human population had increased substantially. Yet the authors claim that 603,550 Israeli men, fit for military service with millions of sheep, camels, goats and donkeys, left Egypt and wandered through the desert, camping for fifty years. Against this immense army the Egyptian pharaoh sent 600 war chariots and his cavalry. As the war chariot was manned by two men, at the most three, the Egyptian army can be estimated at 1,500 charioteers and maybe 5,000 horsemen. So although outnumbering the pursuers 100 to 1, the Israelis flee in terror before Pharaoh's army. But the Israelis are also protected by a giant rotating pillar of fire that separates them from Pharaoh's army. The Egyptians in those days must have been made of sterner stuff than the modern ones that fought the four wars with Israel with disastrous results in the 20th century. The Torah states that an army of maybe 10,000 Egyptians attacked 603,550 Israeli warriors and a population that we may calculate at maybe 2,500,000 people with millions of animals. Undaunted, the bloodthirsty Egyptians are turned back by a gigantic pillar of fire. Even so, apparently accustomed to the sight of enormous rotating pillars of fire, the 10,000 Egyptians pursue the fleeing 2,500,000 people until they are unable to follow them through the huge swampy area known as the Sea of Reeds.

These 2,500,000 people, accompanied by millions of animals, then camp in areas for forty years where there is no food or water available, and have to resort to eating manna. You too can eat manna. In the area a type of plant produces a sticky, slightly sweet substance when pricked by insects that feed on it. Manna has been the name of this substance for thousands of years and has been eaten by the local Arabs when needed or used as sweetener for coffee or tea in the absence of sugar.

Other battles in Israel's efforts to eradicate from the face of the earth the plague of Arabs occupying the houses, water cisterns and fertile fields that the Israelis, tired of wandering in the desert, so coveted are related with equally absurd numbers.

However, the five books of Moses cannot so easily be dismissed as the psychotic rantings of genocidal herder priests. It was common in those days for authors to exaggerate numbers, even distances, by factors of 100, or even 1,000 to 1. The Greek authors did it and other tall tales from that era that have survived show that it was the norm, rather than unusual. There is much to be learned from a careful reading of the Torah about life as it must have been in those times. A reader can see, for example, that the god Malek required the killing of the first-born son on a stone altar or through fire. This is mentioned several times. What purpose could this have served?

Anyone can easily observe that once enough people are convinced to perform some ritual, generation after generation will continue to perform the same ritual without knowing why, much like ants or caterpillars following a circular scent trail until they die. The reader can also see that society was highly patriarchal then, where one fecund man sought to found nations by having as many children as he could, and putting them to work, tending his fields and animals. The reason to have children was to put them to work, increasing the parents' wealth. One of the basic Ten Commandments is 'Honor thy father and thy mother'. Disobedience, slackness at work, insulting the progenitors, and certainly striking the parents were often punished either by the parents killing the wayward child, or the community (of parents, presumably) stoning the offending child to death. In fact the killing of the slack, disobedient child did not disappear among the Jews with the example of Ibrahim. We see that in Deuteronomy 21:18 to 21, 'the disobedient, slack, rebellious child shall be brought before the town elders and shall be accused by the parents, and then all the men of the town shall stone to death' the rebel without a cause. The proper organization of the family structure was of paramount importance in those days. Therefore, the custom of sacrificing the eldest son (presumably in front of the gaggle of surviving children) was probably used to impress upon the progeny the importance of obeying the parents. 'Did you see how Dad cut Junior's heart out with that knife? We'd better do as he says and plant that field!'

This glimpse into life as it was in those harsh, near-desert climatic conditions can be extrapolated into giving the reader a more comprehensive image of life as it must have been for the herding and settled tribes. Here we have a world, not as harsh as the desert Arabs further south, where women may not venture outside the tent or the house unguarded by a male blood relation. The women in the Torah go to the well unaccompanied to draw water. The children are put to work as soon as possible and are kept in that position until they marry. A child disobeying or slacking at his tasks may be killed by his parents, although not with the ease or ritualization common before Ibrahim founded his religion. A stranger who had anything useful to one is to be killed and robbed, and his wife is better killed so as not to corrupt the Israeli man that will copulate with her, and the children as well so as not to give them the chance to grow up to take vengeance for their murdered parents. However, the stranger who dwells among you humbly shall not be oppressed, for the Israelis were once strangers and servants in Egypt and they know what it is like to be a stranger. There are a number of bodies of law that have a kind, humane side: prohibiting sex with animals, incestuous sex, homosexuality, murder, robbery, usury, etc., but probably common to many peoples and their respective religions at the time. So we see a picture from a careful reading of the Torah of a time and a place where human life is anything but sacrosanct, in fact being equivalent to a certain number of camels or goats. Marauding herders invade the land of milk and honey, hardened by a life wandering in search of water and scrub, tired of living on semi-sweet manna, hungry for the milk from the animals that graze on this greener land, which even produces flowers from which the honey bees make the sweet substance. Sugar is unknown in this area at the time, so milk with honey is the equivalent of an ice cream sundae in modern times.

All peoples have their own god; even every town has its own god. Laws vary considerably according to local customs. Encounters between strangers often result in fighting. The father of the family is all-dominant, being allowed to legally kill his children should they refuse to work for him. Anyone who is anyone has bought or taken slaves. A strange man who seeks to pass the night inside some town's walls can find himself the subject of forced sodomy by the male residents. Medical knowledge consists of isolating the leprous or those with dripping sexual organs. Other diseases are treated by killing a white dove and dripping its blood over the patient, while releasing another white dove. The punishment for most crimes is death, usually by public stoning. Most readers would not think twice given the opportunity to convert to this religion. So what is it about Genesis that has had such an impact on the human race that billions of people claim it is the Word of God?

Compared to the other dominant religions at the time it is actually quite a humane, kind religion. Following some of its laws, if generally applied, could lead to a lowering of the death rate and an increase in the average lifespan, and probably an expanding human population. 1) It prohibits the killing of one's children in purely ritual sacrifice (the children can be killed only if they are wanton, stubborn, and slack); 2) it tells the Jews to treat the strangers who dwell humbly among them (as servants) kindly and not oppress them (for the Jews had been strangers in Egypt). Also the widows, the poor, the orphans are to have some consideration; 3) it states that Yahweh is the god that has most stood by His people and has shown the most visible signs and that perhaps He is the father of the gods. If so, can there be any other gods if they were created by Yahweh?

This thought particularly appealed to mankind, where in a world rife with deadly violence the idea that all men are created by one Father God could lead to the idea that all men are brothers. If all are worshipping the One God and following one code of laws, then the violence among people should lessen. This could lead to the sanctity of human life. A worshipper could believe that 'my life is holy because I am surrounded by my brothers and brothers should treat each other kindly'. However, in practice, over the thousands of intervening years, the brotherhood of mankind has been called into question as, through travels, peoples of different races came face to face.

Surely the Europeans considered the Japanese as monkeys in the first decades that trading posts were established in Japan by Portugal and Spain. The Japanese in turn considered the Europeans as unwashed barbarians. The Europeans and the Arabs considered the black Africans as inhuman, fit for legal slavery, until some court decisions in the mid-1800s first established that a black person was not an animal (because the black person on trial could read English). The settlers of the USA considered the native Americans as savages, unfit for anything – 'The only good injun is a dead injun'. The Germans certainly considered the Jewish race as a problem, solvable by efficient gasification and incineration up to 1945. The settlers of Australia considered the Aborigine as a curiosity that could become violent. The Aborigines were exterminated in the island of Tasmania, and some of the skin of the last Aborigine to die there was made into a purse, proudly worn by his white owner for many years. However, all these races could mate and produce half-breed children. So the idea that all humans are brothers still has very much appeal today. One wonders, though, how many Europeans would be willing to mate and have children with the Central African black pigmy, whose three-foot-tall stature is radically different to, say, a six-foot-tall Swede. However mating is possible. In fact, the neighboring Negroes much appreciate pigmy women for their tight vaginas, and it is common to have a pigmy girl as one of the wives.

So is there a line, a gray area, where the humans pass from being brothers (with whom we can have children) to not being brothers, but rather of a different species (with whom it is not possible to birth

36

babies)? Scientists believe that Neanderthal man lived at the same time as our human ancestors and gradually disappeared from the areas where our ancestors lived. It is unproven whether our ancestors mated with the Neanderthals (whether mating was even possible) and the Neanderthal genes eventually practically disappeared, leaving only some slight traces these days, or whether the Neanderthals simply died out as a result of losing the competition with our ancestors for the food supply (surely some antagonism would have developed there and the massively built, extremely powerful Neanderthal race would not have allowed our ancestors to starve them to death without a fight?), or whether our ancestors systematically used their superior intelligence to exterminate the dangerous, much stronger, hair-covered, barely-able-to-speak, killer hunter creatures that the Neanderthals must have surely been. It is unknown whether mating was possible, but if it was, would a Cro-Magnon male have accepted for a mate a hair-covered female, brutally built, with massive strength, a jutting brow ridge, that was capable of uttering few sounds and grunts? Would they have had much of a home life?

Even today, nearly all human males feel a natural repugnance towards fur-covered females. Throughout known history no image of female beauty or attractiveness has been found of a female similar to the Neanderthal female. Yet some fragments of early Greek pottery seem to depict a large hairy man being chased by warriors. Surely a race as numerous as the Neanderthals and as widespread could not have disappeared in a short period of time. Some indications exist that some remnant Neanderthals may have had encounters with civilized peoples as recently as 1,000 BC, about the same time as Genesis may have been written. Some even believe that large, hairy, manlike creatures survive today (like the Yeti in Nepal or Bigfoot in the USA and Indonesia). In any event, the widespread lovemaking between humans and Neanderthals seems unlikely due to the repugnance that most humans feel today at the sight of such a humanlike creature, far more advanced than the apes. And although the Neanderthals surely must have taken human females (by force), recognizing in them a superior genetic line, it is unknown whether birth could issue from such a mating. So the far more likely scenario is that of the Neanderthals becoming extinct as a result of our ancestors preventing them from eating, or of our ancestors chasing and killing them whenever they found them; either way points to a protracted war of extermination between our ancestors and Neanderthals that lasted for thousands of years, even into recent historical times, as scattered remains of the Neanderthal race may have been sometimes encountered in their last remaining hiding places by civilized warriors in the Bronze Age, and killed.

Surely the lifestyles described in the Torah do not point to a kind, gentle, amorous human interested in the welfare of a grotesque, apelike creature, but rather indicate a very long line of descent where killing and despoiling anyone who was not from your father's family was the norm. The enslaving of the vanquished stranger carried with it obvious dangers, so that extermination was frequently the preferred course of action. Surely the Jews did not invent genocide. Many peoples practiced it from before the dawn of recorded history. Perhaps the One God idea represented the brotherhood of all humans, in that all humanlike creatures alive then could successfully mate and produce offspring, as the thousands of years' long war of extermination against Neanderthals was coming to an end and their God ceased to exist.

But the One God idea is not the main attraction of Genesis. Although an influential concept, there is a far more widespread and central concept that directs the life of anyone who reads this book. The reader has had some time to think about it, but this concept is so ingrained in the reader's life that it is almost subliminal and difficult to see, given its unconditional acceptance by nearly every reader. That concept is: *the week*. Yes, the seven-day week. The first thing Yahweh did was work creating the universe for six days and on the seventh day He rested. The Torah is full of references to how the Sabbath is to be kept and no work is to be done on that day. It is one of the Ten Commandments. The penalty for working on the Sabbath is to be stoned to death. But it is not just the Jews that must rest every seventh day. Their slaves, their animals must also be given the day of rest. Even the women are prohibited from cooking, as no fire is to be lit on the Sabbath, and the women are admonished to prepare the food on the day before. The seventh day is to be devoted entirely to rest and adoring Yahweh. The week is also the basis of the Christian and Islamic religions. The Muslims rest on Friday, the Jews on Saturday, and the Christians on Sunday.

In the many other religions current at the time, the slave or the woman had to work, sometimes continuously for months at a time; sometimes they could rest on the feast days of the particular neighborhood gods, and sometimes they worked the entire year without a full day of rest, year in, year out. The concept of the seventh day of rest was so attractive to the oppressed masses that it eventually convinced the entire population that came into contact with it, thus resulting in the structural time organization of the world in which we live in today. It sold the religion to the public more than any other concept contained therein. It was like a little bit of paradise, right here on earth.

The other religions in the area had nothing to offer the masses that could compare. Whereas some had a continuous month of feasts and debauchery after the harvest, none had hit upon the idea of setting up a time rhythm that kept the people working for a relatively short period of days so that a lot of work could be accomplished. The six-day rhythm gave the people an immediately foreseeable reward of a day of rest and feasting. The other religions' holy days were usually arranged to celebrate the recollection of cereals or grapes, etc. The people would work to achieve the goal of the harvest and then they would feast on it. The herders' religions, though, could not offer such a reward. Herding has to be done year round. There is no season of rest in herding. There is, however, feasting any time one wishes to kill one of the animals and eat it. The seven-day time rhythm allowed the people to work hard at anything (construction, factories, crafts), because people can hold out working at that rhythm for all their lives. With the interspersed day of rest coming up so frequently the people can employ a good effort at production as they are always looking forward to recuperating on the holy day, feast day.

In the UK, the mother country of the English language, the word 'holidays' is used instead of vacation. Obviously the holy days were immediately seized by the people everywhere for themselves, as the excuse of adoring the God was used to cover the rest and rejuvenating that the people craved. Throughout the Roman Empire the Romans had temples and housing built at strikingly beautiful natural sites, such as stunning beaches, cool mountain lakes, etc. The wealthy classes would travel to these sites with the excuse of going to adore at the temple of Diana, Neptunus, whatever. Travel in those days was by cart or ship, or on the back of an animal. It took weeks of sitting on the back of a horse or sailing on a small ship to reach some of these temples from Rome. The wealthy would bring servants, slaves, and bales of baggage. Travel was dangerous for the wealthy. Even their very servants and slaves could be rancorous because of their station in life and the injustices heaped upon them by their masters.

In the resort of Cancun, Mexico, the Mayan elite had a temple built (and housing) on a placid lagoon that languishes just beyond the beach line where the ocean waves break. They would travel there in the hot summer with their servants and slaves to worship at the temple. Seven miles offshore, on the island of Cozumel, another small temple was built (with some housing) to which the more adventurous would go to worship, after enjoying the crossing by boat. The island's stark beaches and crystal clear ocean waters today still attract a huge amount of tourists.

It is apparent from examining the far-flung temple sites of these and many other cultures that the upper classes used the cover of going to worship at the temple to justify to their servants and slaves the long, arduous, dangerous voyage that the rulers wanted them to make, carrying their beach stuff, clothes for partying, and food and other necessities. The servants and slaves were many and the owner and his family were few. Religion was used to instill awe and fear in the servants so that they would mostly obey their masters' whims. These beach and lake temple sites were where the wealthy would go to escape the summer heat or to see a bit of the world in a pleasant voyage. They were actually the equivalent of the resort hotels of their era. Religion and god worshipping were used as the justification for the expense and effort of what was in fact a tourist trip.

In the same way, the seventh holy day, where total rest was mandated by Jewish law under the penalty of death for all Jews, their women, their servants, slaves, even their animals, was very attractive to the human race as the holy day was used for rest and diversion from the world of daily work that existed before it. This idea was so powerful that peoples everywhere who had any contact with it were soon converted to it and made up their own religions, which had little or no resemblance to the Jewish religion, i.e. Christianity, Islam, but were based upon resting for a day after six days of work.

The Jewish religion mostly preaches no heaven or hell; they don't know if there is life after death. The Orthodox Jew is mandated to kill all non-Jews who are occupying their promised land (or at least force the current dwellers to leave the area), and to conquer the area that extends from the Nile to the Euphrates, to rest on the Sabbath and also to heed Yahweh's commandments. Islam commands its followers to pray five times per day, fast for one month every year, travel to Makkah once in a lifetime if possible, give charity to the poor, attend the Friday prayer meeting (which lasts about an hour. The rest of the day is for family, feasting and relaxation). The Christian religion commands its followers to attend the prayer meeting on Sunday (which also lasts about an hour, the rest of the day also being for feasting and relaxing with the family) and to obey the Ten Commandments (which are more like 100 commandments if one actually takes the time to read the pertinent passages in the Holy Bible. However the Christians only like ten of them, the rest of the commandments of Yahweh being ignored and disregarded).

The only characteristics these Torah-based religions have in common are the paying heed to somewhat primitive, quasi humanitarian laws – that no government on earth today would be allowed to enact even for one day as the people everywhere would rise up and overthrow that government – that of the seven-day week, and in the case of Islam and Christianity, that there is One God. The Jews are only certain that Yahweh is the god of the Jewish people and that they have been chosen by Him; for what purpose, they don't know.

The commandments aside, and realizing that the seven-day week is the most important element of these religions, there is only one other concept that has been much appreciated by many people. That, of course, is the idea that all humans are brothers, that we were all created by One God, the creator of all things, and that those who follow the One God should treat each other as brothers. Do not be deceived into believing that Islam teaches its followers to treat humans as their brothers. The golden rule of Christ was: treat others as you would like them to treat you. Muhammad's golden rule remained the same as the Jewish rule: treat others as they treat you, do unto others as they do unto you, an eye for an eye, a tooth for a tooth, a murdered wife for a murdered wife. Islam tells its followers to follow certain rules regarding those who believe in Allah and Muhammad, i.e. give hospitality to a fellow Muslim if he asks for it (this was particularly important in the desert), safeguard an orphan's inheritance for when he attains the age of emancipation, without stealing from it, although one may charge management fees (for Muhammad led a warring tribe that created many orphans), but the Holy Qur'an only once mentions any type of commandment, in Sura 6, verses 151–152.

'Join not anything with Allah';

'Be good to your parents';

'Kill not your children on a plea of want; we provide for you and for them' (obviously the killing of one's children was widespread even in this date of AD 636);

'Come not nigh to indecent deeds, whether open or secret';

'Take not life, which Allah hath made sacred, except by way of justice and law';

'Come not nigh to the orphan's property, except to improve it'; and,

'Give measure and weight with justice'.

That's it. That is all that is prohibited to Muslims in social conduct. Far more words of the Holy Qur'an are dedicated to what kind of animals and sea creatures to eat, and how to perform divorces, and the different manners to be displayed under different circumstances when someone goes into someone else's house or tent. The good conduct of Muslims is only regulated as far as it concerns other believers in Allah and Muhammad. Muslims are allowed to treat the non-believers as animals, and may either slaughter them, make them slaves, or convert them to the true faith under threat of death (should they convert they may still remain slaves).

But the people only want one leader. They will not stand for two or three. All countries on earth are lead by one man (some women). Some Greek city-states briefly experimented with two leaders, but nearly without exception all countries, states and provinces, cities and towns are ruled by one man (a few women) and it has been that way for thousands of years. In the Torah we see that the high priest had all the power, serving as both priest and king for Israel. However, there were dozens of high priests, dozens of religions, dozens of gods, just between the borders of Lebanon (ancient Tyre) and the Sinai peninsula. In Egypt there were hundreds of religions and gods. The Holy Qur'an tells us that before Muhammad, up to the year AD 630, there were equally hundreds of gods and religions in the Arabian Peninsula. This situation led to a lot of warfare. In the average lifespan of maybe fifty years in those days, a human might be affected personally by several wars and raids. This of course caused much mayhem, suffering, destruction of one's property, and loss of family and loved ones, as well as personal wounds and psychological scars. It was a terrible situation.

Also, the thousands of gods each had different powers, different ways of worship, different rules and codes of conduct. This led to a lot of confusion and it must have been obvious to any thinking person that this mayhem could not have any basis in reality. Thus the Hypocrites were honored for their attitude and gained converts in the practice of their policy of acting with a soft defense against invading groups and their gods. By pretending to go along with the armed groups that attempted to foist their new god onto the local population, the Hypocrite congregations were far better off than if they submitted or fought the invaders. The Hypocrite philosophy spread throughout the areas of Greek influence as well as at least the Arabian Peninsula and the Hypocrite congregations lived together, defended each other, and held regular meetings for at least 1,500 years. Now a forgotten practice, the Hypocrites have, in any event, achieved the complete domination of the lucrative practice of modern medicine, having even succeeded in making it a crime punishable by imprisonment to practice medicine without a Hippocratic license in all the Western nations.

The confusion of religions continued, as it had since the dawn of history, with the apparent real religion shared by mankind in the Mediterranean region being based on enslaving other humans, stealing their goods and stock animals, or even just exterminating the other human groups in order to occupy their homes and farmlands. Gods and religions were dedicated to attempting to explain the world, such as Yahweh opening the taps of the membrane that separated the waters above (sky) from the waters below (sea), thus causing rain. Other gods could be appealed to by the hapless humans to increase the harvest of grapes (i.e. Bacchus) or to give many children to women (i.e. Isis) or whatever else the humans wanted to happen. Gods have always been conceived as something that is more powerful than humans. Would any human be interested in worshipping a god that was less powerful than himself?

Power is the key to godhood. Some humans were thought of as being so powerful that they became living gods, such as Alexander the Great, or some Roman Caesars. But the vast army of gods in those days did not all have even the power to kill a human. Each god had different tasks to perform, such as control the seas, make the sun move about the sky, bring good harvests or rain, make the goats fertile and birth many kids, etc. – things that humans could not do or control. A distinctive feature of Yahweh was that His main power was to kill humans. He could consume them with fire, bring plagues on them, or illness, open the earth and swallow the humans whole, drown them in a gigantic flood, but mostly he would kill humans by ordering the Israelis (through the priests' words) to take their swords and spears and kill other humans. This was a real killer god. The concept survives to this day in the saying 'a God-fearing Christian'. If you follow Yahweh, you should be afraid of Him.

The Torah says He exterminated life on earth except for Noah and his family and animals. Some people claim that all the ancient cultures in the Mediterranean basin shared a common story about an ancient mighty flood that some people claim validates the Torah's story. A simple explanation for these common stories may be found if we examine the common tales of dragons between the UK and faraway China. How could two regions so far apart have developed such related lore? The simple fact is that in the cliffs of Dover in the southern UK, and other regions, dinosaur skeletons, nearly complete, had been found centuries ago. The people could see that they were gigantic reptiles' skeletons. The fire-breathing story developed as an observation of the fact that reptiles shoot out a forked tongue that could resemble a flame in some eyes. Similarly, in China, the Gobi Desert has long been one of the best dinosaur hunting grounds on earth, as many entire dinosaur skeletons have been exposed by erosion, as in the cliffs of Dover, and are visible to anyone, having in fact been described in Chinese literature as early as 2,700 years ago. However, the Chinese imagination did not lead to the fire-breathing dragon. In fact, powdered dragon bone has long been an expensive kind of medicine in Chinese stores. The people would take the dinosaur fossil bones and sell them to the apothecaries, who would then crush the bones into powder and sell it to the public as a medicine.

Similarly, all along the mountain ranges bordering the Mediterranean Sea, anyone can walk about and find fossil seashells in very high places. It was obvious to the ancients that seashells had to live under the sea. So the ancient cultures developed a story that obviously the sea level must have been higher than where the seashells were, at one time. This gave rise to the story of the flood. We now know that the mountain ranges, even though being thousands of meters above sea level now, were once the ocean floor, and the tectonic plates which cover the surface of the planet forced the present mountain ranges from the sea floor up to their present positions. This is not a scientific theory any more, as the cracks between the plates have been observed and studied and the movement of the plates is under continuous measurement in many countries.

The people only want 'one' now, and this desire became more universal as the peoples in the Mediterranean basin spent more and more centuries in close contact through trade and travel and shared some common governments: the Roman Empire, the Arabs from the Arabian Peninsula, now known as Saudi Arabia, and the Holy Roman emperor, who predominated in Europe. As the groups of peoples and diverse races congealed over the centuries, the One God idea became sought after. This was not so at first. The books following the Torah clearly describe how the Jews, having failed to exterminate the dwellers of their promised land, as ordered by the priests of Yahweh, settled in among the inhabitants where they could and eventually elected judges to rule over them along with the high priest, and then, beginning with Saul, David, Solomon, accepted kings over the Jews who no longer relied on the priest class for their power, but rather on semi-professional soldiers and generals.

The Jews began to worship other gods, as well as intermarry with the local people, and the worship of other gods became somewhat acceptable and no longer punishable by immediate public stoning – in fact, it became for centuries the official religions of the kings and the states of Judah and Israel. So the development of the One God was not a straight line, but rather a complicated process. But as the desire for the One God grew, the Killer God was the logical choice to occupy the position. The other ancient gods had ruled for thousands of years, but their powers were limited. The Greek and Roman gods toyed with people for their amusement but seldom killed them. They were much more bland gods, and you could mess with them a little bit. In a world of killer men they could never have held the attention or the respect of the population for long. The Killer God was needed to impose order in a world in the grips of chaos and genocidal warfare and raids. The Killer God was the only god who could establish order and bring large groups of people into peaceful cohabitation.

The people have become so attached to only having one that in any nation it is a matter of extreme urgency and utmost priority to not be without one, even for a few hours. If a president of a nation demits or is assassinated, emergency sessions of the remaining government are convened to select a new leader. Witness the 2005 demission of the Bolivian president, or the change in government in Ukraine. The US president is whisked away to safety in the event of a threat and the line of succession is clearly marked and followed should he become unavailable. The whole population in any country becomes worried, even wild and uncontrollable, when they know that there is no one in charge, and the new one must be placed into power immediately. They don't want two, they want one. If things are going badly or unsatisfactorily for the nation, the one must be thrown out and replaced with another one. The new one frequently makes some speeches, orders some new programs, and the nation's economy improves for a time. But can one man really be responsible for an entire nation? Is George Bush really responsible for what 300,000,000 US citizens do?

The desire for one could be a rational thought process as a result of mankind's experience with conflicting leaders. Several leaders have often disagreed in the past, leading their different factions into dispute, even internecine battle and warfare. Also, should several fail to agree, this situation leads to confusion as no clear orders, even conflicting orders, will be issued and the people will not know what the leaders want them to do. Also several are more expensive for the people to maintain. More than one rapacious king has been quite expensive to his subjects in the past. Imagine if France had to maintain several Louis XIVs at the same time. However, the Greek city-states and the Roman Senate functioned quite well for many centuries, issuing edicts as a body of dozens or even hundreds of rulers. In fact, the political basis for Western culture is found in these senatorial government systems, not in the rule by one.

But if mankind's desire for one was based on rational memory of past experiences, how do we explain the state of national emergency that overpowers a country when the one is suddenly no more? Why does the population take to the streets, agitating, making noise, even acting wild and out of control? Get us a new one, and we want one now! This behavior certainly resembles the same succession crises that have been observed in nearly all primates: monkeys, chimpanzees, baboons and others. Could this desire for one really be an instinctive need to have a dominant male in charge of the group that we share with the other primates?

Today, the USA is the dominant culture on earth. Its movies and music set the standards for other countries to follow. American dress and style are widely admired. The fact that the USA has developed a five-days-of-work, two-days-of-rest week may be the main factor in selling the American way to the masses. Surely the USA is not admired for its oppressive military power, or for its pseudo-democracy where only the Bush family seem to be capacitated to hold power in a nation of 300,000,000 people. In fact the European political model, where the prime minister can be dismissed in a matter of days, rather than having a guaranteed four-year term like the US president, is far more democratic. No European democracy has ever elected the son of a previous president as president. In fact, only Haiti, India, and the Arab dictatorships have ever done that.

The US is admired for its economic opportunity. Although few become wealthy, everyone enjoys the five-days'-work, two-days'-rest week by law. Europeans still mostly maintain the five-and-a-half-day work week by law, although the 35-hour work week was briefly experimented with in the industrialized countries, where hourly wages are more common. The obvious trend is to work fewer days and take more days of rest, still on the seven-day counting basis. Why not ten days or five days? Because of Genesis.

The Development of the Concepts of God, Day of Judgment and Heaven

As can be seen by reading the Torah or the Bible, the idea of gods was common throughout the area as a sort of template, spiritual mold, a sort of archetype that guided a community or people. Yahweh was the director of the affair of the Jewish people taken as a whole. The Greek, Roman or Egyptian gods (far more advanced civilizations than the original Israelis, who were wandering herders living in tents and tree branch-covered lean-tos called tabernacles) not only enable the existence of peoples and towns, but also families at the micro level (the family god), but also big things at the macro level. Mars was the god of war, Poseidon the god of the sea, Isis the goddess of fertility, Bacchus the god of wine, Thor the god of thunder, etc. These gods got big things done, well beyond the power of a nation or the entire human race.

Some American Indians developed the same types of religious concepts completely independently of Mediterranean civilizations. They believed that the Great Spirit created all, but that mountains had their own enabling archetype, the spirit of the mountains, which allowed the mountains to be understood by man, to have an existence in the material world. Buffalos had their own spirit, which was the template for the physical buffalo, birds likewise, etc. The One God, Yahweh, creator of the gods concept agreed with many religions at the time. The Great Spirit of the American Indians; Zeus, the father of the Greek gods; Brama, the great originator of the Hindu gods in India. The Egyptians toyed with the idea with the brief cult to Amon-Ra, the sun god, but soon dropped the concept and reverted to the multitude of gods religion (but with a father god).

The written tradition states that Yahweh brought death and destruction on the Jews whenever He caught them worshipping other gods, which were everywhere (and many times when they were worshipping only Yahweh as He ordered them, as well). He showed them great signs, spoke to them with a voice like thunder, slew their enemies, etc. However, after the astounding miracles that Yahweh performed in plain sight of the Israelis in aiding their flight from their Egyptian bondage, the first thing the Israelis did was to build themselves a statue of a golden calf to worship. Apparently the Israelis were unimpressed by giant pillars of fire, the seven plagues brought on the Egyptians, and by Yahweh speaking to them in a voice of thunder. Some of them continued to worship the golden calf religion, which lasted for nine centuries as can be read in later books of the Holy Bible.

However, the tribe of Levy had been assigned the enviable position of priests of Yahweh. They don't have to work. The rest of the Israelis have to give them food of all types in prescribed measures, gold and silver, as well as an annual ransom for each parishioner. This religion of golden calf worship represents a serious challenge to the Levites' privileged position, and their food supply as well. In fact, the Israelis give their gold ornaments to the priests of the golden calf religion, gold that the Levites were hoping to collect soon. When Moses descends from the sacred mountain with the commandments, Yahweh becomes aware of Israel's idolatry and Moses orders the Levites to take their swords and kill the Israelis who had transgressed. And so the priests of Yahweh's religion did just that, killing apparently some 3,000 of their fellow Israelis that day with their swords (Exodus 32:1–35).

Verse 34 contains the first and only mention of a Day of Punishment. Verses 32 and 35 mention that Yahweh has a book from which people can be erased. This is the basis for the entire Judgment Day; Book of Life stories developed much later. However, it is connected with the Levite priests establishing their dominant position within the tribe of Israel by killing with their swords their fellow Israelis who sought to set up a competing religion that would take at least part of the gold assigned to them and possibly their food supply.

The next book, Leviticus, is dedicated to the rights of the Levites and exactly how much food and precious metal is to be given to them on a regular basis as sacrifices to their god Yahweh and for their maintenance. In return for this tribute the Levites perform all types of absurd rituals of killing doves in order to cure leprosy and all the illnesses, in that the Levites were the equivalent of doctors and judges for the primitive Israelis. And primitive surely were the methods used as medicine. If the Hypocrites had been around then they should have had a higher curation rate. The Levites also caused the stoning to death of anyone who insulted their Yahweh (Leviticus 24:10–23). What better way to suppress dissent than to kill those who speak out against you? This was a method adopted by Muhammad and very much in use to this day, as Vladmir Putin and others are demonstrating.

The next book, Numbers, contains the only reference to what much later developed into a concept related to the modern-day hell (Numbers 16:30–35). Again, a faction of the priesthood, headed by a man named Coreh, began to agitate to take over Moses' position as top man. Yahweh causes the earth to open and swallow his faction of followers where they are descended alive into Seol. What Seol means is not known by anyone. There is no other mention in the entire Torah of anything mildly resembling life after death, heaven, hell, a Day of Judgment, a Book of Life. These two meager passages containing some thirty words briefly alluding to a Day of Punishment, a book written by Yahweh, and descending into Seol (whatever that may be) are the entire basis for all the much later developed theology regarding these invisible worlds. And these passages are strictly related to power struggles within the Israeli tribe to assume the privileged position of collecting tribute from the other Israelis.

Yahweh Himself never mentions anything else about life after death; Yahweh simply kills those who displease Him. The punishment for sin is only death. This is why the Jews do not necessarily believe in heaven or hell. The Jewish religion does not accept such dogma. The Jews are not certain if there is a life after death. Since they did not accept Christ as a prophet, they are still waiting for someone to appear who can show them something about this theme. Perhaps the generalized financial success of the Jews is due to their being concentrated in material matters, as their religion teaches them that the rewards are given to one while one is alive. Life after death, to the Jews, is at best an unknown, but to the Christians and the Muslims it is a certainty. This certainty, however, is not based on anyone ever demonstrating the existence of any of these things. It is only based on a collection of writings called the Holy Bible and the Holy Qur'an. So would not a believer be well advised to read carefully the holy books that promise him eternity?

Reading on past the Torah in the Holy Bible, the next books tell us that Yahweh, the One God of the Jews, was not that popular with the very Jews for at least the following 900 years after Moses. We can read that the Jews continued to worship the golden calf throughout all this time. The golden calf had a long feast, a holy day in the middle of August. This was the end of the harvest. It would seem that the entire religion was based on the fertility of the fields and stock animals. The calf was one of the more prized stock animals and represented the birth of more stock animals. The feast days from mid-August were timed to allow for the long rest period after the harvest that all farmers enjoyed, and the feasting on the recently collected crops. So this religion continued on alongside the worship of the killer god, Yahweh.

We read that Solomon was the first to build a temple to worship Yahweh (1 Kings 3:1, 2). Before then the Jews worshipped in 'high places' (mounds of fieldstone or earth of up to six levels, possibly resembling the flat top pyramids called ziggurats common to the Babylonian religion, the dominant religion in the area). To build this house were employed by Solomon 70,000 porters, 80,000 woodcutters and 3,200 foremen. It took this incredible workforce seven years to build the famous Temple of Solomon, which was only 112 feet long by 32 feet wide by 48 feet tall, housing roughly 3,500 square feet in the main building. This is further verified by the explanation that the two cherubim's statues that guarded the Ark of the Covenant had wingspans of 16 feet each, and their combined wingspans reached from wall to wall of the temple, so that their wingtips touched the walls and each other. Also, the altar was so small that the popular sacrifices had to be performed in the front plaza of the temple, because the altar was not big enough to hold a large animal such as a cow. The Israelis used a measurement called an elbow, which is roughly equivalent to 1.61 feet. Another sign of primitive backwardness in those days, as the people had not the intelligence to use the king's foot as the standard of measurement.

The famous temple of Solomon was smaller than many single family homes in the USA. This is not unexpected. If one examines the great temples such as the Mayan Chichen-Itza, or the Valley of the Kings temples in Egypt, one realizes that the interior covered spaces were tiny. The same was true for the magnificent Roman villas. The rooms are the size of large closets these days. The people in those days did not have the technology to enclose sizable covered areas with a roof. Solomon's temple could house about 500 worshippers standing shoulder to shoulder. So one is asked to believe that 150,000 workers took seven years to build this construction; another example how authors in those days multiplied facts by 1,000. You can read all these supposed facts for yourself in 1 Kings 5 and 6.

Solomon built his temple so that 'all the peoples would know that Yahweh is God and there is no other'. However, we then find out that Solomon himself worshipped other gods and built temples to them as well. We read he worshipped Astoret, Ilcom and Quemos, that Solomon built a temple for Moloc (this was the old god Malek of the Malequites, that required the sacrifice of one's child) (1 Kings 11). Solomon was the last king who was actually all Jew. His descendants who reigned after him were derived from concubines who were not Jewesses, were in fact foreigners and adored other gods (1 Kings 16:29–32). In fact, the famous Jezebel was one such wife, and she remains famous to this day as a traitor because, as the wife of King Acab (1 Kings 18:4), they not only worshipped Baal (Baal Zebub, Baal Peor, etc.), but they also ordered the killing of all of Yahweh's priests. The king after Solomon was named Jeroboam and he revived the cult of the golden calf (1 Kings 12:28–33) and he ordained a new set of priests who were not Levites, to serve the two golden calf temples that he erected.

The famous Baal Zebub (later changed into Beelzebuz, a powerful demon, in the New Testament) was only one of the Baal gods. There was a Baal god for every town named Baal, which were the towns where the worshippers of the Babylonian religion lived and presumably of Babylonian lineage. He was named after the town of Baal Zebub and was the god of that town only. He became famous because he is mentioned in the first paragraph of 2 Kings 1 and 2. Simple-minded people read only a few paragraphs of the holy books and saw his name and he became famous. However, Baal Peor is the god of the much larger city of Baal Peor and is repeatedly mentioned throughout the Torah and the later books, but has never enjoyed the same fame as his cousin Baal Zebub because his name is not head-lined in any book, but rather one has to read the entire book to find it.

Reading on, we find that 800 years after Moses it is revealed that Moses himself had left the Jews a bronze serpent god that they worshipped (2 Kings 18:3, 4) which was destroyed at that time. In 2 Kings 16:3, 4 and 17:9–12, 16, 17, we get a good picture that the Jews worshipped Moloc by burning their sons and daughters in sacrifice to him; in fact the king himself performed such a sacrifice with some of his children. In Jeremiah 7:8–32, the Jews worship Tofet and burn their sons and daughters to him. The golden-calf harvest fertility cult was going strong 800 years after Moses. All these books were written by the priests of Yahweh, the Levites, and one can see how the holy author describes how the king anointed priests for some other cult from the 'low people', not Levites (2 Kings 16:29–32). Obviously, all these books are slanted to favor the Levites and their god Yahweh, who proclaimed that the rest of the Jews had to pay regular tribute to and give food daily to the Levites.

We see that the power of the Levites was, in fact, miniscule, espe-cially after Queen Jezebel ordered them slaughtered. The Temple of Solomon, the House of Yahweh, was shared by many gods (2 Kings 23:4). The cult of the goddess Asera shared the temple and her holy prostitutes worked there (2 Kings 23:6, 7). Solomon had built other temples and places of worship to Astoret, Quemos, Milcom, but also for sun worship and to Moloc for the sacrifice of children (2 Kings 23:10, 11). The Bible also tells us that Jews worshipped lush trees and offered sacrifices under their shade (understandable in a semi-desert region, 2 Chronicles 28:1–4). So the Bible tells us that the early Jews who witnessed the most grand, awesome displays of power by the god Yahweh, were not impressed and continued to worship all the other gods of the region (including trees), in fact, at times attacking the priests of Yahweh and trying to do away with them and their religion.

The One God religion had a difficult time getting started.

Throughout all this time there appears no mention of life after death, heaven, hell, or a Day of Judgment. Rather, the only mention of a Day of Punishment, as before said, is when the Levite priests attack with their swords the priests and worshippers of the golden calf religion and kill some 3,000 of them in one day. Another odd thing is that Aaron – the brother of Moses and head priest of Yahweh, from whom descended all the head priests of Yahweh – is also the one who ordered the people to give him (Aaron) their gold and he himself builds the golden calf and the altar to worship it on (Exodus 32:1–6). Moses also had built a serpent god at that time to whom the Jews would pray so as not to be bitten by snakes.

Just about every other book of the Old Testament mentions other gods and exhorts the Jews to stop worshipping them. The main reason why the writings exhort the Jews to worship only Yahweh is to keep their race pure and not take wives from or mix with other peoples. Other peoples in the area are now to be dominated or enslaved. The Jews, having failed at committing the complete genocide on the native dwellers of their promised land as ordered by Yahweh in the first five books of the Holy Bible, are now to collect tribute from the outlying peoples and enslave the foreigners among them (2 Chronicles 2:17, 18). The killer god Yahweh now begins to be called the God of the Armies (or the watered down version, Lord of Hosts, in English). The Jews, having become the dominant power under Solomon, collect tribute from their empire, from as far away as Ethiopia. However, modern-day Iraq (Assyria, Babylon) and Egypt remained far more powerful, both militarily and in terms of having a more advanced, stable civilization. So Egypt and Babylonia would occasionally send armies into Israel and Judea (ancient Israel was two kingdoms) to enforce their superiority and collect tribute. One of these Babylonian kings, Nebuchadnezzar, decided to end the Jews' rule over the area and decimated the population, destroyed the Temple of Solomon, tore down Jerusalem, and took all of the Jews who had any property into captivity in Assyria, leaving only the poor people behind. They were forced into all types of slavery there (just as they had been in Egypt earlier) and remained as servants of the Assyrians for seventy years. Eventually the Persians and the Medes conquered Babylonia and established the very long-lasting Persian

Empire. Then the Jews passed from being slaves to just being discriminated against by the local peoples among whom the Jews now lived.

Apparently a Jewish girl, Esther, was chosen by a Persian king, Asuero, as his number one wife. Shortly thereafter, some of the peoples agitated with the king to be allowed to exterminate the Jews in Babylonia and take the property they had accumulated. Esther interceded with her husband, the king Asuero, and he decreed that it should be the Jews instead who could exterminate those peoples who planned to attack them, and that the Persian army and officials were not to interfere. So, armed with this decree, the Jews fell upon their enemies on the 13th and 14th of the month of Adar (part of February and March) and slaughtered some 75,000 people in those days. This is celebrated today by Jews as the feast of Purim (Holy Bible, Esther 9:20–26). The Jews grew in stature in the Persian Empire and the Emperor Xerxes II issued an order that the Jews were to be allowed to return to their land and rebuild Jerusalem and the Temple of Yahweh. The first group, comprising 42,370 men, 7,337 slaves and many pack animals, etc. arrived in Jerusalem (Holy Bible, Ezra 1:64–67). Before the attack of Nebuchadnezzar the census showed some 2,500,000 Jewish men lived in the two kingdoms of Israel and Judea (this would be more people than live in Israel today, about 6,700,000). This now much decimated population set about rebuilding the walls of Jerusalem, but when the peoples of Jordan saw this they came to order the Jews to stop their construction work and made a plea to the new Persian emperor, Darius, to search in the official records and notify them if indeed the Jews had a decree to be allowed to restore Jerusalem and install themselves there. Darius ordered a search of the archives and confirmed that such a decree did exist. Another Persian king, Artaheres, sent another migration of Jews back to Jerusalem. The Jews rebuilding Jerusalem had to mount guard continuously and work with their weapons at their side, as the local peoples were not happy to see them return to the area and threatened them continuously, obviously preserving a memory of the Jews' warlike and terrible treatment of their forefathers.

The Jews themselves began to practice racial purity again. They sent away their foreign wives and children by order of the new governor of Jerusalem, Ezra (Holy Bible, Ezra 10). That is what Yahweh wanted, for He would not be God to other peoples or mixed Jews. The Jews kept a record of paternal descendants and any Jews who could not find their continuous family line in this record could not become priests. This is probably where the Book of Life came from. Even so, to take a census of the population was a great sin, as the King David witnessed when he ordered a census (Holy Bible, 2 Samuel 24). (This is possibly because the census gave the king some power over the people. Government registration was more than a bother in those days, as it led to oppression without benefits.) So in the second year of Darius's reign, the returned Jews began to rebuild the Temple of Solomon and that's where the story of the Old Testament ends. For the next 400 years, until Jesus Christ, the history and writing of the Jews has been suppressed from the Holy Bible.

All the remaining books of the Old Testament were written during the captivity in Babylon, or during the period shortly after the return. The real interest of humanity in the Old Testament relates to the fact that is a collection of very early stories and history of mankind dating back to the Bronze Age, before iron was invented. If Bible timelines are reliable, the stories date back to over 1000 BC. But until the writings about Jesus Christ there is no mention of, 1) life after death, 2) paradise, 3) hell, or 4) Judgment Day, that has any emphasis or credibility. None of these things were believed in at the time. In fact, there was not One God. There were still many main gods in the area right up to the time the Old Testament ends. And it ends with the Jews returned from captivity in Babylon, now much decimated and reduced to a small fraction of their pre-slavery population, being grudgingly permitted to rebuild the defensive wall of Jerusalem and start work on rebuilding Solomon's Temple by the local population, who keep a wary eye on them, remembering the Jews' enslavement and domination of them, seventy years before. The Jewish God Yahweh nearly got the whole race exterminated; their power and domination were long gone and now they were humbled and weak, and they never regained the status they had before. Let us examine nearly all the instances of life after death, paradise, hell and Judgment Day mentioned in the entire Old Testament of the Holy Bible.

The word Seol appears several times. It relates to the grave. It may have been similar to the Greek Hades or the Egyptian Underworld, but it seems to be much more like death and sepulcher; no life after death here. Psalms 30:3 mentions Seol. In Psalms 88:3 Seol seems to refer to grave, but no fire here. Psalms 137 tell us that that the entire book was written during the Jews' captivity in Babylon. In Psalms 137:7 we find the Edomites (one of the peoples oppressed by the Jews) fought with Babylon against the Jews. In Isaiah we see the evil and the holy both go to Seol. The living, not the dead, can worship and exalt Yahweh (Isaiah 38:18–20). In Isaiah 27:1 and 9 we see the Jews are still worshipping Asera (and her prostitutes) as well as the sun, and also Leviathan, the Great Serpent or Dragon. The Leviathan cult was quite widespread in the entire area and apparently came from the deserts of Babylon or thereabouts. The name has survived to this day, as if there was something to it. Could it be dinosaur skeletons exposed in some desert or cliff? Just as Islam has become the most popular religion because there is a meteorite at its heart, so Leviathan may have survived, along with dragons, because of dinosaur skeletons. Also at this time was the beginning of the Iron Age. Up to the time of Nebuchadnezzar, the Bible mentions only bronze. Iron was introduced into the area from what is now Turkey in about 620 BC. From the book Isaiah onwards, the Bible mentions iron and ironworkers.

Seol is mentioned in Job 11:8, although the entire book is obviously a parable, a tale of morality, dedicated to long discourses on the power and might of Yahweh and how insignificant man is compared to this power. The entire writing style in Job differs dramatically from the other books and seems to have been written by a Hellenized Jew who had training in Greek oratory. In Job also appears the only mention of Satan (related to Satyr the Greek mythical figure, half man, half goat?). In Job, Satan is the creature that uses his power to cause Job's calamities. Satan is something that sits and talks with Yahweh and also wanders the earth. There is also the barely mentioned tradition of cherubim in other books, such as the two statues of cherubim standing over the Ark of the Covenant in Solomon's temple. Right at the beginning, in Genesis, cherubim guard the entrance to Eden and prevent Adam and Eve from going back in once

God evicts them. In Hosea 13:14, Seol is equivalent to death; Yahweh will save his worshippers from Seol. Very little other mention of Seol is made, all in the same context.

The first mention of a punishment in a burning oven is in Daniel 3. Nebuchadnezzar has built an 85-foot-tall golden statue and orders all people to adore it. Three of the Jewish leaders refuse to prostrate themselves before the idol and Nebuchadnezzar orders them thrown into an oven, but they remain unharmed and then he has them taken out, realizing that the power of their god Yahweh has saved them from the hot fire. This is the entire basis for the burning hell stories. The only other mention possibly related to the theme is in Malachi 4, where a day will come that is hot as an oven. We also see in Daniel 6:10 that Jews prayed three times per day facing Jerusalem while captive in Babylonia. Muhammad, 1,200 years later, ordered his followers to pray every day facing Makkah.

The entire Old Testament is filled with admonitions about and ridiculing the worship of statues. Yet if one enters any Catholic church today, one will see it is filled with statues and people will be kneeling before them, worshipping them.

In Isaiah 40:22, Yahweh is the creator of the round earth. In 40:28 Yahweh is eternal creator. The Greeks popularized the knowledge that the earth was round. This was probably due to the high mountains in Greece that have a view of the sea. If the reader has ever had the experience of climbing a mountain of, say, 5,000 or 6,000 feet with a view of the sea, then the reader has seen the curvature of the earth; an experience which many people have had when flying in airplanes. The Greeks didn't need airplanes or spacecraft to see the curvature of the earth. They could just climb a mountain and see that the earth was round. In Isaiah 44:5–7, Yahweh proclaims Himself the only God. In 45:12 Yahweh is the original creator. Further along a few words (Isaiah 45:14), Yahweh prophecies the conquest of Egypt and Ethiopia by Israel and Israel's enslavement of its subjects. That hasn't happened in the ensuing 2,600 years. Maybe we should continue to wait. Perhaps Israel has an invasion plan prepared to conquer Ethiopia, although what benefits that would bring are somewhat obscure in the present times.

In Isaiah is also the prophecy of a birth of an Emanuel from a virgin, a prophecy that is referred to in the New Testament in the gospel of Saint Matthew. Most of the prophecies in Isaiah are, however, dedicated to the destruction of all the surrounding nations, conquest and wars, most of which have not happened since that time.

In fact, most of the Old Testament is devoted to threats from Yahweh and his priests of all kinds of killing, maiming, destruction, slavery, famine and illnesses to be wrought by Yahweh upon the Jews who do not worship Him and his priests, and on the surrounding nations whose land, riches and stock animals the Jews might crave. If someone would take the trouble to count what percentage of the words in the Old Testament are actual threats from Yahweh, one would find that is quite high. And what does the reader have to do to avoid all this suffering threatened by Yahweh? Maintain the racial purity of the Jews. Dominate the conquered lands and expel the non-Jews. Sacrifice animals and give bread to the priests of Yahweh who wrote these books, and also give them gold and silver. Not work on Saturday and, most of all, not worship other gods.

After the Torah, the ambitions of the priests of Yahweh are scaled down. The extermination of all the men, women and children of the peoples living in the promised land and the conquest of the area between the Nile and the Euphrates, not having been carried out by the Israeli tribe, the new plan is more to dominate the lands around the Jewish kingdoms and exact tribute from these peoples and enslave the remains of the conquered tribes which survived the Jewish invasion. The conquest of the entire promised land now depends more on Yahweh than on the force of Jewish arms, and is seen as being in the far future.

But if one follows in the path of Yahweh, obeys his commandments, sacrifices his food to the priests and worships Yahweh as the only God, then one may hope to avoid some of that death and suffering, mainly as Yahweh, God of the Armies, will fight the invaders or at least give strength to the Jewish armies to overcome their enemies. The only other blessings from Yahweh are lots of sons and daughters, rain and crops, and plentiful birth of stock animals.

In a land where human life was frequently taken by a sharp piece of bronze or iron, where medicine consisted of spilling the blood of a killed dove over the patient, where lions and other wild beasts attacked humans, where rainfall was scarce and survival was uncertain, and where milk with honey was the very apex of pleasure, the living of life was not worth much. The threat of death, or even prolonged suffering while alive, was not frightening enough to break the will of many people. Something more fearful was needed to keep the people in line. People looked at death as an escape from the suffering of their lives. To truly convince people, the taking away of this escape, even if only in thought, was a very powerful motivation. By convincing people that if they obeyed, once dead they would enjoy an everlasting ecstasy, and if they disobeyed they would suffer an everlasting pain of burning throughout their entire body, one could expect people would be more likely to obey.

Also the idea of the One God was a very powerful attractor to give the different peoples the opportunity to think of each other as the sons of the One God, all worshippers of the same God, and therefore the peoples should treat each other as brothers and respect each other. Also, the people wanted to think that a super-powerful creature was watching them and protecting them from harm. In the event of being seized by an adversary, the loser could say, 'Don't do harm to me, as God is watching us right now and if you harm me he'll make you suffer badly. Not now, because he won't interfere in events here, but in an invisible world that you can't see right now, he is preparing a dreadful punishment for you that you will suffer from forever, once you die.' Although it may not have convinced too many aggressors, it at least had to make them stop and think for a second.

All these powerful human urges crystallized in the writings about the life of Jesus Christ. The four official (or canonic) gospels suddenly appear in the Bible as the New Testament with all these (and other) ideas more or less developed. And although many of the miracles performed by Christ are not described in all four gospels, the radical change brought about by these ideas, as compared to the prevailing ideas and lifestyles in the area at the time, represented a substantial improvement in the human condition.

However, Christ was not the first to perform these types of miracles in the Bible. We find that Elijah and Elisha, who were high priests of Yahweh and at that time appointed the kings of Israel, also performed similar miracles. Samuel was the first high priest of

Yahweh from whom the people required that he appoint a king to rule over them (1 Samuel 8). Before this, the people resorted to judges to sort out the conflicts among them. The next high priest, Elijah, brings fire down from heaven to consume fifty soldiers sent to fetch him, twice (2 Kings 1:10–14). Elijah also parts the River Jordan so he can cross on foot (2 Kings 2:7–8). Elijah then ascended into heaven in a chariot of fire pulled by horses of fire (2 Kings 2:11). His successor, Elisha, also parts the River Jordan to cross on foot (2 Kings 2:12–15). Elisha sends two bears to kill forty boys who had taunted him (2 Kings 23, 24). Elisha makes water potable for a city (2 Kings 2:19–22). Elisha makes an endless supply of oil from one jar for a poor widow (2 Kings 4:1–7). Elisha revives a dead child and brings him back from the dead (2 Kings 4:31–37). Elisha makes poisonous porridge edible (2 Kings 4:38–41). Elijah multiplies loafs of bread to feed 100 men (2 Kings 4:42–44). Elisha cures the general of the Syrian army of leprosy (2 Kings 5:9–15).

The striking resemblance between these miracles and those attributed to Christ could be more than coincidental. The authors of the canonic gospels were familiar with the Jewish scriptures and make references to Christ fulfilling the prophecies of Isaiah and Elijah, although the authors were not familiar with Christ. The names of three of the authors, Mark, Luke, and John, do not coincide with the names of any of the apostles. Matthew, the fourth author, is the name of one of the apostles, but it is not thought that they were the same person.

Jesus Christ also converted water into wine, similar to Elisha and the empty jar of oil, and the conversion of the city's water supply into potable water. Christ walked on water, similar to Elijah and Elisha crossing the River Jordan on foot. Christ also cured the son of a foreign official, similar to Elisha curing the general of the Syrian army. And of course Christ revived a dead young man, just as Elisha did, and Christ multiplied loafs of bread to feed multitudes, just as Elisha did. Christ also ascended to heaven, though not in a chariot of fire like Elijah.

So we see that at the end of the Old Testament the returned Jews are trying to rebuild Jerusalem, but have no hope of regaining their former domination of the native peoples of the Jews' promised land, such as the Philistines (known as Palestinians today; the Philistines were actually the descendants of an invading tribe from Greece that settled in the area now known as Palestine. The Bible says some of them were blondes and giants, like Goliath. Teutonic Germanic tribes were among the ancient Bronze Age Greeks). The local tribes, warily and with misgivings, now permit the Jews to continue to return and rebuild their capital, only because the Jews are protected by the Persian Empire, the dominant force in the area. The Jews, under their new governor Ezra, set about purifying their race by sending away the wives who were not Jewesses as well as the mixed children. The Jews also expel from the congregation of Yahweh the Moabites and Ammonites, as a result of reading in Exodus that these peoples had attacked Israel when Israel had escaped from Egypt and was crossing their lands. The Jews also expelled all those among them who were mixed with foreigners (Nehemiah 13:3).

Even so, when the governor, now Nehemiah, goes on a trip to see the king of Persia, when he returns he finds that the temple is abandoned and that the people have stopped giving food to Yahweh's priests, which caused the priests to go work for food. Nehemiah remedies this by making the people bring food to the temple's storerooms. Also, he finds the people are going shopping on the Sabbath, a practice that he prohibits. Nehemiah finds many of the Jews left behind have taken non-Jewish wives and have children, some of whom speak foreign languages. He has some of them whipped and their hair torn out.

So Yahweh's religion is clearly meant for only the Jews, right through the entire Old Testament. The most important aspects remain, 1) not to work on Saturday; 2) to maintain racial purity; and 3) to give food and money to the priests of Yahweh.

Where then are the concepts of, 1) the one God; 2) the last day of earth and the Day of Judgment; 3) heaven and hell; 4) eternal life; and 5) good and evil, that form the basis of today's Christian and Muslim religions? Nowhere in the entire Old Testament will the reader find any concepts of this nature.

Not all peoples felt a need to worship the One God, to believe that all men were created by One God, or to think that all men were brothers. The American Indians, the Africans, the Indian Indians and the Orientals never developed these concepts. Only at the crossroads of three continents, where the trading routes between India and China, Europe, Africa and the Arab world met did this brotherhood of man idea arise. The Chinese, however, never developed the concept of God at all. The two main ideas in China are, and have been for 5,000 years, Taoism and Confucianism, not religions, but more like advice on how to live a prosperous and successful life. The two philosophies are based on a very ancient book called *I-Ching* (*The Book of Changes*) in which there is no concept of God. Rather, there is a concept of a creative force acting on a receptive force, encountering difficulties in manifesting its intentions.

The Inventor of Hell

The title of this chapter is misleading. Jesus Christ did not invent hell. Actually, the Bible tells us that he was born into a world where people were possessed by demons, which caused some diseases such as madness, muteness, blindness and epilepsy. Also, the concepts of a God ruling over an army of flying angels in the sky and a devil ruling over an army of demons in the bowels of the earth had already acquired some acceptance among the followers of Yahweh. These groups of Jews were known as Pharisees. The dominant group among the Jews and the priests of Yahweh were, however, the Sadducees, who did not accept any concepts of life after death, armies of angels or demons, or even absolute good and evil (Luke 20:27). The Sadducees outnumbered the Pharisees' sect by several times. Their religion, Judaism, remained based on the writing of the Jewish tradition, the Old Testament, plus the missing parts of the Old Testament that have been eliminated by Roman Emperor Constantine. This refers principally to the Maccabean scriptures and other books which covered the 400 years from the end of the Constantine Old Testament, which is official today, to the time of the birth of Jesus Christ. These missing 400 years of Jewish history are not missing in the Jewish writings. They have the books. Only in the official Holy Bible have these books not been included.

Muhammad's religion, further south, incorporated the local lore of the Jinn (Jeenies). Unfortunately for the Jews, these magic beings didn't travel far enough north to grant their three wishes. The minority Pharisees, into whose tradition Jesus Christ was born, mostly could not read. Hardly anyone in those days could read. There were very few books. Books consisted of scrolls of sheepskin and were copied by hand. There was a class of people who could read. They were called scribes. Their position had gained importance over the centuries, changing from similar to secretaries or bookkeepers to, in Jesus Christ's time, interpreters of the law. Since they could read the written books, they were the ones who could tell others what the written laws meant. The laws and the other written traditions of the Jews, the books of the Old Testament, were read out loud to the congregations on the Sabbath for a few minutes, were copied by hand to be passed to new synagogues, and were told as stories in religious meetings or study groups. Over 400 years of story telling, some changes were introduced into the story telling (oral tradition).

There have been stories among primitive men since men could speak. Thousands of tombs have been excavated from as early as 10,000 BC, in which humans are buried with possessions and treasure, even sacrificed dogs, horses, and human servants or concubines. The reason behind burying a useful weapon, tool or valuable treasure with its dead owner is the belief that the dead owner will have a new life after death and will use his things in the afterlife. This belief in an afterlife was common among prehistoric men in vast regions of the planet and still is today. However the Jews, as represented by the Sadducee sect in the time of Christ, never held this belief in their 3,000-year history. The Jews are only certain of what can be known through reason, rather than having faith in some invented stories, of which there were thousands in the time of Christ, some of which were better known and had more believers than others.

The Pharisees, however, had come under the influence of one of these stories. Although there were no official writings, the prophets of Isaiah, Ezekiel, etc., who wrote during the time of the invasions of Babylon and of the seventy-year captivity in Babylonia and upon the return of the liberated Jews to Israel, began to allude in scant passages to a burning hell, a final day, armies of demons under the dominion of the devil. This happened to be the religion of the dominant power in the area, Babylonia, who several times invaded the area and took the ruling Jewish elite as captives (2 Kings 17 to end; 2 Chronicles 28 to end; Jeremiah 52:1 to end). Babylonia left a puppet king over Judea, who foolishly appealed to Egypt to send troops to help Judea rebel against Babylon (Ezekiel 17:12–17). This caused Nebuchadnezzar, King of Babylon, to destroy Jerusalem completely and take all the Jews who had any property as slaves to Babylonia, leaving behind only the landless to serve as farm labor to the immigrants that he sent from his dominions to repopulate Judea.

It seems the captive Jews, having been taken by force as slaves into Babylonian lands to serve their masters, obviously would have regular contact with their masters' religion. In what is known today as the Stockholm Syndrome, some of them came to accept their masters as their friends. This process was made all the easier by a seventy-year captivity, in which two entire generations were born in Babylonian lands. Under these conditions it was remarkable that the original captive Jews could have such influence over their progeny born in Babylon to even maintain their traditions and religion, rather than being completely absorbed by their masters' ways and religion.

The Babylonian religion was just what the Pharisees believed in. It was one of the thousands of primitive stories that were common before the Iron Age. The story was that there were two great forces in the world, an absolute good and an absolute evil, that the evil was operated by a powerful general, who commanded armies of demon spirits, and the good was run by an equally powerful general who commanded armies of angels. These armies fought it out on earth as well as in the spirit world, and mankind was under their influence. The Pharisee sect of the liberated Jews who returned to Israel had, as many kidnap victims do, come under the influence of their masters' vision of the world and continued to tell these stories after being liberated by the invading Persian Empire, who allowed the Jews to return to their homeland. These ideas of demons, at least, may have been brought to Babylonia in commerce from India, where the earlier Hindu religion had demons, although they were giants with red skin, measuring 30 feet in height.

So the kidnapped Jews, once freed, mainly returned to the practices described in their books. However a minority, the Pharisees, continued to tell these stories of armies of angels and demons commanded by a good and evil spirit. If the Jews had been kidnapped by the Australian Aborigines they would have told stories of a giant turtle holding the world on its back; or if they had been kidnapped by the Arabs further south, they would have believed in Jinn that had supernatural powers. If they had been kidnapped by the Barbarian tribes further north, they would have believed in not washing, letting their hair grow, and killing a dead man's concubines, servants and animals and burying them with him for continued service in his afterlife. But this was the sect into which Jesus Christ was born and, since that time, billions of people have been looking for these angels and demons and trying to decide what is good for all humans and what is evil for all humans.

The Pharisee branch of Judaism did not commit their vision of the universe to any formal writing, although the find of the Dead Sea Scrolls in the 1950s, which seems to be an extensive, very large library of the Essenian sect, would be in this tradition. Rather, the Pharisees told these stories verbally and loosely anchored them to a few scant words found among the prophetic writings of Isaiah and Ezekiel, which we shall later examine. Perhaps this was due to suffering persecution from the mainstream Jews who controlled the temple and the synagogues, the Sadducees, and perhaps because very few of them had mastered the art of writing or reading, which was a rare skill in those days. In any case, even their tradition of storytelling was only more or less formally committed to writing by followers of Jesus Christ. It still remains as an oral tradition today among billions of Christians and Muslims who have lived since then.

It too is an idea that has *always* appealed to mankind. Like the great ideas that mankind has had – the One God brotherhood of man, resting on the seventh day (or more frequently if possible), getting rid of the capitalist owner of the factory and having the workers divide his profit among themselves, men thinking about women when they have free time, the fear of burning, the uncertainty of what happens to a human after death, etc. – mankind has always looked at the sky and birds as admirable and the earth and its dwellers – worms, maggots, insects – as unpleasant. Man, when seeing the relative mobility of birds, the quickness with which they travel and the apparent ease, imagining how exciting the view while flying is as well as the pleasure of the physical sensations, the freedom displayed by birds in both escaping so quickly from threats, moving from place to faraway place and being able to see so much... It certainly is an apparently enviable life. Thus were born angels. A man who had wings and could fly would obviously have a tremendous advantage over normal humans. Who has not spent some time of their lives wondering what it would be like to be able to fly? If superior beings go up while flying, obviously paradise must be up, not down. If fact, down is an obviously unpleasant place. Falling down is unpleasant, even dangerous or deadly. Digging in the earth immediately reveals what an unpleasant, impossible environment it would be to live in. In fact, it's where humans bury their dead in great parts of the planet. The creatures that live in the earth, slimy worms, creepy insects, crawly snakes, maggots, certainly have never inspired the admiration of mankind. Being in the earth is certainly to be avoided at all costs. So therefore paradise is in the sky and the human dead, decomposing in the earth, go down to Seol, Hades, the Underworld, eventually a burning hell, where even the dead will not escape eternal excruciating pain. Another great idea of mankind – fear the priest who can make you suffer eternal burning, just as you thought you could escape your human tormentors by dying.

In reality, this idea is so natural to mankind that the fact that it is barely written down in the New Testament, although Muhammad elaborates upon these ideas in the Qur'an, has in no way prevented Christians from believing in it. The only references found in the Holy Bible to this imaginary world of a good God sending angels to do his bidding and a Satan living in the bowels of the earth ordering forth demons to do battle with angels are the following:

Matthew 1:20, an angel appears to Joseph in a dream and speaks to him; 3:16, Jesus sees the spirit of God like a dove that descends from the sky and alights on him and a voice is heard from the sky; 4:1–11, the devil approaches Jesus, speaks to him, transports him to Jerusalem to the pinnacle of the temple, then to a very high hill. Then angels come to serve Jesus; 8:28–34, two Gadarenes have their demons expelled by Jesus into pigs.

Mark 1:9–11, Jesus sees the sky open and a spirit like a dove descends over him and a voice comes from the sky; 1:12–13, the spirit impulses Jesus into the desert where he is tempted by Satan and the angels serve Jesus; 1:21–28, impure spirit expelled by Jesus in synagogue; 1:32–34, Jesus cures many illnesses and expels many demons; 3:11–12, impure spirit prostates itself before Jesus and says, 'You are the son of God'; 3:14–15, the apostles had the authority to cure illnesses and expel demons; 4:15, Satan comes and takes away the holy words; 5:1–20, one Gadarene has a legion of demons expelled by Jesus into pigs.

Luke 1:11–25, Angel Gabriel speaks with Yahweh priest Zacharias to announce the birth of a son, John the Baptist, to him and his elderly wife. As Zacharias questions this possibility, Angel Gabriel makes him mute; 1:26–38, Angel Gabriel is sent six months later to speak with Mary to tell her of the conception of Jesus Christ. She too questions this but Angel Gabriel doesn't harm her; 2:8–15, an angel, as well as a multitude of celestial hosts, appear to some shepherds; 3:21–22, Holy Spirit descends upon Jesus in the form of a dove and a voice speaks from the heavens; 4:1–13, the devil speaks to Jesus, then takes him to a high hill and to the pinnacle of the temple. No angels come to serve Jesus in this gospel; 4:33–37, Jesus expels impure spirit from a man in a synagogue in Capernaum; 8:26–39, Jesus expels a legion of demons from one Gadarene into pigs.

John 1:29–34, John the Baptist says that he saw the spirit descend from the sky like a dove and remain above Jesus; 1:51, Jesus says to a disciple that he shall see angels if he follows him; 5:4, at a pool of water near Jerusalem some blind, lame, paralyzed people would sit waiting for an angel who would occasionally come and stir up the waters. The first one in the pool would then be cured; 7:20, a crowd accuses Jesus of being demon possessed; 8:44, Jesus accuses a crowd of being sons of the devil; 8:48–52, Jesus has an argument with a crowd of Jews about whether he is demon possessed; 10:19–21, a crowd debates whether Jesus is demon possessed.

Matthew 12:43–45, the impure spirit leaves a man and finds more spirits worse than him and returns to live inside the man with the other spirits; 22:29–30, in the resurrection there will be no marriages, but will be like the angels in the sky; 24:29–31, the son of man will come above the clouds and he will send his angels with a great voice of trumpet and will unite the chosen ones from the four winds; 25:31–46, when the son of man comes and all his holy angels with him, he will place the people who helped their fellow men on his right and they will inherit the reign of his father. He will say to those on his left, 'Cursed, to the eternal fire prepared by the devil and his angels.' They will go to eternal punishment and the just to eternal life; 28:1–10, Mary Magdalene and the other Mary (presumably the mother of the apostle Jacob as in the other gospels) see an angel of the lord descend from heaven, remove the sealing stone from the sepulcher and sit on it. His aspect is like lightning and his clothes as white as snow. The Roman guards tremble and are frozen with fear, but the angel speaks to the women.

Mark 6:7–13, Jesus expelled many demons and cured many illnesses and gave authority to his disciple over demons; 9:14–29, Jesus is asked to cure a boy who probably suffers epilepsy but says that this type of demon will not come out except by prayer and fasting; 12:25, the resuscitated dead will be like the angels who are in the skies in that they won't marry; 13:24–32, Jesus preaches that the son of man will come and his angels will unite the chosen ones from the four winds, but even the angels in the sky do not know when that day or hour will be; 16:4–8, Mary Magdalene, Mary mother of Jacob, and Salome go to the sepulcher of Jesus and see one young man seated dressed in long white robes who speaks to them.

Luke 9:1–6, disciples of Jesus are given authority to cast out demons and heal diseases; 9:37–42, Jesus expels a demon from a probably epileptic boy; 10:17–18, seventy apostles dominate demons; 11:14–23, Jesus expels demon from mute; 13:15–16, Satan is responsible for an illness; 20:34–36, Jesus preaches that the resurrected dead are equal to angels in that they don't marry, nor can they die, and are sons of God; 24:1–12, Mary Magdalene, Juana, Mary mother of Jacob, and other women who followed Jesus are spoken to by two men with shining clothes at sepulcher of Jesus.

John 20:11–18, two angels dressed in white appear to Mary Magdalene at sepulcher of Jesus and speak to her.

One can read that the only times any angels make any appearances in the canonic gospels are before Jesus Christ is born, after he dies, and when he has fasted for forty days in the desert. Apparently, being alive and not delirious from hunger is not conducive to seeing angels.

From these scant words, the oral tradition continues to grip the mind of Western man, conjuring forth an entire invisible world that no one has ever seen. Flying is great, heaven is up, being buried in the earth is bad, hell is down, an idea that reaches its limits when man flies high enough to experience lack of oxygen and deadly cold. Not much of a paradise in dying asphyxiated and frozen.

So there was already a prevailing oral lore among the Jews that admitted the existence of this invisible world when Christ was born. However, the emperor Constantine and the Council of Nicaea in AD 325 decided not to incorporate into the Bible the 400 years of history after the return of the Jews from captivity in Babylonia. An entire 400 years just lopped off the Holy writings, the Word of God. The gap in the writings makes it appear to a casual reader as if Jesus Christ was the one who originated these concepts, the good going up to be with God in heaven when they die – the bad being cast into an oven or burning inferno, the angels carrying out the orders of God, demons working tirelessly to possess men and make them suffer. Why would Constantine want to create this appearance, when in reality these concepts were promulgated by a heretic Jewish sect who had been indoctrinated into the Babylonian religion during their captivity, 400 years earlier? Perhaps a passage from Saint Lucas (12:4–5) best expresses the intent of Constantine. 'Do not fear those who can kill the body, but can do nothing more afterwards. I will teach you who you should fear. Fear he who, after taking your life, has the power to cast you into the inferno.'

If the beleaguered Roman government of the time could instill this concept into the population, it would certainly make crowd control a lot simpler. It would be a lot easier to control the populace by preaching to the masses a fear of an everlasting burning pain, rather than physically having to inflict a beating on large numbers of people who might fight back. One preacher could convince hundreds of people to obey, even thousands, whereas a man armed with a sword or a spear could only be counted on to intimidate a few people before he might be overcome by resistance. Another suspicious fact is that Constantine decreed that Christianity, or his version of it, would become the official religion of the Roman Empire, or Roman Catholic, as it is known today. This religion was imposed by force of law. Rome had tolerated dozens of religions previously, only persecuting those sects that created problems or violated Roman morals at the time. There really had never been an official Roman religion before that was imposed by law. Was Constantine so concerned that his subjects would be cast into hell upon dying, rather than arising into a blissful paradise? Or was he a pragmatic politician seeking to extend Roman rule for a time more in the face of overwhelming invasions and political pressures? In any event, the strategy failed, as Rome was soon conquered and the empire overthrown by Teutonic Barbarian tribes, and those tribes were the ones who went on to effectively impose Christianity on a conquered European population.

So what happened in those 400 years of missing Jewish history between the time of the release of the captive Jews from Babylon, their return to Israel and rebuilding of Jerusalem and the Temple of Yahweh, and the New Testament compiled by Constantine beginning with the birth of Christ? As the reader can see, the returning Jews at the end of the Old Testament are mainly concerned with maintaining racial purity, expelling the non-Jews or half-breed Jews from among them, and convincing their own not to even go shopping on Saturday, to do nothing on Saturday, and to give food to the priests of Yahweh so that they don't have to work.

Suddenly in the New Testament, 400 years later, the reader is faced with a totally different world. No longer do lions, leopards, and desert wolves seem to be feeding on the human population, as these creatures are not mentioned in the New Testament. In the Old Testament these predators are mentioned several times as living among the humans, and challenge the human domain of the land right up to the end of the Old Testament. The Old Testament tells us that the Jewish population, before the defeat by Nebuchadnezzar, the Babylonian king, was larger than the current population of Israel, some 6,700,000 people. How could these predators have lived among and fed on such a large human population when these animals need vast hunting grounds in order to hunt enough food to survive? Obviously the typical exaggeration of army and population numbers that was common among authors and storytellers of those times. In any event, at the time of Christ the human population has obviously increased as those animals have been exterminated by humans over the ensuing 400 years. Another major change is that the poor, ignorant Jews who were left behind by the conquering Babylonians have racially mixed with both the remnants of the peoples that the Jews had tried to exterminate, but who survived, and with the new settlers that the Babylonians had transplanted into the area (2 Kings 25:1–12) in order to break the Jewish traditions and ethnic pride.

In fact, the old kingdom of Israel is now populated by such a mixed race of peoples with varying creeds that the hardcore Jews who maintained their racial purity during the captivity in Babylonia and returned to repopulate Jerusalem, capital of Judea, have no dealings with the people of Israel, now known as Samaria, not even speaking to them or drawing water from the same well (John 4:7–9). Samaria was between Judea and Galilee, where Jesus Christ's family was from and lived, and the Jews who kept their family line pure continuously doubted Jesus Christ's credentials to be a prophet because nothing good could come from Galilee, nor had there ever been a prophet raised in Galilee (many citings in gospels too numerous to mention). So, although the Jews are still a majority in Jerusalem and the kingdom of Judea, in Israel, Galilee and the remainder of their old empire under Solomon there are a great mixture of peoples, principally Babylonians, Greeks, Macedonians, Romans and the pre-Jewish invasion tribes that survived the Jewish genocide and subsequent wars.

Another major change is the religion. In the Old Testament there is not one mention of demons possessing humans and living inside them. 400 years later, somehow, demons are jumping around everywhere. They take over people but only Pharisees, the minority Jewish sect, as the Sadducees didn't believe in demons, and cause them to be mute, deaf, lame, paralyzed, to act out of control and suffer some other diseases. Now there are demon expellers everywhere, some of whom make a living from their profession, some even traveling about seeking the demons continuously, known as traveling exorcists (Acts 19:13–17). There are also magicians, some of whom have big names and international fame. Simon the Magician had a large following in Samaria and the people thought his magic came from God (Acts 8:9–18). There were many magicians and magic books (Acts 19:18–19). Religion was big business and employed many people. The Temple of Diana in Efeseo was one of the seven wonders of the ancient world and supported a great many workshops of manufacturers of miniature copies of the temple or of the statue of Diana or of other religious trinkets, as well as the owners of stalls and salespeople who sold the artifacts to the public. Just like one will find today outside the Vatican or in Makkah. When Paul came preaching to Efeseo, a near riot broke out among the people employed in this industry, who demonstrated, shouting, 'Great is Diana of the Efesios!' (Acts 19:23–41) and forced Paul to flee for his life.

Also, the disciples of John the Baptist continued to go about preaching after Jesus Christ's death, not following Jesus Christ. Freelance demon exorcists had success, not just Jesus Christ and his disciples, and actually expelled these demons from the possessed people (Mark 9:38–40; Lucas 9:49–50).

There were also Hypocrites everywhere. Hippocrates' teachings were introduced by the conquering Macedonians, led by Alexander the Great. Jesus is credited with using the expression hypocrite as an insult (Matthew 7:5; Matthew 6:1, 2, 5, 16; Matthew 23 is all about Hypocrites; Lucas 11:37–53; 12:1–3; Mark 7:6; Matthew 15:3–7; Matthew 16:1–3). Even the apostle Paul accuses Peter of practicing hypocrisy (Galatians 2:11–14) when Peter sits and eats with Paul's Gentile disciples in Greece, but when some important Jews arrive from Jerusalem, Peter avoids contact with the Gentiles so as not to be ostracized by his fellow Jews. The Hypocrites must have been following Hippocrates' teaching of pretending to believe in the dominant religion in order to gain advantage for themselves. They also practiced the medical knowledge that had been taught to them, part of which was the cleaning of the eating plates and drinking glasses, washing the bedclothes, washing their hands before eating, practices which Jesus Christ disapproved of (Mark 7:1–23), even attempting to convince the Pharisees to give up this practice by equating cleanliness with hypocrisy and against the true religion (Matthew 23:25–26; Lucas 11:37–40).

However, the Hippocratic medical knowledge was extremely limited at this time and apparently ineffective, as the Jewish priests continued to practice the killing of a dove and dripping its blood over the patient and releasing another dove as a means to cure diseases. This practice was ordained in the early books of the Old Testament and is evidenced to continue in the life of Christ by his evicting the sellers of doves from the temple, even addressing them directly as more serious offenders than the money changers (John 2:13–16; Matthew 21:12, 13; Mark 11:15, 16). In any event, Yahweh, God of the Armies, is gone. The Jews have no armies at this time. In fact, the entire area is under the dominion of the Roman Empire and its gods, who however have no influence over the psyche of the Jews, as the Romans allow freedom of worship within the empire, so the Jews continue in their ways.

So what happened in Israel and Judea during the 400-year history suppressed by Constantine and missing from the Holy Bible? Quite a lot. Briefly, the Jews mostly remained quiet as many great empires came and went in the area. Firstly the mighty Persian Empire, of which King Cyrus had defeated the Assyrian, Babylonian Empire, and given the Jews the choice of returning to Jerusalem, was eventually attacked and defeated by Macedonian Greek armies under the command of Alexander the Great. After Alexander's untimely death, his enormous empire was broken up into three and ruled by the three principal generals of Alexander. The area of Israel was near the border between the Ptolemy dynasty descended from General Ptolemeus who ruled in Egypt, and the Seleucid dynasty, which ruled in Persia. The two generals and their descendants fought among each other and Israel was passed from one empire to the other several times. The area was composed of small, insignificant kingdoms. The Jews were a majority in Judea with its capital Jerusalem, but the kingdom of Israel had come to be called Samaria and was a very mixed land. Further north, the small province of Galilee had strong Jewish influence. The Philistines, descendants of Greek Teutonic Barbaric tribes that had come to the area in boats perhaps 2,000 years earlier, remained in their coastal area of Palestine (as they do now, Palestinian = Philistine) and the Lebanese remained in their coastal area centered around their cities of Tyre and Sidon. The Jews had also emigrated quite a bit and Jewish communities could be found in Iraq (Babylon, those who chose not to return), Egypt (especially in Alexandria and the delta area, again those who did not follow Moses' exodus) as well as the Greek cities in the Turkish coast.

The area itself became strongly Hellenized as it came under the dominion of the Greek culture. Many Jews came under the influence of Greek customs and ideas. This trend was accentuated by Antioc, king of one of the factions that the Seleucid Empire had broken up into. As ruler over Judea, Antioc sought to erase the Jewish religion by converting the temple in Jerusalem into the Temple of Zeus, the principal Greek god. Antioc also sought to destroy the Jewish writings, although there were too many copies for this to be possible, and he abolished the Sabbath, as well as circumcision. Antioc also tried to force Jewish priests to eat pig but, in general, they refused even when tortured by the Seleucid soldiers, and some became martyrs. This situation shortly led to the forming of a guerrilla force led by a family of brothers named Maccabee.

Due to the weakness among the Seleucid army due to constant internal warfare, the Maccabee fighters eventually succeeded in conquering the area, entered into Jerusalem and restored the Jewish cult. This date is today celebrated by the Jews as Hanukkah. The three main Jewish holy days are Passover, when the Jews sacked their Egyptian masters and escaped from slavery; Purim, when the exiled Jews in Assyria slaughtered 75,000 residents throughout the area with the approval and non-interference of the Persian armed forces; and Hanukkah, when a Jewish guerrilla force expelled the Seleucid army from Jerusalem and restored the cult at the temple. They are not very similar to the Christian holy days of fattening up for the winter during the Christmas feasts and celebrating the coming of spring with painted eggs and palm fronds.

The Maccabees succeeded in establishing a dynasty of kings and eventually gained the support of important factions combating between the Ptolemy and Seleucid Empires, and were allowed to re-establish a nominal empire dominating many of the surrounding peoples. Soon the Romans became influential in the area and conquered nearly all the old empires that Alexander had left behind after his death. At the time of Christ's birth, the Romans had troops stationed throughout the area, as well as a Roman administrator. The Jews were not allowed to have any kings, so high priests served the same function in the subjugated Jewish society. The high priests had for some time become shrewd politicians who were accustomed to forging alliances with invading forces against other Jewish pretenders to their position and practiced murder among themselves and betrayal.

There arose messianic fever among the Jews at the time of Christ's birth. A messiah was awaited who would lead the Jews in a revolution, like the Maccabee revolution 165 years earlier, to evict the Roman invaders and restore a Jewish kingdom. Many Jews conspired to organize revolutions and formed secret societies and religious sects, even small guerrilla forces with the purpose of animating resistance against the Roman occupiers. Sects of Sicarius arose that used daggers to assassinate political figures. Also sects of Zealots formed, who refused to pay tribute to Rome and maintained that any Roman who entered the temple should be killed. These words have survived to our day in many languages, i.e. in Spanish a *sicario* is a paid assassin; in English, to 'zealously' guard something.

Another sect that developed was the Essenians, who were commune-living faith healers, who expelled demons and practiced the laying on of hands to cure illness, but allowed no women among them. Jesus Christ borrowed much of his philosophy from this sect.

This missing 400 years of Jewish history was censored by Constantine and the compilers of the Roman Catholic New Testament because it showed only too well to the careful reader the development of the ideas that comprised the new official religion of Rome. It also showed the Jews' struggle against Hellenization and the very Roman Empire that Constantine was the emperor of, and was therefore likely to undermine Roman authority. But by eliminating the availability of this background information, Jesus Christ appeared to the average convert to be the divinely inspired predicator of this brand new world of an absolute good and an absolute evil, armies of angels and demons commanded by God and the devil doing battle, and mankind caught in the middle in the field of battle. The Jews have preserved all these books. It is their history. This is why they did not accept Christ, nor do they believe that he was even in the line of prophets. They can read the Jewish history books and see the environment into which Jesus Christ was born, the development of the ideas of those times, and where Jesus Christ's head was at when he developed his philosophy.

In fact, upon reading the official books of the Holy Bible, one can see that nearly all the miracles attributed to Jesus Christ were copies of miracles attributed to Elijah and Elisha, ancient prophets, as discussed in the previous chapter. One can also see the early germinating ideas that infiltrated the true Jewish religion, beginning with some scant passages in Isaiah, who wrote at the time that Judea asked Babylon for military assistance upon finding itself attacked by their fellow Jews from the kingdom of Israel. Babylon sent an army, but also occupied Judea after defeating Israel and its ally Syria.

Isaiah 2:19–21, the people will hide from Yahweh when His day comes. They will hide in caves and spaces between rocks and will throw their silver and golden idols to the moles and bats; Isaiah 6:1–3, Isaiah sees the Lord seated on a throne with seraphim above him. Each seraphim has six wings, with two they covered their faces, with two they covered their feet, and flew with two while they shouted; Isaiah 24:21–23, Yahweh will destroy the earth and will punish the armies of the heavens in the sky and the kings of the earth in the earth; Isaiah 26:19–20, the dead will live, their cadavers will resuscitate. Yahweh will come out of His place to castigate the dweller of the earth, and the earth will no longer cover her dead.

That was the beginning of it all. From a total writing of some 30,000 words attributed to Isaiah in the Holy Bible, some 250 words (less than 1%) describe this new heretic world, never before written about in the previous 600 years of Jewish writings. It seems that Isaiah was exposed to the conquering Babylonian's religious ideas, but only slightly influenced by them. The remaining 29,750 words are nearly all the standard fare of traditional Jewish writings, warning of the death and destruction to be wrought by Yahweh on just about everyone that Isaiah had ever heard of. The killing desolation, maiming, burning, bringing on of plagues, drought, warfare and slaughter that Yahweh will descend on all those who don't give food and treasure to the priests of Yahweh. In Isaiah's writings, mostly fire will be employed by Yahweh to eliminate the people that Yahweh disapproves of. In the earlier books of the Holy Bible, Yahweh will kill the hapless humans by using other humans formed into invading armies. Since at the time of Isaiah the Jewish armies are overwhelmed by all its neighbors, Isaiah resorts to fire, probably influenced by the dominant Babylonian religion. In Isaiah 27:1,

Yahweh will castigate with his hard sword Leviathan, the serpent dragon that is in the sea. Another reference to a religion (also Babylonian?) based on exposed dinosaur skeletons? These ideas of Isaiah form the basis for the last book of the Holy Bible, Apocalypses.

Isaiah's book is also the basis of the supposed prophecies of the birth of Jesus Christ, or so state the writers of some of the canonic gospels, when they claim that Christ's life went certain ways to fulfill some prophecy that had been written long ago. Isaiah 7:14–16, a virgin will birth Emanuel and while he is a toddler, the land of Syria and Samaria will be abandoned. This referred to the alliance that Samaria (Israel) formed with Syria to attack Judea. In any event, while Jesus Christ was a toddler, Samaria and Syria were certainly not abandoned nor suffered even a war or revolution; Isaiah 8:1–4, the Prophetess will birth a son to be named Maher-Salal-Hasbaz and before he can talk, the king of Assyria (Iraq) will take away the riches of Damascus (Syria) and Samaria. Is this another example of how ignorant people are? Billions of people say that verse 7 is the prophecy of the birth of Jesus Christ, even though he never acquired the name Emanuel, but in the next verse the prophecy of a prophetess birthing Maher-Salal-Hasbaz is of no importance.

The only difference between the birth prophecy in verse 7 and the next verse, verse 8, is that the verse 8 name is more foreign sounding than Emanuel and the mother is a prophetess rather than a virgin. So billions of people have selected the virgin rather than the prophetess. This is another great idea of mankind, at least Western mankind: the worship of the virgin mother. In fact, it is the major cult within the Roman Catholic religion, exceeded only by the cult to Jesus himself. Many people want to think of their mother as a saintly virgin. It is important to many people to visualize their mother as holy and pure, rather than committing the necessary acts of fornication to become pregnant. Try it yourself. Can you bring yourself to imagine your mother having sex? Don't you feel a natural revulsion that quickly leads you to become violent? Can this reaction be a natural instinct that all offspring feel in knowing that their mother's sexual activity could soon lead to another sibling being born who will compete for essential food and attention?

However, Jesus Christ's mother, the Holy Mary, was not the ideal mother that a son might wish for. In fact, although some confusion arises as to whether a brother of Jesus Christ named Jacob became an apostle (Galatians 1:18–19), Jesus Christ's parents and brothers strongly disapproved of Jesus Christ's preaching, at times trying to remove him from the temple and his preaching activities which were causing a dangerous (for Jesus) commotion (Luke 8:19–21; Matthew 12:46–50; Mark 3:31–35; Luke 2:41–50) and when Jesus's insistence on continuing his preaching had caused a death warrant to be issued for him by the Jewish council and high priests, his brothers actually taunt him as to why he does not come with them to Jerusalem for the annual feast of the tabernacles and risk being killed by the Jews, because his family do not believe in him (John 7:1–9). In the town of his family's home, Nazareth, Jesus Christ is unable to perform miracles as the people did not believe in him and had no faith that he could perform miracles in front of them (Matthew 13:53–58). This passage names Jesus's four brothers as Jacob, Joseph, Simon and Judas, and states that he had several sisters as well. It is clear that if Mary, mother of Jesus, had a virgin birth with Jesus, she certainly then took up copulating with her husband Joseph in a serious way, bearing at least seven children more. It is unclear in the Bible whether any of these brothers and sisters of Jesus were older than him. Jesus could not perform any miracles in his home town and was astounded at the incredulity of the people there (Mark 6:1–6). This passage again names the four brothers of Jesus as Jacob, Joseph, Simon and Judas. The English Bibles translates Jacob as James, which is completely incorrect, as the name James did not exist in those times. In fact, Jacob and Judas were the most common names among the Jews then, as the Jews were descended from the patriarch Jacob and were all sons of Jacob and were known as the people of Jacob. Judas was named after the kingdom of Judea and the people Judeus of that kingdom.

Only one of the four canonic gospels claim that Jesus's family were present at the crucifixion and none that they came to the funeral (John 19:25–30). Jesus's mother and her sister (Jesus's aunt), Mary mother of Cleofas, are introduced to the male disciple that Jesus loved at the cross. The other three gospels do not mention that anyone from his family was present at the crucifixion.

The following is a list of women present at Jesus Christ's crucifixion and burial:

Matthew 27:55–56, Mary Magdalene, Mary mother of Jacob and Joseph (probably Jacob, an apostle son of Alfeo, Matthew 10:1–4), and the mother of the sons of Zebedeo (the apostles Jacob and John, Matthew 4:18–22); Mary Magdalene and the other Mary (mother of Jacob abovementioned) were sitting in front of the sepulcher (Matthew 27:61); the two Marys abovementioned go to the sepulcher on Sunday morning (Matthew 28:1).

Mark 15:40–41, Mary Magdalene, Mary mother of Jacob the Minor and Joseph, and Salome are observing from far away the crucifixions. Mary Magdalene and Mary mother of Joseph see where Joseph of Arimethea places Jesus Christ's body (Mark 15:47); Mary Magdalene, Mary mother of Jacob, and Salome buy aromatic spices and go to the sepulcher where they find it empty except for a young man dressed in white who speaks to them. The women run out of the sepulcher and say nothing to anyone because they are afraid (Mark 16:1–8); the resuscitated Jesus appears to Mary Magdalene, from whom Jesus had expelled seven demons, and she goes to tell those who had been with Jesus, but they don't believe her (Mark 16:9–11).

Luke 24:10–12, Mary Magdalene, Joanna, and Mary mother of Jacob return from the sepulcher to tell the eleven apostles and the others of having seen two young men in the sepulcher with shining clothes. They are not believed.

John 19:25–27, mother of Jesus and his aunt, Mary wife of Cleofas, Mary Magdalene, and a male disciple that Jesus loved are next to the cross. Mary Magdalene goes to the sepulcher early on Sunday morning (John 20:1–2); Mary Magdalene sees two angels at the sepulcher (John 20:11–18).

So we see that Mary Magdalene is mentioned by name eleven times, Mary mother of Jacob and Joseph is mentioned seven times, and Jesus's mother Mary is mentioned once. Mary Magdalene is certainly expressly pointed out in all four gospels as a very important person to

Jesus, a fact that Dan Brown's famous book, *The Da Vinci Code*, has seized on to claim that Mary Magdalene was married to Jesus Christ and was pregnant with his child.

Jesus Christ's body is claimed by Joseph of Arimethea, and Nicodemo, members of the Jewish council. Jesus Christ's family is in no way mentioned as going to see him at the sepulcher or being involved in the burial in any of the four gospels. The question arises as to whether Jesus's family had washed their hands of him and wanted to avoid trouble with the authorities and the angry Jews, thus staying away from the execution and certainly the burial.

Yet the cult of the Virgin Mary is the strongest within the Roman Catholic religion, another example of how when an idea appeals to the psychic makeup of a large human population, people will make that idea true, regardless of whether there is any logical reason to believe in it. It is as if people look for some tenuous connection to some rational story in order to base their inherent archetypal idea and flesh it out, as though it had been real in the material world. When people are predisposed to believe in some concept due to their physical makeup or mode of life, or an instinct, they will be easily susceptible to any storytelling or teachings that claim that this basic concept was indeed true in the material world, even if it was in a faraway place, thousands of years ago.

This is how great ideas spread among humans, as well as scientific achievements. People will avidly look for new processes or products that will make their lives easier or give them more power over the material world. Also, when people hear a story that fits into a belief that they are predisposed to have due to their psychic condition, they will grasp this story as the material (real) reason why their belief should be true, and many of these converts will then preach the story to other people, thus causing the story to become more true as more people believe in it and support their own belief on the fact that other people also believe the same as them. Like a virus spreading among communicating computers, these great ideas among mankind are spread simply by the fact that, once originated by one human who communicates it to others, the other humans have a place in their psyches prepared to accept the idea. What makes an idea, story or moral great is the fact that many humans are predisposed to accept it.

Thus, even though the Bible tells us that Mary, the mother of Jesus Christ, and the rest of his family did not believe in him, that Jesus's brothers taunted him, tried to convince him to stop preaching, and certainly played no prominent part in supporting him at his crucifixion, not even appearing at the tomb, the cult of the Virgin Mary has become the strongest in the Roman Catholic religion. The virgin mother of whom? The saintly mother of every believer in this idea. Even the African Americans say that talking about one's mother is reason for a fight.

Another question arises. If Mary and Joseph were warned by angels that their child was engendered by the Holy Spirit and would save His people from their sins (Matthew 1:18–25), would reign forever over the people of Jacob (Luke 1:26–38) and Jesus Christ's birth was attended by three kings, angels, celestial hosts, shepherds who adored him (Luke 2:8–20; Matthew 2:1–12), why then, eight days later when Mary and Joseph take the baby to the temple to be circumcised, are they amazed because an old prophetess named Ana and a pious man named Simeon make short speeches declaring that the baby shall be glory to the people of Israel and the redemption of Jerusalem (Luke 2:21–38)? Were not the amazing supernatural beings that had manifested themselves eight days earlier more awe-inspiring than two very old Jews who hung around the temple a lot?

But back to Isaiah's writings. Isaiah was a prophet to King Hezekiah of Judea, who reinstated the cult of Yahweh (2 Chronicles 29 and 30). There were many seers, fortune-tellers, priests, and prophets who had served the previous king of Judea, or who served the king of Samaria (Israel), who did not worship Yahweh but rather worshipped other gods (Jeremiahs 27:9–10; prophets, enchanters, augurers, fortune-tellers, dreamers). Isaiah writes about his time and the warfare among the Jews and the changing alliances between Judea, Israel and Syria, and Iraq, the dominant power in the area. Isaiah was called upon by King Hezekiah of Judea to curse the Assyrian troops who had set siege to Jerusalem's walls (2 Chronicles 32:1–23, 2 Kings 18:13–36 and 19:1–37). Prophets served several functions in those days. One function was as fortune-tellers, as the kings, amongst others, would consult them for predictions on the outcome of future wars. Another was as cursers. The king would call upon them to curse the enemy so as to animate the people into fighting the enemy troops. The prophet's professional curses would both inform the people as to why they should take up arms and fight, and also animate them with predictions of victory. The curses would denigrate the enemy and his fighting capabilities in the eyes of the people so as to give them courage to take up arms. Sometimes they would curse the enemy directly, so as to discourage them, from the city's besieged walls. It was like a modern national government launching a propaganda campaign. The prophets' curses were the ancient version of a media blitz and press conferences launched by modern governments to prepare their peoples for an upcoming war. So their writings are a collection of all the great curses that they had thought up. Large portions of the Old Testament of the Holy Bible are simply the collections of the curses that famous prophets had written down. It is similar to classic advertising campaigns or propaganda preserved through thousands of years. Great curses such as Deuteronomy 28:56, 57, where the wives of the errant Jews shall secretly eat their own placentas and newborn babies after giving birth so as not to share them with their hungry husbands and children, express concepts and elevate cursing to heights seldom witnessed in other writings. It is curses such as these that make the Bible memorable. Whether people want to believe that the prophets' cursing constitutes an ability to predict the future, even after 2,500 years have passed without their predictions coming true, is a testament of how effective government propaganda can be.

Isaiah also wrote the original version of the Day of Judgment or Punishment. Isaiah 14:9–23 reads, 'The Seol awakened its dead so that they came to greet you. Your pride and the sound of your harps descended to Seol, worms will be your bed and worms will cover you. How you fell from the sky, Lucero, son of the morning. Dashed to earth were you who weakened the nations. You who said in your heart, "I will rise to the sky. In the heights, next to the stars of God, I will raise my throne and in the hill of testimony I will sit in the extremes of the North, over the heights of the clouds. I will rise and I will be similar to the Lord." But you are dashed down to Seol, to the most profound of the grave.' The whole of Isaiah verses 13 and 14 are curses against Babylon (Assyria), Syria and Israel. It was changed over hundreds of years of storytelling into the story of how Lucifer (Lucero, which means 'source of light') became the angel fallen to earth because of his pride and presided over the dead. It actually refers to the various kings of Babylon, who repeatedly invaded Judea and took away all the elite and property owners as slaves to work in Assyria. Isaiah was a top prophet and well-known curser. Obviously if the priests of Yahweh were paid with food to spare and treasure, the top prophets also were paid for their fortune-telling or cursing, and dedicated themselves professionally to these tasks, certainly not having to farm or herd goats to sustain themselves. So that one must assume that Isaiah was paid by the kings of Judea for his cursing and writing. Again, this cursing was directed against the enemies of Judea, as, at this time, Assyria (Babylon) was asked by Judea's king to attack Israel (Samaria), which had formed an alliance against Judea with Syria, and after vanquishing both Syria and Israel, the kings of Babylon, Salmanasar (2 Kings 17:1–6) or Tiglath Pileser (2 Chronicles 28:16–22) set siege to Jerusalem and made Judea pay a huge ransom to avoid being sacked by the supposedly allied Babylonian troops that had come to rescue them.

The entire Lucero passage is directed clearly against the Babylonian kings. Storytellers changed the names and the facts over hundreds of years of telling the story. Thus was born Lucifer, the top bad angel. Of course, with some modern translations of the Bible the words are completely changed so that the new translations have less and less relation to what was actually written back then, and more and more resemble the oral tradition that has become prevalent among the converts. The promoters of the modern translations want to leave no possibility that the reader might actually be able to read the closest possible translation of the ancient writings, but rather work the translation in ways that eliminate the obvious inconsistencies, weak points and outright nonsense.

What keeps the true believers from printing condensations of the Holy Bible, where they simply promulgate the parts of the ancient writings that tell the believer exactly what he is supposed to believe in? Why do the translations include all that ancient history? Why not just print the dogma and the supporting writings that are related to the oral tradition and leave out all that extraneous Word of God material?

Satan was also born in the same way. In Ezekiel 8:7–18, Jazzanias, son of Safan, is found by the visionary Ezekiel in one of his dreams when Ezekiel enters a hidden room through a door that he had to excavate from a wall. Inside he sees paintings of abominable beasts and reptiles covering the walls and seventy elders of Israel are burning incense and worshipping the images. Ezekiel also curses those who worship the sun and writes how Yahweh will kill them all and bring on the last days (Ezekiel 14:21–23), where war, famine, pest and beasts will destroy Jerusalem. This is the precursor to the four horsemen of the Apocalypse. Also, the roll written on both sides mentioned in this passage is copied by the author of the Apocalypse.

Over hundreds of years of storytelling, Jazzanias, son of Safan was changed into Satan or son of Satan and became mixed up with the Aramaic and Hebrew word for adversary. The hidden room with the paintings of the abominable beasts and reptiles was changed into the illustrations of Dante's *Inferno*. Ezekiel also curses people who practiced sex on top of altars in front of a congregation (Ezekiel 16:16–23), as well as those who decapitated their children and burned them in sacrifice to idol gods. Ezekiel had been a prisoner in Assyria, thirteen years when Jerusalem fell to Nebuchadnezzar, King of Assyria (Ezekiel 33:21–22), and when he wrote his book, so obviously he was under the influence of the Babylonia religion.

Beelzebub was already the prince of the demons (Luke 11:14–23) and the law interpreters say that Beelzebub was the prince of the demons (Mark 3:22). Pharisees say Beelzebub was prince of demons (Matthew 12:24). Obviously, Jesus did not invent this lore, but rather came into a world where it was fully developed. Beelzebub had been changed from Baal Zebub, the Baal god of the town by the same name. Since his name appears at the very top of the second book of the Kings Book II the storytellers and the congregations more easily remembered his name, as the prolonged reading of the lengthy books probably put the congregation to sleep, and so he became the prince of demons, because people remained alert during the first paragraph or two of the readings, then slowly drifted off into a stupor, thereby missing the names of all the other wondrous gods.

The changing of the pronunciation of names is inevitable as languages change over 400 years or in translations between languages.

Try to pronounce the name of the new king of Saudi Arabia. If you try Abdulah, Ahbdalah, Abdlah, Abduhlah, you still won't have it right, but at least you'll be getting closer, a name you should try to pronounce correctly as he is supplying most of your gasoline and petroleum by-products. The old king was known as Fahd in the West, but was actually closer to Fehad. And so was Ibrahim changed into Abraham and Gott changed into both God and Goth, as well as *Godo* in Spanish.

And so Jesus Christ was living in a world where demons caused many diseases. He dedicated himself to expelling demons and curing diseases in direct competition with the Hypocrites, thus his many derogatory references to them. They were in competition for followers who would supply their food and other needs. Jesus Christ was a faith healer. He practiced the Essenian cult's laying on of hands to expel the demons causing the disease. Every time he heals someone he says, 'Your faith has healed you.' His main miracles are expelling demons to cure diseases. In his home town, before his own family and neighbors, he cannot perform any miracles as the people have no faith in him. As we have seen, Jesus Christ was not aware of the germ theory of disease, as he righteously states that bathing and cleaning one's used glasses and dishes are hypocritical (Mark 7:1–23; Matthew 15:17–20). His philosophy is anti-Hypocrites. These days, people who go about not washing and expelling demons are locked up in mental hospitals. In those days, however, where life was much crueler, those people could be crucified.

John the Baptist followed in this tradition as he went about dressed in camel skin. He too was executed by the authorities. There was a type of legal war between demon expellers, exorcists, magicians and the Hypocrites for control over the means of curing the sick. This war was fought again at the beginning of the 19th century between the Hypocrites and patent medicine makers, as the Hypocrites succeeded in outlawing patent medicine makers and having them branded as charlatans and quacks. Severe legal punishment is meted out on those who try to cure people these days with non-regulated, non-hypocritical methods. The Hypocrites also won the war for the very profitable healing business over the Christian sect, as, although Jesus and the twelve apostles (and many other magicians and demon expellers) cured some demon-infested people, as the religion spread to areas where people didn't believe in demons, there were no more cures. In fact, the next generation of Christians gave up on expelling demons or curing diseases altogether and dedicated themselves to helping people avoid the burning hell once they died, an even more profitable business as we shall later discuss.

So the demon expelling business was a tiny blip in the history of mankind, lasting only some fifty years, perhaps, and limited only to Galilee (an area about 50 miles by 25 miles) and some surrounding areas, not even succeeding in Judea or Samaria and certainly not in areas not under the influence of the Essenian or Pharisee sects of Judaism. But that was how Jesus Christ got his big start. And as we all know these days, Hypocrites do all the healing by law in the industrialized countries.

The gospels tell us that Jesus was a direct descendant of King David and thus was a rightful heir to the combined throne of Judea and Samaria. In Matthew 1:1–17, there is a genealogy of Jesus Christ leading back to King David, and in Luke 3:23–38 there is a different genealogy, but also leading back to King David, another example of facts being fabricated to fit a story previously believed in. We also see that John the Baptist was a direct descendant of Aaron, the first high priest of Yahweh (Luke 1:5), and was thus qualified to be high priest of Yahweh. So Jesus Christ was a legitimate heir to the throne and John the Baptist was heir to high priest. Jesus Christ then spends his childhood in Egypt (Matthew 2:14–15). When Jesus Christ's life becomes public, he is mostly expelling demons and curing diseases, but he also manages to copy the miracles performed by Elijah and Elisha in 1 Kings 17 to 2 Kings 8, on a grander scale, which seems appropriate since they were only prophets and Jesus Christ was the son of God. Unfortunately, none of the four canonic gospels seems to have been written by anyone who actually saw Jesus Christ.

Although Matthew was the name of an apostle, the author Matthew claims that Matthew was the name of the publican (tax collector) called by Jesus Christ (Matthew 9:9–13) whereas in Mark 2:13–17 and Luke 5:27–31, the tax collector's name is Levy. The author Matthew in fact demonstrates a lack of familiarity with the geography of the land he writes about, whereas Mark and Luke are much more specific about the names of the towns, etc. John seems to write about stories that he has heard. No writings by Jesus Christ are ever mentioned anywhere, unlike the Qur'an, which was codified by the senior followers of Muhammad a decade after his death and preserved in its original language. It is strange that there are letters written by Peter, John and Judas, apostles who spent several years with Jesus Christ, but none of them felt moved to write a gospel of the life of Jesus or even summarize his teachings. This task was left to unknown authors who lived hundreds or even thousands of kilometers away and many decades after Christ's death, and who never had any direct experience of the events they wrote about. Could it be that Jesus Christ, being a simple carpenter, never learned to write?

When Constantine and the council of Nicaea selected the gospels and other writings to form part of the new official Holy Bible and words of God, a number of gospels were also left out, besides the 400 years of missing history of the Jews. Constantine selected these four gospels from among possibly more than eighty other gospels, many of which are still available today in the Vatican library, or other sources, and which are known as the Apocryphal Gospels. Apparently the suppressed gospels were either badly written, preached heretic creeds, or were just plain silly. So the four canonic gospels are the least silly of more than eighty other possible gospels relating the life of Jesus Christ.

So Jesus Christ did not invent hell, and the paradise he taught us about was not as vivid as Muhammad's paradise. In fact, whereas Muhammad's paradise was mostly about having sex, in Jesus Christ's paradise there is no sex (Mark 12:25; Matthew 22:29–30; Luke 20:35). Jesus Christ's hell also is pretty undefined, not necessarily involving eternal burning. Often it seems to be an oven (Matthew 13:37–43 and 47–50), or burning straw (Luke 3:17, Matthew 3:12). In fact, the Greek story about Hades is still very influential in the New Testament (Matthew 11:23; Luke 10:15) and in Luke 16:19–31, a rich man and a poor man die and go to Hades, where they can see each other. The rich man is tormented by flames and asks the poor man, Lazarus, to bring him some water, but Abraham explains to Lazarus that he cannot cross to the other side because they are separated by a big *sima* (unknown word). The poor man's joy consists of being with

Abraham and the holy prophets. This story also confuses the story of Lazarus returning from the dead in John 11.

In Luke 7:11–17, Jesus Christ brings back from the dead a young man, the son of a widow. The Lazarus revival is not mentioned in any other gospel, nor is the son of the widow's revival. One might expect that bringing a person back to life would be a feat generally talked about, and not just mentioned in one sole gospel.

In Mark 9:42–50, hell is an inferno where the worm doesn't die and the fire never goes out. In Matthew 25:30, the useless servant is thrown out into the darkness, obviously no fire there. In fact the only mention of everlasting fire is in Matthew 18:8–9 and Matthew 23:33 where inferno is mentioned. So the entire burning hell story is based really on Matthew 25:31–46, 'Cursed, to the eternal fire prepared by the devil and his angels'. A total of twelve words which formalize the Christian concept of burning hell, devil, and demon angels held by billions of Christians since that time. More than 100 words are used by Luke to describe Lazarus's stay in Hades, the Greek Underworld. This is the very definition of an oral tradition. All the eternal burning hell and purgatory stories have simply been related orally for 2,000 years. They are not actually written anywhere. It's simply a story that people tell, passing it on from generation to generation, just like the Santa Claus story.

Why has this oral tradition taken such a hold on mankind's imagination? Because it is another of the great ideas that human brains are prepared to believe in. Many people want the existence of a killer God, to judge and punish the harmful acts performed by others against us. The burning hell is the most painful punishment conceived by man. Just the possibility of the existence of the killer God and his burning hell can be useful to a human when faced with someone who is about to harm him, as by trying to convince the aggressor of this terrible punishment that awaits him, one can often avoid harm. In fact, the human desire to set up a hierarchy of judges and punishers over human societies is paramount, as every nation has had a court system, police, and prisons for the last 100 years or so. For the thousands of years before police were funded by the state, punishment for harming a person depended a great deal on the status of the person who had been harmed. But even so, the desire for an all-knowing, all-powerful punisher of those who harmed one has been an overwhelming need of mankind throughout the planet. So the myriad gods in the ancient world didn't fit this mold. They were bland gods, seldom killing humans. Once Yahweh, God of the Armies, became mixed up with the Babylonian general of the flying angels and the burning oven was elaborated upon in the teachings of Jesus Christ and his disciples, then was the formula created for a truly successful invisible world. A very deep human need for an all-good, all-powerful, all-knowing, omnipresent God who punished those who did one harm with the pain of burning for eternity seemed to be fulfilled by a few words committed to sheepskin rolls or papyrus leaves, and the legend was passed on from person to person, generation to generation, because if every human believed in this story then all the people would treat each other with consideration. Unfortunately, if some humans didn't believe in this story, or just not in the same way, then those humans would have a very big material advantage over the believers. They would be like wolves among a flock of sheep, doing pretty much what they wanted. In fact, an entire religion was created designed to take advantage of this very bad structural flaw in the Christian doctrine: Islam.

Jesus Christ's religion was originally intended only for the Jews (Matthew 10:5–6). Jesus Christ refers to a Greek woman as a dog (Matthew 15:21–28). Paul was the disciple who was accepted by the apostles Jacob, Cefas and John, to preach to the non-circumcised, while the apostles continue to preach to the circumcised (Galatians 2:1–10). Paul accuses Peter of practicing hypocrisy when Peter eats with Paul's disciples regularly, who are all Gentiles, but when Jacob and other Jews arrive, Peter stays apart from the Gentiles for fear of what the other Jews might say (Galatians 2:11–14). However, in Matthew 8:5–13, Jesus Christ, impressed by the request for healing from a Roman centurion, states that the reign of the heavens will have many non-Jews in it. Paul was the apostle who allowed non-Jews into the Nazarene cult. The original apostles, following Jesus Christ's prejudices, did not.

Paul became the most important preacher of the Nazarene cult, as early Christians were known. People were so prejudiced in those days that even the city where one was born was of utmost importance, even becoming attached to one's name. In fact, those living in a city shared the cult of the city's god and were obligated to live by the city's morals, so that everyone from a particular city was pretty much like everyone else and thus could be typecast easily. It was Paul who gave Christianity the impulse that allowed it to break out into the wider world and become popularized among many peoples. If it hadn't been for Paul's drive and organizational skill, the cult of the Nazarene would probably have remained a minor footnote in history, lost in the dusty archives of history buffs, just as the Essenian and the Sadducee cults' histories are. Paul wrote nearly all the epistles in the Bible. Peter, the founder of the Roman Catholic Church, only two. Peter was a simple fisherman. Paul had military training and captained a troop of guards that were formed by the Jewish council of Jerusalem to suppress the heretic Nazarene cult that insisted on invading their temple and preaching to the congregation. This would be like a layman frequently entering a Christian church today during mass and insulting the priest and deacon and preaching, let's say, the Hindu religion to the congregation. Paul was even sent on at least one military expedition to Syria in the pay of the Jewish council, to imprison the upstart Nazarenes who were invading the synagogues in Damascus. On the way to Damascus, he became blinded for several days and during his blind spell converted to Christianity and recuperated his sight.

Or maybe not, as Paul himself never mentions this in his epistles, actually stating that 'when it pleased God to reveal His Son in me so that I would preach among the Gentiles, I was in no hurry to consult with flesh and blood. Neither did I go up to Jerusalem to see those who were apostles before I, but rather I went to Arabia and then again to Damascus' (Galatians 1:15–24). Quite a different story from the miraculous conversion in Acts 9:1–25.

After three years, Paul met Peter in Jerusalem and Jacob, a brother of Jesus Christ, but apparently not an apostle. Paul then began to gather followers among the Gentiles, who preached with him, and returned to Jerusalem after fourteen years (Galatians 2:1–10). After some friction with the supposedly important people in the sect and with false brothers who had introduced themselves into the sect, Paul received a handshake from three of the apostles, approving his mission of preaching to the Gentiles. Paul then organized churches in at least Rome, Corinth, Galatia, Efeseo, Filipos, Colossus, Thessalonica, cities which were many of the major centers of civilization in the northern Mediterranean. Peter seems to have organized churches among the Jews in Ponto, Galatia, Capodocia, Asia Minor and Bitinia.

There were far more Gentiles than Jews and so the possible convert base was so much larger for Paul's preaching than for all the other Jewish apostles that Paul became the dominant influence in the organizing of the international Christian sect. Paul set up bishops and deacons who ran the local churches, and maintained traveling preachers who would go from church to church checking that the parishioners did not institute new or unapproved practices and did not follow other early Christian preachers who preached unapproved doctrines, as well as collecting the yearly payments from each local church to bring back to Paul's central command post. Paul names the traveling overseers of his as Tito, Timothy and Appollos. Paul's military training allowed him to set up the structure of the church in a way that functioned. This structure has survived to this day and its success is based on it being constituted as a conquering army, a spreading empire, that has its central command center, the Vatican, and the local commander, the parish priest, collecting tribute from the population and remitting a portion of the collection up the ladder of command for the maintenance and profit of the commanders. It really was efficiently set up as an army to conquer men's minds.

And the tribute was unlimited. The early Christians were communists and were prohibited from having any personal property. They sold their property and donated all their money to the twelve apostles, who used the money collected to support the community, who didn't work (Acts 5:1–11; in this passage God kills a couple who sold their property and lied about the price to the apostles so as to keep some of the money). So this practice became far more profitable than expelling demons. Whereas a demon expeller might collect a gift from the patient's family and a free night's lodging with a meal or two, the preacher who convinced a new convert to join the religion got all the new convert's property! The trick was to convince the new convert that he would not be needing his house or his land or his treasure because the end of the world was coming. In his lifetime

Jesus Christ would come back and the stars would fall from the sky and the earth would be burned and only those who had given their property to the Christian sect would have a new eternal life of bliss in Jesus's new kingdom, whereas those who didn't would be placed in the oven of fire and cooked and burned forever. Paul and Peter and all the writers in the Bible after Christ's death write of the approaching end of the world, as this generation would not pass before the earth is completely destroyed by God and his angels.

Paul expected the end of the world, the revival of the dead, and that he and the other believers would be taken alive up to the sky to live in the clouds as Jesus had said, 'This generation shall not pass without the second coming of the Son of Man' (1 Thessalonians 4:13–18). 'The end of all things approaches' (1 Peter 4:7). 'The sky and earth that exist now are reserved by the same word, reserved for the fire on the day of the judgment and the perdition of the unholy men' (2 Peter 3:7). 'Then the heavens will disappear with great thundering noise, the elements will burn and will be undone, and the earth and the constructions that are upon it will be burned' (2 Peter 3:10). 'But we await, as by His promises, new skies and new land, in which justice will live' (2 Peter 3:13). 'Sons, now is the end of time. As you have heard that the anti-Christ will come, now have arisen many anti-Christs, for this we know that it is the end of time' (1 John 2:18). 'When the Lord Jesus manifests himself from the sky with the angels of his power, in a flame of fire, to give retribution to those who did not know God nor obeyed the Gospel of our Lord Jesus Christ' (2 Thessalonians 1:7–8).

The last book included in the Holy Bible, appropriately, is Apocalypse, great parts of which were copied from earlier prophetic books, mostly Isaiah and Ezekiel. Apocalypse (or Revelation) of course seeks to describe and give credibility to the imminent cataclysm that would put an end to the entire world, an event difficult to conceive of given the technology of the time. Thus the entire gist of the sequence of books is 'the end of the world is upon us'. So this teaching was very profitable to the early Christian Church and caused its success in the world that, after all, didn't end. But even though the very reason for its being – its main prediction, to warn mankind about the upcoming end of the world in that generation – never happened, the church just kept on going and became big business. This was due to the massive income generated by convincing converts to give to the church all their possessions. And, of course, everyone is afraid of death and a personal death is like the end of the world for that person, so the religion was soon changed more to the fear of what will happen to one when one dies, rather than to the fear of the imminent end of the entire world.

So we see that many people of all types were quickly attracted to this new religion, many of whom seemed not to be acceptable to the established leadership. Various Church leaders appointed by Paul abandoned the faith and introduced their own creeds (2 Timothy 2:16–18). Anti-Christs were everywhere, renegade converts to Christianity were preaching alterations to the apostles' teachings (1 John 2:18–19). Early Christians wanted to follow those who baptized them (1 Corinthians 1:10–13), also used the communal supper, now the Holy Mass, to get drunk and stuff their faces (1 Corinthian 11:17–34). False apostles sought to take over the Corinthian church (2 Corinthians 11:1–15), others preach false gospels to Galatians (Galatians 1:6–9), Paul is still persecuted for not preaching the need for circumcision (Galatians 5:11–12). Others preach the end of the world is near (2 Thessalonians 2:1–4). Paul writes to Timothy, 'When I asked you to stay in Efeseo, when I went to Macedonia, so that you would send some who don't teach different doctrines, nor pay attention to fables and interminable genealogies' (1 Timothy 1:3–4), was Paul referring to the gospels of the New Testament and the two different genealogies of Jesus Christ that both lead back to King David?

'Some will lose the faith listening to lying spirits and doctrines of demons, from hypocrites and liars. These will prohibit marriage and will order the abstaining from certain foods' (1 Timothy 4:1–5). 'Some of the supposed converts serve only their own bellies' (1 Romans 16:17–18).

There were false teachers among early churches, even negating the existence of Jesus Christ (2 Peter 2:1–3), for the purpose of avarice they will make merchandise of the converts (1 Peter 2:3). Many false prophets have come out in the world (1 John 4:1–6). Many preachers have come out in the world who do not confess that Jesus Christ has been incarnated (2 John 7 to 11). John recommends the replacement of a church leader, Diotrefes, as he has rebelled against the central leadership (3 John 9 to 12). Some men have entered secretly into the church preaching false doctrines (Judas Apostle Epistle 4 and 12). 'We are not as many who benefit themselves falsifying the word of God' (2 Corinthians 2:17). 'And from among you will rise up men who will speak perverse things to gain disciples for themselves' (Acts 20:30).

So we see that the credulity of the converts and Paul's organization of the congregations to collect donations and give their goods to the leadership led to a situation in which many preachers joined the early churches with the intention of benefiting financially from their positions as preachers, even attempting to take over the control of some churches entirely. It was like a deregulation of preaching. The basic Christian credo, combined with the killer God Yahweh and the Babylonian angels, demons, heaven and hell, was a triumphant thought pattern that found a receptive spot in many human psyches. The credo opened up opportunities for small-time operators to compete with established religions.

Many early Christians took advantage of the faith-based religion to pervert the apostles' intentions for their own gain and profit. The apostles had a difficult time trying to maintain control over the entire Mediterranean basin, considering the slowness and difficulty of communications in that era, and the dispersal of the rapidly expanding congregations. Was the Roman Catholic Church one of those perversions of early Christianity?

In fact, whereas the early Christian Church solicited donations from the congregation and required the converts to contribute all their worldly goods to the apostles, this practice was voluntary. The Holy Inquisition, however, instituted by the Roman Catholic Church, was not an organization that gave its victims the option of contributing or not. For five centuries, between 1200 and 1600, the Vatican, in league with governments in Portugal, Spain, France, the Netherlands, Belgium, Italy and the Germanic states, assassinated some 10,000,000 people in Europe, nearly all of whom suffered excruciating deaths from torture or from being burned alive. The reason for this mass murder was to expel from the lands Arabs and Jews and to exterminate any sects that opposed the authority of the

Vatican. The practice of confiscating all of the victim's property led to an orgy of torturing and killing on the part of the Holy Inquisitors, as the confiscated treasures and properties enriched those in power in the Holy Inquisition and consolidated the Roman Catholic Church as one of the richest and most powerful organizations on earth. Even the name Holy Inquisition stands out as an abomination. They were 'inquiring' as to whether one really believed in Jesus Christ and the invisible world associated with his religion, or one was merely pretending to.

Does the reader believe that if the Holy Inquisitors, who were mostly descendants of the God tribes, had not murdered 10,000,000 non-worshippers during 500 years, the reader today would still have the belief and fear of God that the reader has probably has through-out his life? or that the belief and worship of God would be so widespread? Was this conscientious, concerted, continuous mass murder of opponents to the ruling status of the God tribes during those 500 years not the real reason why there are so many worship-pers of God today? It became so dangerous to *not* worship God for so many centuries that eventually the population surrendered and obeyed, and that fear of being tortured and burned alive still propels many Christian sects today, and is the root cause of their existence.

If one would argue that the murder of 10,000,000 people was ordained by the God in heaven rather than just by the descendents of the ruling God tribes here on earth, does the reader want to worship with the followers of a God that has done such terrible things while, at the same time, preaching brotherly love and peace on earth? If so, is that not the definition of hypocrite rather than Christian?

Muhammad's history was also similar to the experience that Paul and the apostles had in setting up their organization. Muhammad also relied on a traditional body of superstition, conquering the lucrative site of the annual pilgrimage to Makkah and incorporating the widely diffused belief in Jinn, as well as the traditional Babylo-nian, and then Christian lore of angels and demons. The Christian preachers had done a great job for the preceding 600 years of laying the groundwork for the acceptance of this belief in an all-good God and his army of angels, doing battle with an all-evil devil and his army of demons in all the Middle East and Egypt (where the vast majority of peoples were Coptic Christians before the Muslim conquests), throughout modern-day Turkey, and of course Christianity had become the official religion of both the Western and the Eastern (Byzantium) Roman empires.

Muhammad basically taught that one must submit to Allah (that's what Muslim means in Arabic), and that the Muslims must have a spirit of community, and Muhammad galvanized his followers into attacking and conquering non-believers. Immediately upon Muhammad's death, his followers degenerated into just plain attacking and conquering anyone who might pay tribute, regardless of whether they were believers or not.

Muhammad also expanded upon Jesus Christ's ephemeral concepts of heaven and hell and made them much more real and easier to understand. In paradise one would have cool underground water, shady gardens, desert fruits and many virgin women to copulate with. These days, the underground water, the shade, and the desert fruits have been completely eclipsed by many virgin women as the main selling point of Islam's paradise.

Hell was also quite clear. Allah would set one's skin on fire and the skin would grow back and burn off again, and so on for eternity. Muhammad made quite clear what he was selling to his congregation. Hell is described graphically some thirty times in the Holy Qur'an, and paradise some thirty-six times, unlike the twelve words dedicated to the entire concept of hell in the Holy Bible.

And so Paul's organizational skills allowed the Christian concept to take root and expand into the minds of the Mediterranean population. The siphoning off of the converts' contributions to unscrupulous preachers became a major problem. Another problem that arose was the fornicating among the congregation. Jesus Christ had lived a life in which unmarried men and women were allowed to mix, and traveled with him, camping together. Many women followed Jesus Christ from Galilee, serving him (Matthew 27:55–56) – women who followed Jesus Christ and served him (Mark 15:40–41), women who supported Jesus Christ with their goods (Luke 8:1–3) and the women who had followed him from Galilee (Luke 23:49). This is not allowed in Islam, being a great sin; a woman may not even speak to a man who has not been previously introduced by her family, nor may be in public with any man who is not her husband, brother or father. Jesus Christ also sought to abolish the practice of stoning to death an adulteress (John 8:1–11), in effect de-penalizing what was a crime punishable by death. Mary Magdalene is identified in Luke 7:36–50 and 8:1–3, John 11:1–2 and Mark 16:9 as a prostitute who had seven demons expelled by Jesus and became his near constant companion.

Jesus Christ also sought to eliminate the practice of divorcing a wife by giving her a letter and thus avoiding any financial responsibility or payments of alimony, so that many women were attracted to this new religion that gave them some measure of equal rights. In fact, women were allowed to be deaconesses in the Christian churches (Romans 16:1).

However, Paul soon came to disapprove of this coming out of the women, which apparently led to fornicating in the congregations (1 Corinthians 5:1–13). In fact, one of the many heretic sects of early Christianity was the Nicolites, which practiced orgies and ritual copulation. These practices were unpalatable to Paul, who himself abstained from sex and recommended that the Christians may want to follow his example as the end of the world was near and they could avoid carnal problems by holding out for a little while (1 Corinthians 6:12–7:40).

In fact, Paul orders that women not be allowed to speak to the congregation (1 Corinthians 14:33–35) and also that they must cover their hair when attending mass (1 Corinthians 11:2–16). So Paul rolled back the rights that women had acquired in the early Christian churches and also, due to his personal dislike for sex (it seems all the other apostles were married, 1 Corinthians 9:3–5), Paul reprimanded sexual activities among the early Christians. This passage seems to confirm that the apostle Jacob, who accepted Paul as apostle to the Gentiles, was not Jacob the brother of Christ, whom Paul also met, and that, therefore, of the brothers of Jesus Christ none became apostles – Jacob was the most popular name in Judea along with Judas.

Paul's orders to the congregation formed the basis for the celibacy vows of the Roman Catholic sects, such as monks, nuns, and of course priests and their hierarchy. In fact, Paul even recommends, as did Jesus Christ (Matthew 19:11–12), that a true convert may want to consider castrating himself and become a eunuch. So Paul's writings demonstrate that he was anti-sex, anti-women, and a very motivated organizer. The other apostles, the ones who had actually spent three years with Jesus Christ, were not, but it was Paul's military training and mindset that forged the Christian Church and allowed it to remain unified, thus his influence formed the basis for all of the existing Roman Catholic Church structures.

The main thrust of the teachings of Jesus Christ was the Golden Rule. Love God with all your being and love your neighbor as you love yourself (Matthew 22:34–40; Mark 12:28–34; Luke 6:27–36; John 13:31–35). Paul saw his purpose in life somewhat differently, adding 'vanquish evil with good' (Romans 12:21). That is to say that his irreproachable good conduct was an effort to win over the minds of men from the evil they were immersed in, once again revealing his military training and his outlook on life as a battlefield. This attitude is appropriate for missionary preaching, but the 'love your neighbor' attitude is quite different to 'vanquish evil with good'. Whereas we all have neighbors and can choose to love them, the main thrust in Paul's preaching was that there was an absolute good and an absolute evil, prepositions that are debatable.

For example, imagine the reader is a survivor of a boat sinking and is marooned in a life raft, and there is a person who did not survive also in the raft. The reader has no food or drink and is starving to death, and the dead person is the only possible source of food or liquid. Would the reader be good to die of thirst and hunger? Would the reader be evil to eat the dead person and drink his fluids? If the person was not quite dead but was obviously dying soon, would the reader be evil to kill the dying person in order to eat and drink him?

If the reader came to a water well in a burning desert and there was only enough water to allow one person to survive the trip to the next well, and another person arrived at the same time in the same situation of serious dehydration, would the reader be good to let the other person drink all the water available and cause the reader to die of thirst? Would both people be good to divide the water between them and both die of thirst during the trip to the next well? Would the reader be evil to drink all the water available and cause the other person to die of thirst?

The Christian nations espouse the belief that everyone that has been born, or has the possibility to be born, must be kept alive by the good humans, utilizing any means possible, including machines that do the living for the clinically dead. This concept is known as the sanctity of human life. Supposedly a human life has no price. Legally, however, a human life when lost due to the negligence of a culpable party has a price equivalent to a certain amount of currency and this price varies considerably from, let's say, $10,000,000 for a US citizen victim of the Boeing 747 Lockerbie bombing (which was the figure legally agreed to by the Libyan government, the other governments involved, and the victims' families), to less than $100 for a traffic accident victim in many poor African countries. In any event, this concept leads to other concepts logically deduced.

If a situation required the trading off of one human life for two human lives, are the two priceless human lives worth more than the one priceless human life? If a human dedicates himself to killing other humans, does his priceless human life become valueless?

The concept 'priceless' really means eternal. If something is so valuable that its price has no limit, then its price is a figure eternally large. So the reason that a human life has an eternal value is the belief that human life is eternal. If it was doubtful that a human life is eternal, but rather possibly ends at bodily death, would a human life become less valuable? Many people say that the lynchpin of the Roman Catholic religion is the belief among Catholics of the dogma that Jesus Christ was crucified, was dead for three days, then resuscitated from the dead and appeared to his disciples. Then Jesus Christ was ascended into the heavens (where possibly he died from asphyxia and cold, since he hasn't been heard from since). Paul himself, the creator of the Roman Catholic Church's structure, states that, 'If the dead do not resuscitate, then Christ also did not resuscitate, and if Christ did not resuscitate, our faith is in vain... If only in this life do we await Christ, we are the most deserving of pity among men' (1 Corinthians 15:12–19). If Christ was crucified on Friday and died Friday evening (Luke 23:54; John 19:31; Mark 15:42; Matthew 27:62–28:1) and was then resuscitated by Sunday at dawn, when Mary Magdalene went to the sepulcher (Luke 23:55–24:3; John 20:1; Mark 16:1–4; Matthew 28:1), then Jesus Christ was dead for two nights and one day, not three days as the prophecies and the very same gospels state.

In Luke 23:26–24:12, the sun darkens and there is darkness over the land and the veil of the temple tears in half. Christ expires on the cross. The centurion states that, 'Truly this man was just.' Then, Joseph of Arimethea, who was a member of the Jewish council, asks Pilate for the body of Jesus Christ, which he then places in a sepulcher. After the Sabbath, Mary Magdalene, Joanna, Mary mother of Jacob, and other women go to the sepulcher and find it empty. Then two young men with shining clothes come and speak to them. The women then tell the apostles the news, who think they are mad and don't believe them. Peter, however, goes to the sepulcher and finds only the linens inside.

In John 19:17–20:18, Jesus dies on the cross without any supernatural manifestations. The soldiers break the legs of the other two crucified but do not break the legs of Jesus Christ because they can see he is already dead, but one of them pierces his side with a lance. Then Joseph of Arimethea and Nicodemo, both dignitaries of the council of Jews (John 3:1–15), ask Pilate for the body of Jesus Christ and place the body inside the sepulcher. On Sunday morning, Mary Magdalene goes to the sepulcher and sees the sealing stone removed. She then runs to tell Simon and the disciple that Jesus loved, who then run back to the sepulcher and find only the linens inside. Then Mary Magdalene sees two angels with white clothes who speak with her. She then confuses the gardener with Jesus Christ revived from the dead.

In Mark 15:21–16:10, Jesus Christ dies on the cross without any supernatural manifestations, except that the veil of the temple tears in two and the centurion says, 'Truly this man was the son of God.' Joseph of Arimethea, member of the Jewish council, asks Pilate for the body of Jesus Christ. Pilate is surprised that Jesus Christ is already dead and asks the centurion for verification, who informs him. On Sunday morning, Mary Magdalene, Mary the mother of Jacob, and Salome go to the sepulcher and find the sealing stone removed and a young man dressed in long white clothes who speaks to them. The women run away from the sepulcher and tell no one because they are afraid. Mary Magdalene then tells those who had been with Jesus Christ, who do not believe her.

In Matthew 27:32–28:15, there is darkness over the land. Jesus died on the cross, the veil of the temple tears in two, there is an earthquake, rocks break open, the tombs open and many of the dead saints rise up and, after Jesus is resuscitated, come out of the sepulchers, go into the holy city and appear to many. The centurion and those who were guarding Jesus Christ, seeing the earthquake and other things, full of fear said, 'Truly this was the son of God.' Joseph of Arimethea, a rich man, then goes to Pilate and asks for Jesus Christ's body. On Saturday, the principal priests and the Pharisees met with Pilate and asked for a guard to seal the tomb of Jesus Christ, saying, 'Sir, we know that liar while alive said, "After three days I will resuscitate." Order therefore that the sepulcher be sealed up to the third day, so that his disciples do not go there at night, steal the body and say to the people, "He has resuscitated from the dead," and the last fraud will be worst than the first.' They then go and seal the sepulcher and place the guard. On Sunday at dawn, Mary Magdalene and Mary (mother of Jacob the apostle) go to the sepulcher. There is a big earthquake because an angel descended from heaven, removed the sealing stone and sat on it. His aspect is like lightning and his clothes as white as snow. The guards were so frightened they were trembling and like the dead. The angel speaks with the women, who go running to tell the disciples. The women meet Jesus on the way and he speaks to them, and they hug his feet. One of the guards goes to the city to notify the principal priests, who then give the soldiers a lot of money so that they would say 'his disciples came at night and stole the body while we slept'. The guards take the money and say what they had been told. This saying is still current among the Jews up to the day the gospel is written.

It is amazing, the power of money. After witnessing two earthquakes, unexplained darkness over the land and an angel whose aspect is like lightning descending from heaven, the guards give false testimony in exchange for money. There are few things all four gospels concur in. One is that Joseph of Arimethea asked Pilate for Jesus Christ's body, and took it to the sepulcher. Joseph was a member of the Jewish council and also a disciple of Jesus Christ. Mary Magdalene was the woman who first spread the story about Jesus

Christ's resuscitation, and she is the only one in all four gospels who sees one or two angels. This woman is identified in the same gospels as being a prostitute and having seven demons expelled from her by Jesus Christ. Being a prostitute, one would have to deduce that the demons neither caused her deafness, blindness, lameness nor muteness as these conditions would have made it difficult for her to carry on her profession. The only other conditions caused by demons identified in the Holy Bible are epilepsy and madness. The fact that the disciples do not believe Mary Magdalene would seem to point to her lack of credibility among them. One could be led to deduce that Jesus Christ resuscitated from the dead was a story that was first propagated by a mad (or epileptic) prostitute as against the other story propagated by the bribed Roman guards that the disciples of Jesus Christ came and stole his body while the guards slept.

There was obviously a rift among the Jewish council that condemned Jesus Christ to death. At least two of its members, Joseph of Arimethea and Nicodemo, were disciples of Jesus Christ and immediately seized his body from the cross, obtaining permission from Pilate. The other two crucified with Jesus Christ were not dead, as the soldiers had to break their legs to accelerate their death, but Jesus had died unusually early, thus the soldiers did not break his legs. Pilate is in fact surprised that Jesus Christ had died so early (being an old hand at crucifixions, one would assume Pilate knew how long it took for a person to die on the cross) and receives only the word of the centurion as verification of the death, the same centurion who states, 'Truly, Jesus Christ was the Son of God.' Pilate himself had been reluctant to order the death of Jesus Christ, preferring to release him or at the most have him whipped, but finally gave in to the insistence of the Jewish majority.

It's as if the gospels were written to deliberately cause confusion as to whether Jesus Christ was dead on the cross or was taken by his disciples before he died, or whether his body may have been stolen by the disciples from the sepulcher. The few remaining words of all four gospels pertaining to the manifestations of the resuscitated Jesus Christ and the ascension into the heavens are even more wishy-washy and inconclusive.

In Lucas 24:13 to the end, one unnamed disciple and one named

Cleofas walk with a stranger whom they do not recognize and are about to eat some bread with him inside a house when the stranger disappears. The disciples then return to Jerusalem to speak with the eleven apostles about their belief that the stranger whom they did not recognize was in fact Jesus Christ (maybe wearing a disguise). Jesus Christ then appears to the eleven apostles, speaks with them, shows them his wounds in the hands and feet and eats some bread with honey. Afterwards, Jesus Christ goes with them to Bethany and is raised up into the sky.

In John 20:19 to the end, on the same Sunday night the disciples are together in a place with the doors closed, for fear of the Jews, Jesus Christ arrives and speaks to them and shows them his wounds on his hands and side. Apostle Thomas, who was one of the twelve apostles – not eleven as in the other gospels (since Judas Iscariot was no longer with them and in fact in Acts 1:12–26, the twelfth apostle is selected by the name of Matias, after the ascension) – is not present and doubts the veracity of the other apostles. Eight days later Jesus Christ appears to the disciples again, this time with Thomas present, and speaks to them. Afterwards, seven disciples fishing from a rowboat see a stranger on the shore who later shares a roasted fish with them and speaks with them. They then decide that he too was Jesus Christ. The end is about the disciple that Jesus Christ loved, the same man who, in the last supper, had lain against Jesus Christ's chest, and that he is the one who gave testimony to these occurrences and the writers know that his testimony is true. No ascension mentioned here.

In Mark 16:12 to the end, two of the disciples claim that they saw Jesus Christ in another form but no one believes them. Finally, Jesus Christ appears to the eleven apostles while they are seated at a table and tells them to go all over the world preaching, baptizing, expelling demons, laying hands on the sick, speaking in tongues, and taking poisonous snakes in their hands. After he speaks with them Jesus Christ is received up in the sky and sits at the right hand of God (Yahweh is not mentioned at all in the New Testament). In this ascension, Jesus Christ does not go to Bethany or even leave the locked room.

In Matthew 28:16 to the end, the disciples go to Galilee to the hill where Jesus Christ had ordained them, and when they see him, they adore him although some had doubts. Jesus Christ speaks to them. Also, no ascension to heaven here.

The only eyewitness testimony of Jesus Christ being recognized in the same body that everyone knew him by are from the mad (or epileptic) prostitute who was Jesus Christ's companion, Mary Magdalene, the eleven apostles in a locked house mentioned in three of the four gospels (although in John it is twelve apostles, which contradicts Acts). But in one gospel, Matthew, Jesus Christ appears to his disciples on a hill only, and some of them do not believe it. If one sees a person one believes it; why would some not believe it? Ascension to the heavens is only mentioned in two of the four gospels. In Acts, many occurrences stated in the gospels are completely contradicted. Now in Acts 1, the author Teofilo claims Jesus Christ appeared to the apostles for forty days before Jesus Christ was ascended to a cloud in the sky and two young men in white robes spoke with the disciples. Also, that Judas Iscariot bought a field with the money he received for turning Jesus Christ into the guards from the Jewish council, and that Judas fell on his head in that field and broke in half and his intestines spilled out, and that field is now used as a cemetery (Acts 1:16–20). In Matthew 27:3–10, Judas throws the thirty pieces of silver he received at the priests of Yahweh and then hangs himself. The priests then buy a field for a cemetery for non-Jews with that money.

In 1 Corinthians 15:3–8, Paul states that Jesus Christ appeared to Cefas and then to the twelve. Afterwards, Jesus appeared to more than 500 brothers at a time, many of whom were still alive. He then appeared to Jacob and afterwards to all of the apostles and lastly Jesus Christ appeared to Paul. In three, Paul states, 'I have taught you what I myself have received just the same.' So besides the contradictions, we see that in the gospels Jesus Christ, resuscitated, appeared to eleven apostles once or twice. As the authors in the posterior books get further away in time and lack supposed personal experience of the events, Jesus Christ now appears for forty days and before up to 500 people at a time.

In fact, in the actual epistles included in the Holy Bible, which may have been written by apostles who actually lived with Jesus Christ for three years, Peter, John and Judas claim no miracles, resuscitation of Jesus Christ from the dead, or ascension to heaven. In fact, Peter states (1 Peter 3:18) '…Christ […] being in truth dead in the flesh, but unified in spirit' and in 2 Peter 1:16–18, 'We have not given you the knowledge of the power of the coming of our Lord, Jesus Christ though artificial fables, but as we have seen ourselves with our eyes his majesty, for when he received from God Father honor and glory, was sent to him from the magnificent glory a voice that said "this is my loved son in whom I take pleasure." And we ourselves heard that voice sent from the sky when we were with him on the holy hill.' The only miracle that Peter claims to have witnessed is this voice from the sky. Peter then states in the next verses (19 on) that they also base their belief in Jesus Christ on the prophecies (as the only other proof they have) and that false prophets had appeared among the people as there will be among you, who introduce secretly destructive hearsay. Surely Peter must be referring to the storytellers who copied Jesus Christ's miracles from the miracles of Elijah and Elisha, and started the stories of the appearance of Jesus Christ after being crucified and the ascension to heaven (also copied from Elijah who ascended into heaven in a chariot of fire)? In fact, the only doctrine written by the three apostles who lived with Jesus Christ for three years is: 1) the devil is the cause of man's sins; 2) angels strive against demons; 3) Jesus Christ was born from a loving God to redeem the believers into a spirit life after bodily death; 4) his doctrine is to not reply to faults against oneself with retributions but rather with acceptance and good behavior; and 5) the end of the world is imminent and the resurrection of Jesus Christ, that the world had been destroyed by water before and this time it will be destroyed by fire.

As we have discussed, the world having been destroyed by water before in the Great Flood is probably a generalized story among mankind based on the finding of fossilized seashells on mountain ranges driven up by the drift and collision of the continental plates.

In 1 Peter 5:1–4, Peter states that he was an eyewitness to the suffering of Jesus Christ and participant in the glory that will be revealed when the prince of the shepherds reappears. At no time do any of the apostles claim to have seen a resuscitated Jesus Christ or any ascension to heaven. Rather, the resuscitation is to be at the upcoming end of the world. All the apostles' epistles in fact are warnings directed against false prophets and tellers of fables who introduce heresies and silly genealogies into the true gospel. So are all the claims of miracles, resurrections, ascensions into heaven claimed in the four canonic gospels and all other books of the Bible those very heresies written by the false prophets?

What do we know about the books of the Bible? We know that they were written by unknown authors who lived hundreds or thousands of kilometers from Galilee and decades, even hundreds of years, after the death of Jesus Christ. We know that none of these authors ever saw Jesus Christ, and they were merely putting into writing stories that had been told and retold among people in those times, many of whom took advantage of the popularity of the Christian religion to gain followers who would give them donations. These false prophets had every motive to embellish the story of Jesus Christ and make it as fantastic as possible in order to convince the simple-minded to pay tribute to them. The more powerful and miraculous the sales pitch was to the possible converts, the more earnings the false prophets could receive. It's more difficult to convince people to donate their property to one by preaching a philosophy and an invisible world than to claim hundreds or thousands of witnesses to supernatural events.

We also know that the books of the New Testament directly contradict each other on many important points. Two of the gospels, in fact, contain the very absurd genealogies that the apostles point out are invented by false prophets, genealogies which don't coincide but both lead back to King David, so that one of the genealogies is obviously false. Obviously the intention behind the genealogies is to make Jesus acceptable as an object of worship among the Jews, since he was supposedly a descendant in direct line of the kings of Israel and had a legitimate claim to the crown.

The claims to the appearance of Jesus Christ after his crucifixion are so unclear and barely mentioned in the gospels, almost as if some of the authors were ashamed to dedicate twenty to fifty words describing the resurrection from the dead. The impression the reader gets is that some of the authors are sorry to tell the readers this lie but it is better if the readers believe it.

We also know that the books of the Holy Bible were selected from as many as eighty other similar writings by a politically motivated Roman emperor who ordered the religion to become the official religion of the Roman Empire, and then that official religion carried out the mass murder of tens of millions of people in Europe in order to steal their property. These were true murders. The victims were not armed or offering resistance. Most of them were dragged from their homes in the middle of the night and tortured for weeks, then burned alive in front of crowds. How did these mass murders, carried out for five centuries, fit in with the philosophy that Jesus Christ and the official religion taught?

There are two kinds of people who will read this book. One kind couldn't care less about religion and wouldn't bother to look up the references in the holy books here given. Another kind will already be highly offended at the statements contained herein and shocked at the possibility that everything that has been hammered into their heads since childhood is based on an ancient pagan Babylonian religion, perverted by primitive Jewish tribes and continuously twisted through 500 years of storytelling, as the people were too ignorant to be able to read or write, to create an imaginary world into which Jesus Christ was born. Then Jesus Christ's actual teachings were seized upon by a multitude of false prophets who sought to take advantage of the new religion's popularity by gaining followers for their own purposes, and embellished his life with a multitude of contradictory supernatural events. That then the Roman government, and the Germanic tribes that seized power in Europe after it, used the religion as a means to impose obedience and docility on the subjugated peoples of Europe by the force of arms, as the philosophy made control of the masses much easier than other philosophies of the time (as you could mess with the old gods a little bit and man had some freedom of action under them). Then the central Church leadership in Rome organized the mass murder of opponents and eventually just plain people whose property it wished to steal, thus enriching itself with the seized properties and becoming one of the wealthiest and most powerful organizations on earth, a status which it retains to this day. This offence or mental shock possibly precludes the reader from looking up the references given in this book for the Holy Bible.

Author Dan Brown's book, *The Da Vinci Code*, is statedly a work of fiction. In it, Dan Brown exposes some half-baked theories and supposed facts that are pure fabrications of the author's imagination. The success of the book is based on debunking the silliness of the Roman Catholic religion and the false history that it presents to the public. In *The Da Vinci Code*, Brown alludes to a body of writings that he has never read, and to supposed alternate histories based loosely on secret societies' lore, to which he has no access. The concepts presented therein are a creation of fiction. Anyone can make up stories saying Mary Magdalene was a descendant of Jewish royalty, married Jesus Christ, and had a child from him, but where does Brown get any indication that this was so? Leonardo Da Vinci's painting, 'The Last Supper', was described in writing by eyewitnesses in the 1700s as being so damaged by humidity that it was just patches of colored paint, unrecognizable as human forms. Today's painting is entirely the work of several restorers, and early restorations were done in primitive times with unscientific methods. Few things are known about Da Vinci's private life. One is a court indictment when he was twenty years old, charging him with sodomy, which was a crime punishable by death, for which he was obviously not executed. It is also known that he never had a wife or a girlfriend and through his life kept young boys in his house as assistants, eventually trying to adopt one of them as his legal son when Da Vinci was in his sixties, and to whom he left his estate. The adoption was denied, probably because Da Vinci was unmarried.

So to Brown, Da Vinci is the grand master of a sect which promotes the divine feminine and ritually copulates with his wife on an altar in front of the congregation. *The Da Vinci Code* reminds Christian followers that there were goddesses before the One God became dominant. The divine feminine has disappeared because of the spread of Christianity and Islam, which follow a male god. As the vast majority of book buyers are women, it would seem that the readers took a liking to Brown's concepts (and his wife's, who suggested them) as the thesis of the book promotes the divinity and power of the feminine. As the female readers became enthusiastic about this book and told others about it a snowball effect developed, which resulted in increasing sales of the book.

Brown also states that Constantine, the emperor of the Roman Empire who made Christianity the official religion of the empire, was also the high priest of the pagan Roman religion and its pantheon of gods. This was not so. The Roman emperors held purely secular offices and were not priests. Many religions existed in Rome. Christianity was the first Roman religion to be declared exclusive, in that other religions were not tolerated legally.

Christianity today resembles much more the religion of the God tribes; evergreen tree worship before the winter (as the evergreen does not lose its leaves and die a small death during the winter); through feasting to fatten up for the cold, hungry months ahead; the spring festival with painted eggs symbolizing the birth and hatching of new life in the spring. What did Jesus Christ have to do with evergreen trees and painted eggs?

The Da Vinci Code, even though it is based on complete nonsense, has become a worldwide phenomenon because it questions the oral tradition of Christianity (supposedly based on the Bible) that has been passed from one person to another for 1,800 years. People today are wondering if all those billions of people that told this story could have been wrong. If one looks at the hundreds of other religious stories that were told by billions of people for thousands of years that were later decided to be complete nonsense, one has to wonder why the particular Christian story, even though it is refuted in the very writings that it claims to be based on, has become so popular. The reasons are that Jesus Christ represents peace among all men on earth and the tranquility a Christian can feel when he has faith that upon dying he will rise to a paradise. Right now, peace among all men on earth is under attack by Islam, which professes violence to subjugate others and suicide attacks to kill others. So Christian-thinking people are reexamining their attitude, and wondering if peaceful intentions really will win out in the end and eventually convert the whole world into a peaceful cohabitation of all humans. *The Da Vinci Code* fits into this deep spiritual wondering that many people are experiencing now.

In this book there have been no references to materials, supporting its own conclusions, that the reader cannot read for himself. Although there exist eighty-three other known gospels – of which only a few have survived – that Constantine decided not to include in the official Holy Bible because they were not compatible with the religion that he was trying to create, these Apocryphal Gospels have not been explicitly referred to in this book as they are generally inaccessible to the public. It would be unfair to quote from and use such material knowing full well that the reader may not easily be able to investigate further – although many of these gospels are now posted on the Internet. Therefore a conscious effort has been made to keep the book within the boundaries of the accessible and refers only to the official holy books. From these writings all conclusions can be drawn without having to refer to what imaginary gospels might have said.

So to those readers who are firm believers in the established Catholic hierarchy, a warning. If this book is successful, the Vatican will probably ban it and condemn its readers to a burning hell upon their deaths, as it did to *The Da Vinci Code*. So you should hurry to finish reading the book, as the Pope's condemnation of hell cannot be retroactive, so that if the reader finishes the book before the banning, the reader will escape the everlasting burning pain ordered by the Pope on future readers.

So what central elements have contributed to the Holy Bible's success as the number-one bestseller and the most printed book in the history of mankind? Besides the fact that its dissemination was promoted by European governments, the stories of the Bible also appeal to nearly all of mankind's most basic desires. There are only three things that humans are truly interested in. They are sex, violence and un-catalogued information. The central cortex of the human brain (the brain stem), the basic reptilian part of a human brain that controls the most important functions of human life, besides dominating the human body with the fight-or-flight response to violence and the reproduction drives, also catalogues every item in the human's experience into categories, so as to make rapid identification of a new item that enters the human's sensory field possible. This is necessary for the human's survival, so that the category of items that the new object fits into can allow the human to determine if the new object is a threat, or possible food, or innocuous. So when a human perceives any new object that does not fit into a recognizable category, the human brain automatically dedicates a lot of attention to the new item to determine where it should be catalogued. New items of supernatural nature are extremely interesting to the human brain. So the Bible appeals to all three of the most basic human instincts.

The Bible has lots of violence and lots of sex, with Lot mounting his two daughters, Abraham lending his wife out to all the local chieftains and kings and pharaohs. The Old Testament tells us that in many walled towns in the area of ancient Israel and Arabia, it was common for the men of the town to sodomize any strange man who sought to spend the night lodged within the town. And of course the Bible has many supernatural un-catalogued events.

The New Testament also expounds a philosophy that was quite different to other philosophies that were common throughout the region before it. The Christian philosophy was that God was not Yahweh of the Armies, but rather that God was love. That if believers love their neighbor as they love themselves and seek credit here on earth to achieve a future life of holiness in the soon-to-be-established kingdom of God that would be created after the upcoming destruction of the earth by fire, then the world would be a better place to live, possibly.

This philosophy of replying to personal offences with passivity and peaceful behavior was introduced by the colonizing Europeans into the lands where they sought to dominate the natives. The colonizing, conquering Europeans sought to convert the natives away from their primitive religions and into this policy of accepting slavery, disadvantageous commercial relations, or outright pilfering and theft, as well as a lower social standing when compared to the dominant European, with this new holy Christian attitude. The natives were taught to accept personal affronts amicably and with docility. However, should a native cause a personal offence to a European the result could be immediate death. So it was the natives that were to earn the credits on this earth with their passive behavior that would lead to their reward in the invisible heaven after their death. The dominant Europeans wanted their rewards right here on earth.

The original, official Christian religions were to lead to a brotherhood of man and peace on earth. In fact, the West uses the Gregorian calendar as the means to mark the new beginning of this era of peaceful Christian influences among Europeans and to differentiate this new age from the classical, primitive thinking of pre-Christian Europe. But, in reality, the Christians have invaded the Americas and decimated its peoples, have enslaved great numbers of Africans, and have, for a time, colonized nearly all of Africa and India, and have politically dominated great parts of Oceania and South-east Asia. Some of the highest crime rates in the world are in nominally Christian countries, such as Columbia, Ecuador, the USA. In the Muslim world, with its harsh laws and acceptance of violence, the crime rates are much lower.

The old gods have not been supplanted completely by the One God. If one flies on the airline Egypt Air, for example, one will see Horus, the bird god, painted on the airplane, as if to protect it during its flight. So the old gods are still respected in some ways. However, the methods used in their worship and the stories associated with their religions have been collectively determined by people to be complete nonsense these days. In essence, people today think that all the billions of people who in the past spent their time sacrificing to and worshipping these gods were complete primitive fools. There were many stories of gods that became super popular and are now totally discredited. Could Christianity and Islam not become totally discredited some day?

Jesus Christ represents the idea that mankind can live in peace and that, upon death, man will predictably rise to a paradise if he has followed a certain code of conduct faithfully. In reality, much more peace has been imposed on peoples with the advent of large nations ruled by national governments, court systems, state-funded police, medical assistance, humanitarian aid, United Nations forums, etc. These systems, although taken for granted by many people in the First World, were not available even to the grandparents of many people alive today. However, as beneficial as most people would agree these current systems are, the large-scale organization and standardization of today's world has also resulted in much more organized large-scale warfare, proliferation of nuclear weapons, and the development of insidious deadly means of waging war. Far more people were killed in the recent World Wars I and II than in previous wars. The numbers of dead were probably unimaginable to peoples who lived in the 19th century. So the religion supposedly related to Jesus Christ really has not resulted in an unarguable betterment of the human condition at the present time, even though it has been followed for some 1,700 years now.

Hypocrites have been quietly making substantial progress in taking over the minds of many humans over the past 150 years. Whereas Christianity teaches humans that if they behave kindly towards others and treat others as they would like to be treated then the world will be a better place to live and upon death the Christians will rise to a paradise, Hypocrisy teaches humans to take a wait-and-see attitude, to observe carefully, to experiment and analyze. Hypocrisy has developed into science that teaches the same but adds that humans should develop codified series of actions that can be taught to other humans that, once followed, will result in predictable effects. A scientific human believes that anyone can cause the same reliable results by following a predetermined series of actions that can be taught and were developed by careful observation and controlled experimentation on the basic nature of material things. This belief has resulted in the proliferation of manufactured goods and the incredible increase in the power of any modern individual. This belief is somewhat mirrored in some ancient yogic teachings that can be summarized as 'be here now'. However, it differs considerably in that the observer is also an actor that is trying to dominate the world around him through his actions and knowledge, in order to make himself more powerful and satisfied.

So the Christian set of procedures ordained to be followed by people continues to exist alongside this new set of concepts, known as the scientific method. Science, however, has thus far proven to be such a more visibly effective means of obtaining desired results than any previous system of beliefs that many people are convinced that it is unarguably the final word in the development of the human belief system. Many people think that if we have science and scientific predictable results, do we need any of the old religions that, after all, have failed to deliver the promised results after more than fifteen centuries? Whereas religions are mostly used by humans to regulate the personal conduct between humans, could scientific methods not be applied some day to develop a code that describes predictable human reactions to particular actions, and thus supplant the varying religious traditions throughout the world that continue to regulate the interactions among humanity? Could scientists not develop an international code of conduct that would do away with regionalized morals and religions?

Are People That Ignorant?

If you live in Western Europe or North America, you are probably aware of what a privileged position you find yourself in. Not just in terms of the geographical location in which you are, but also in terms of the time in the history of mankind in which you live. You must be aware that nearly everywhere else on the planet earth, the other people that share this time with you have a lower standard of living. This means they may have a shorter lifespan due to lack of availability of food or Hippocratic medical care, or unsafe hygienic, dietary and medicinal practices. They don't have access to automobiles, refrigerators, televisions and radios, toasters and blenders like you do. They don't have much opportunity for education, either through books and teachers, or through the Internet or reading magazines or watching educational programs on television. They don't have access to communications through telephone lines, web cams, Internet chats. You are among the elite of the planet. In great parts of the rest of the planet such as Africa, Central and South America and China, people risk their lives and a percentage of them die trying to reach your area, where they know they will have a better opportunity to improve their standard of living.

So you can imagine how bad life is in, say, Cuba or Morocco, where people crowd onto anything that floats with the possibility of entering illegally in the First World and brave a dangerous sea voyage that often ends in tragedy. But all is not perfect in the first world. There are many serious problems that are the direct result of people's manifest ignorance.

Take, for example, the large drug problem that affects the rich countries. The prisons in these countries are crowded, not with criminals, but with drug traffickers and importers. The illegal drugs, such as cocaine, opium, morphine and heroin are derivatives of the coca plant or the poppy flower and are naturally occurring substances of great value in medicine, but have been stigmatized by the pressure from people in governments, mostly the USA, so that the private, unprescribed use of these drugs is penalized with serious long sentences in prison. The same is true for mescaline or cannabis in all their forms. However, tobacco or alcohol, which kill thousands of times more people yearly and ruin many more lives, are taxed by these same governments. Not only that, but it is demonstrable that in Mexico, for example, it is the Mexican army that controls the smuggling of illegal drugs and, in the USA, the CIA has been importing these illegal drugs into the country for decades in huge quantities in order to supply the minority populations with substances that allow the government to maintain better control over them.

These government programs are a copy of an ancient policy of the British Empire, as the British navy in the age of sail ran on grog (named after Admiral Grog, who ordered it), a mixture of rum and water, that was obligatory to the sailors to drink three times daily under penalty of being whipped, in order to keep the impressed, unruly sailors groggy and easier to control by the officers. This is where the word groggy comes from.

If alcohol and tobacco are tolerated and provide a great source of tax income for governments, why shouldn't the comparatively small number of people that desire the ingestion of these other drugs not be allowed to use them as well and contribute to the nation's well-being by paying taxes on the purchase of these substances, instead of making up the majority of the population of the prisons in Europe and the USA and being such a drain on the economy? Why is death by cancer or drunk driving more acceptable than the very rare overdose one might face from the use of purified cocaine or opium? Especially as the vast majority of overdoses are caused by poisonous additives used to dilute the drug.

Coca-Cola used to contain cocaine until it was made an illegal substance. That's why it is named Coca (from the coca plant) and Cola (from the kola nut). Were people dying from drinking overdoses of Coca-Cola? The main problem is that the law enforcement against drugs has had the opposite of the intended effect, increasing the consumption by hundreds of times what it was before the prohibition. People want to take the drugs, even though they are diluted by sometimes dangerous substances, much more since the drugs were made illegal than they did when the drugs were available in pure form and were inexpensive, solely because of the cachet of using an illegal substance. The government's policy has also led to huge increases in crime, as mafias and organized gangs have sprung up to take advantage of the importing and marketing opportunities. The illegalization and persecution of users has led to dramatic increases in prices, where recently a few kilograms of cocaine were seized hidden inside an earth-moving machine that was being imported through customs. The value of the few kilograms of cocaine was higher than the value of a brand new excavating machine and it was worth to the smugglers the risk of losing the machine for the sake of getting a few kilos of cocaine past customs. This situation is similar to the tulip bulb mania in Holland a few centuries ago, where a single tulip bulb was briefly valued at more than the price of a small sailing ship, that could transport tons of tulip bulbs or other cargo. Of course, the market soon collapsed and tulip bulbs became valueless as the people regained their senses.

But the market for illegal drugs shows no signs of collapsing due to the government's efforts aimed at maintaining the artificially high price. What can be bought at the source in Peru for a few pennies from the poor coca farmers is sold for tens of thousands of dollars in the USA, probably the highest mark-up of any substance on the planet, due solely to the government's prohibition. The purified versions of opium, morphine and heroin are used daily in hospitals and sell for a reasonable price, but once they are on the black market their cost increases a hundred fold.

It would seem that the government's intention was not to increase the use of these drugs incredibly, or to fill the prisons to overflowing with non-violent people that use or deal in these drugs, or to create an environment that fostered the creation and rise to power of some of the richest mafias ever known to mankind. Yet all these things have happened and continue to happen but the government's policy doesn't change and a noticeable percentage of the federal and local budgets of the USA continue to be spent on so-called drug enforcement. So even though the government's efforts have the apparently opposite effects of the intended, the efforts are increased.

On the other hand, large multinational drug laboratories produce artificial mood-altering substances which are far more dangerous and addictive than the illegal drugs, yet which are licensed and taxed by the governments and marketed with multi-million-dollar advertising campaigns, such as Diazepam, quaaludes, Benzedrine, Methedrine and Valium. Many of these substances are highly physically addictive, as the reader may have experienced in person if one has ever taken certain sleeping pills for even a few weeks. Yet it is the natural drugs that are produced in other countries that are demonized by the governments, whereas the US- or European-manufactured synthetic drugs are idealized and marketed, and the distribution is regulated by the governments.

Just recently the Mexican government has taken the brave step to legalize the private use of marijuana, peyote, cocaine, heroin, ecstasy-type drugs, etc. Now the world will have a realistic opportunity to see if this approach is a good step in solving the problem of criminal drug trafficking or if it will exacerbate the drug addiction problem to intolerable levels. Bolivia, also, has elected a government that consists of coca-growing farmers. It would seem that the USA's efforts to eradicate coca growing in Bolivia will take a turn for the worse. The USA would do well to closely observe the results of these experiments as it may benefit immensely, and do the world's peoples a great favor if the USA government decides to give up its ill-conceived crusade against natural drugs that it began at the turn of the last century (when the problem was minuscule). The USA seems to be unable to judge a policy by its results. Rather, it insists on continuing to judge a policy by the original intention that was sold to the public as the purported reason for instituting that policy, namely that people would be healthier, work harder, and be happy and chipper if they only consumed the manufactured drugs.

The real reason for the factory manufacturing of the modern drugs is that this method assures a standard dose with predictable effects. The natural drugs can be taken in varying quantities with results ranging from negligible to a deadly overdose. However, the standard pill or capsule cannot be appropriate for a ninety-pound female as well as for a 200-pound muscular man. Whereas natural drugs in the past were dispensed by drug stores where the clerk may often have taken into account the size and sex of the person requiring the treatment when prescribing the dosage size, today's standard pills and capsules are designed for a hypothetical average-sized person. Does this standardization really represent an improvement over mankind's thousands of years of experience in consuming natural drugs? Even if it does, is that a reason to punish those who choose to consume natural drugs with twenty years to life imprisonment?

In the USA, medicinal drugs were sold in drug stores until recent times. As Coca-Cola became popular, those drug stores changed into soda shops that dispensed beverages from the soda fountains. When cocaine was outlawed and was removed as an ingredient from Coca-Cola, the soda shops with their soda fountains quickly disappeared, as no one wanted to sit around the soda shops drinking soda that didn't give them a high. Cigarette consumption went up dramatically, as the cigarettes did have mood-altering properties. People in the USA and UK have sought out drugs as a way to pass the time and amuse themselves, much more since they acquired sufficient free time from the necessary survival activities. When society was poor and people had to work long hours in order to earn enough food to survive, drug use was not a problem. At most, people would get drunk on a Saturday night, knowing that the next day was devoted to the Lord and rest. But as society became wealthy and people had more free time, then people turned to partying on Friday as well as Saturday night.

Some people abuse drugs almost daily and their drug use noticeably degrades their ability to perform enough work to trade with others for their survival necessities. Yet, society is so rich that these unproductive, drug-consuming individuals are not only allowed to survive but are also fed and even housed by society. Drug use has been demonized by the USA government. What 2,000 years ago seemed to explain the bad things that happened to people – demons – now has been characterized by the US government since the 1970s as 'controlled substances'. It's as if the US government has decided that drugs are the main cause of the bad things in its society. What demons were to the Babylonian religion have been replaced in US society by illegal drugs, at least as far as attempting to explain why people refuse to work hard and commit petty crimes in order to meet their small daily needs. So, by US laws, when a person consorts with the demon drugs, he must be punished almost to the point of being killed.

Another problem is food distribution. Whereas some countries produce and discard large surpluses of food, and also pay their food producers not to produce food so as to not cause a collapse of that particular food's price in the market, the world is facing now and frequently faces mass starvation in parts of Africa. Indians, Bangladeshi, Burmese and other peoples are chronically undernourished. Even though the food is produced and is frequently discarded, the costs of transporting or the effort of distributing the surplus food to the starving people is not worth it. So many Third World peoples suffer from starvation, whereas the First World gives the food to microbes and fungi. But the good thing is that the microbes and fungi that dispose of our surplus food so quickly disappear once the food has been absorbed by them. Whereas if the food was given to the people in the Third World, there would then be more people there who would then need more food.

So the First World today has few problems arising from ignorance. However, the First World comprises less than one-tenth of the total population of the planet. The vast majority of the other nine-tenths of the humans on the planet today suffer serious problems every day in their lives precisely because of ignorance. The science and knowledge that has allowed the First World's peoples to eliminate illness, hunger, lack of energy, etc., has not been effectively communicated to the rest of the humans. The Third World peoples mostly live in a technological time before the industrial revolution of the mid-1800s. The fact is that the average ten-year-old child in the First World today has more knowledge and is capable of producing a bigger impact on his environment than the leaders and sages of all of mankind up until the time of the industrial revolution. A well-educated ten-year-old child would seem like a god to the people who lived even a few hundred years ago.

As we have seen, the Bible attributes to Christ the teaching that one need not wash his hands before eating, or to wash the eating utensils, jars, cups and such. It's enough to empty them. One need not wash one's sheets or pillowcases. Nothing that enters the body through the mouth can do it harm, as it goes to the belly and comes out in the latrine. The following of this concept is one of the major causes of illness, infections and death in the Third World. Muhammad required his followers to wash their hands up to the elbows and the feet before praying five times per day. He also required the washing of the crotch before attending the communal prayer meeting every Friday (and presumably every day), as the parishioners line up a few inches from each other, face to butt raised up in the air. However, if water is not available the Muslim may clean himself with sand. At last, 650 years after Christ, one of the most important concepts known to man, probably far more important than all the billions of hours spent in God worshipping up until then, had started to take root, but not among Christian Europe, where the yearly bath remained the custom for 1,250 years more.

The main interest of mankind remained, until the full development of the industrial revolution, to enslave other groups and force them to work for the masters in exchange for food to survive on, and the rudimentary necessities as far as clothing and bedding. When people saw that the machines worked at a smaller cost per unit produced, then slavery became illegal, as it was no longer cost-effective, and the oppressed slaves were freed from the hands of their masters, as the cotton gin machine in the USA picked the cotton less expensively than a mess o' Negro slaves.

Since the Age of Enlightenment in Europe, the ignorant masses had acquired enough knowledge to not require a ferrous control over their lives. Prior to the Enlightenment, as is known the epoch when the ancient Greek and Roman books were rediscovered and the classical knowledge was once again disseminated among Europe's elite, the predominant social system in Europe had been feudalism. After the Enlightenment, the social system changed into a mercantile society, a system in which money became widely accepted among peoples. Even the concept of financial credit was developed and the Rothschild family organized the first European international banking system, where money was deposited in one country and then could be withdrawn in another country, even though it had not actually traveled there but was merely a book-keeping arrangement among members of the Rothschild family living in those different countries. Of course, the Arabs had developed an international banking system some 800 years prior to the Jewish family, the Rothschilds, importing the idea into Europe.

Quickly, money and the procuring of an advantageous commercial relation with other people or peoples became the preferred means to enslave others and make them do one's bidding. If one could accumulate money, as long as the financial system continued to function and people had confidence in it, then one could trade the money to other people who would then give one the goods in their possession or their labor. This was far preferable to the feudal system imposed upon the conquered Europeans by the Gods. The feudal system depended solely on which group of armed men could strike more effective blows with their swords, axes and other weapons. If one was not among the well-armed warriors, called lords in English, but 'sons of the Gods' in Spanish and Portuguese (Hidalgos, Fidalgos), or *Herr* in German, or *Heer* in Dutch (which also means 'god'), then one was a type of slave, called a serf in English (related to 'serve').

The system was simple and easy to understand and actually represented an improvement over the previous classical system of formalized slavery. The serf only had the obligation to feed his masters, work for them when called upon, and remain living on his master's land, but was expected to feed himself and his family, and could acquire goods and occasionally his own plot of land. The slavery system was far more dehumanizing. The master owned the slave and any meager possessions the slave might have acquired, and could legally strike or kill the slave at any time without reason. The slave had no rights at all, not even to feed himself.

The mercantile society allowed far more people to enter into the game of bettering their status in life by acquiring an advantageous commercial relation with other people. European nations found it more equitable to develop commercial relations with other nations and peoples than to send armies there to occupy and intimidate the vast local populations, forcing the local people to work for them and give them their goods. By trading with other peoples, the same objectives could be achieved without the enormous expense of having to send armies to fight in foreign lands. Of course, the desired advantageous commercial relation frequently required a military lesson to be taught to the weaker trading partner, whose raw materials the well-armed nations wanted. This resulted in what became known as gunboat diplomacy, where short, mostly naval wars were fought by the European powers and the USA against the nations from whom they wished to acquire raw materials and products at an advantageous price. This policy continues today, although the Arab nations sought to resist by forming OPEC, throwing out the foreign oil companies, nationalizing the oil reserves and the installations of the foreign oil companies in their territory and, in the beginning, booby-trapping the oil well heads with explosives so as to dissuade military intervention from the stronger commercial partner nations. However, the need for oil and the advantageous commercial relation continue to impel the stronger nations into enforcing their rights to obtain the petroleum at a price their people can afford, now with full-scale invasion and occupying armies.

So in Europe the system progressed from slavery under the Roman civilization, to semi-slavery as serfs under the conquering Gods, to a mercantile society, as the oppressed conquered peoples gradually intermarried with the Gods and were allowed to rediscover the knowledge and science of the Roman Empire which the Gods had suppressed.

Then came a major challenge to the mercantile society in the form of communism. A disgruntled unemployed writer had written a book called *Das Kapital*, in which he abhorred the near-slavery conditions that predominated in the early factories as the industrial revolution was in full march. The workers, although voluntary, were working long hours for survival wages. Marx thought that the owners of the factory, the capitalists, were earning a far greater wage than was rational for the amount of effort they employed, and enjoying a far better lifestyle than the workers, to the point where the situation was abusive. Karl Marx recommended that the workers didn't need the capitalists and that the workers should seize the factories, the means of production, that had been ordered to be built by the capitalists, and continue to produce solely for their own benefit. By eliminating the huge wage of the owner of the factory, the workers could then divide that wage among themselves and increase their wages accordingly. Karl Marx was not an organizer, a politician, a speech-maker, nor did he make any headway in his lifetime in convincing people to do as he had written. His idea simply was so appealing to so many people that others seized upon it after his death and popularized it.

Eventually the idea became dominant over the social system of billions of people. Like the idea of the seven-day week, the idea of the One God brotherhood of man, the idea of winning over violence with peaceful behavior, the masses who came into contact with these ideas were so convinced that the ideas themselves spread through the minds of mankind, although impelled by powerful political figures in all cases. Great ideas are like a virus that replicates itself in the minds of people and causes them to alter their behavior and to communicate the idea to other people.

However, Marx's idea has been pretty much discredited these days, as billions of people tried his idea for eighty years and found that the mercantile society with its capitalists, its advantageous commercial relations, and its wars by trading partners in order to maintain the advantageous trading relations, gave the people a far more comfortable lifestyle and opportunities for individual freedoms and personal satisfaction. Muhammad's idea, namely that by acting violently towards other people to force them into an advantageous trading relation, or slavery, if adequate to the time and place, has not at all been found as wanting as communism. For the past 1,350 years, violence or the threat of violence has made the Arabic world function. Although the oppressed masses are worse off than their counterparts in even South and Central America, and certainly the First World nations, the oppressors are better off economically than most of the top capitalists in the First World nations. Also they are not encumbered by morality rituals common among the Christians. A truly wealthy man in the Arab world is expected to live as if he was in paradise on earth, giving himself the most ostentatious luxury, the finest pleasures, the most servile attendants. The oppressed masses tolerate these excesses among their wealthy and their leaders, not just because of the fear of violence against themselves, but also as a matter of custom and racial pride, in that by accumulating their wealth and combined power in the hands of one man, great amazing things can be accomplished in the style of the Arab race.

So how do we know that people are astoundingly ignorant?

The fact that billions of people tried communism, killed tens of millions of people to convince them that communism was a better way, then collectively decided that eighty years of trying had been wrong and that the mercantile society had been better after all. Would a truly advanced race of, let's say, extra-terrestrial beings have done that? Would they not have organized the experiment on a smaller scale under controlled circumstances to determine if this new social system would be satisfactory or not?

What about the people who smoke cigarettes? They know that they are killing themselves but they want to do it slowly. They use cigarettes as an escape from the small pressures of everyday life or even boredom. They must think, 'Let me fill up my lungs with slightly poisonous smoke and that way I don't have to face my reality as much because I can look forward to the day when I finally kill myself.' Are there any readers that could argue that smoking cigarettes is not harmful to their health?

The military efforts to enslave other peoples or gain an advantageous economic relation are among the wisest things people do. The advantages of forcing other people to work for oneself or give one their goods are certainly obvious to most people and most would see it as a desirable thing. Witness the popular motto in the USA that arose spontaneously during the first US–Iraq War, 'Kick their ass, get their gas'.

However, the consumption among Americans of a huge percentage of the world's fossil energy reserves certainly is a form of dangerous ignorance. With most statistics showing that planetary oil reserves will be totally exhausted in fifty years (this at the present rate of consumption, which is certain to increase, perhaps substantially), the fact actually is that much less, probably twenty years, is all that is left of useable oil reserves.

As the easier-to-extract reserves are used up, the day will soon arrive where the remaining oil reserves cannot be extracted profitably. This will be independent of whether people will be willing to pay $100 or even $1,000 for a gallon of gasoline. The physical fact is that, when the process of extracting a barrel of petroleum, and turning it into a refined, ready-to-use, distributed product, uses up more than a barrel of petroleum's worth of energy (because of the difficulty of accessing the remaining remote reserves), then there is no commercial reason to extract the petroleum because it will always cost the producer more to deliver the product than he will charge for it. From that perspective the planet's oil reserves dwindle to maybe twenty years of supply at the current demand rate.

But even so, why are people burning petroleum when it is used in the manufacture of nearly everything around us these days, from plastics, to paint, appliances, computers, watches? If all the petroleum is burned up generating energy, how will these myriad products be manufactured?

Also, why are Americans in denial about their being the biggest contributors to global warming? The current US president, George Bush, or Bushie, as he is known among the intelligence community, recently stated that global warming was not going to be a problem because US scientists had successfully genetically altered trees so that a certain species of tree would grow four times as fast, and that these trees could be planted to absorb the excess CO_2 in the atmosphere, rather than reducing the CO_2 emissions. But he failed to mention where this massive reforestation of the US landscape was going to take place. He presented no figures on just how many billions of these trees would be needed, how they would be planted, and on what land they would be planted in order to begin to make a reduction on the continuing increase of CO_2 emissions by Americans. Also, what about the ecological consequences of planting billions of one type of tree that would reach full growth in five years? It must absorb from the soil the same amount of nutrients that would have taken twenty years. Will the soil be able to supply those nutrients on a massive scale, never before seen by mankind?

As far as Bushie is concerned, the problem of global warming has been solved by American ingenuity and the new genetically altered tree. The US Secret Service has an unofficial motto, 'You elect 'em, we protect 'em'. But it is the ignorance of the American public that drives this kind of thinking. If Bushie was to implement a solution to the CO_2 emissions similar to what European governments have implemented, which is a 300% federal gasoline tax, thus increasing the price of a gallon of gasoline to nearly $8 per gallon (which is what Europeans pay now), he would not be allowed to even finish his term in office and would be lucky to not be lynched on the White House lawn.

Americans, in their ignorance, really seem to believe that the space exploration program is going to open up a solution for them to the problem of running out of petroleum on earth. It's a science-fiction fact to many people that soon the earth's population will be traveling among other solar systems, where humanity will find room to expand, and find useable energy sources. The fact that the entire scientific community of the planet has not been able to design a space orbit vehicle that carries more than seven people at a time seems to preclude a mass migration of the nearly 7,000,000,000 people alive on earth now. Even assuming the eventual development of, let's say, a vehicle capable of traveling in the solar system carrying seventy people at once, millions and millions of these vehicles would have to be built to ferry even a small percentage of the earth's population to another planet or moon, far more incredibly expensive, highly complex space vehicles than all the airplanes that have ever been built in the history of mankind. It is clearly a ridiculous concept that the already taxed resources of the planet could ever provide the material needed to ferry such a large human population to another planet in the solar system. Only a tiny, insignificant fraction of mankind can expect to visit other planets or moons, for many centuries to come. This planet is all we've got and all we're going to have for all practical purposes as far as a home. Yet Americans, in their ignorance, seem intent on burning it up, digging out its resources, in order to rush off to another planet, where the grass will be greener, supposedly.

But in reality there won't be any grass there, or any other living thing. The atmosphere will be unbreathable and the temperatures deadly, so that it is impossible to venture out of a protective enclosure for even one second unless completely sealed off from the lethal environment in a protective and bulky space suit. Yet the Bushie administration insists on Americans' right to cause climate change over the entire planet earth and on the viability of evacuating the earth to some other home in space, should the earth become unpleasant to live in due to extreme weather and increased temperatures.

Many people believe that when they die they may attain admission to a paradise where they will have everything that they want. But if one thinks about it, the obtaining of everything that one wishes for will not seem a paradise for long but will soon turn into a living hell.

Imagine how one's life would be if everything one wished for rapidly materialized. After the novelty wore off and one had experienced every thrill one could imagine, an incredible boredom and lack of purpose would soon develop. It is resistance to obtaining what one wants that makes life interesting. Imagine being forced to play a game that one always wins and everything goes in one's favor. No human could continue to play a game such as that for very long. A human needs adversity and resistance in order to feel fulfilled. By this definition we are already living in paradise, as there is plenty of resistance and lack of what one wants here on earth.

Traditions are a sign of people's ignorance. Roman Catholics ritualistically carry wooden statues through the streets in processions. They no longer know why they do it or what purpose it serves. They just do it because it was done before. Jews and Muslims don't eat pigs. There is no health reason not to eat pigs. They just do it because it seemed wise to prohibit it 3,000 years ago. The maintaining of inherited monarchies in many European countries is another tradition. The kings and queens and their families are a noticeable drain on the national economy and produce nothing of the slightest use to people, yet some nations continue to maintain the royal families, maybe with the expectation that some day the king will make a wise decision about something important.

But as we regress in time into the history of our civilization, the ignorance of the earlier humans becomes astounding, when seen from an educated modern viewpoint. The death and destruction brought on humanity and its cities by countless wars over the millennia certainly point to a less than enlightened attitude. Surely a wise race would have found less destructive methods to achieve their goals, whatever the goals might be.

The witch-hunts in New England and Europe, the Holy Inquisition by the Roman Catholic Church and the religious wars in the UK take our thoughts back to a time when most people alive today would state earnestly that those people were truly ignorant. Of course, the Dark Ages brought on by the Gods stand out, as the name implies, as an era when Europeans' minds went into the dark, and reached levels of ignorance not seen by mankind since the Bronze Age. Life was difficult and cheap then. An author, Sir Thomas

Moore, wrote a book called *Utopia* in the mid-1500s. It too was one of those ideas that spread like a virus, galvanizing the minds of people who came into contact with it. Utopia was a word coined by Moore and has become part of international vocabulary. It was actually the supposed name of an idealized town, or country shire, where people could live in a near-perfect world and indulge in a satisfactory life-style, but the word 'utopia' now means a sort of paradise on earth, an idyllic dream to many people. But what did Moore actually write about?

In Utopia, the country people lived in the feudal system and were subject to their lord who lived up in the castle. However, the people had a fertile, green and pleasant land and they grew enough food so there was no hunger or want among them. The people worked the fertile, well-watered fields and lived a wonderful life enjoying the pleasures available to them. And what were these pleasures? Why, eating three meals per day in the village long house and having the opportunity to sit by the village elders (since it was a communal meal) and listen to them speak in their wisdom and experience. They could even swig ale in moderate quantities and should any of them have the need to travel to another shire (for it was prohibited to leave the valley without permission), he could put the request to the elders who, if considering it wise, would eventually meet with the lord and ask permission on behalf of the villager.

The other great pleasures in life were urinating and those nice, long, satisfactory defecating sessions that humans so enjoy. Upon reaching maturity, the young men would seek out a wife, perhaps even from another shire, if allowed to travel by the lord for that purpose, and upon approval of the elders could settle down to married life and producing future townspeople. For this was paradise on earth in those days. It certainly gives one a glimpse of how ignorant people were back then.

But people were even more ignorant in the Bronze Age. The writers of the Old Testament, upon which are based the Jewish, Christian and Muslim faiths, lived in an area and a time where next to nothing was known by people about anything. Thunder and lightning, rain, waves, the movements of the sun and the moon, the birth of people and stock animals, natural occurrences that most educated ten-year-olds understand today, were complete unexplainable mysteries to every person then. They had to deal with lions, leopards and desert wolves for dominance of the land. They didn't have the technology to heat furnaces sufficiently to distil iron. They had no idea about illnesses but knew leprosy and sexual diseases were contagious. Starvation was a frequent problem, much like some of the primitive African tribes one sees on television nature programs.

So these primitive farmers and goatherders came face to face with the One God, 3,000 years ago, and witnessed astounding miracles which they wrote down on sheepskin rolls. And after 3,000 years of studying their writings, no such miracles have been witnessed again, and still today hundreds of millions of people wonder if these writings were truthful or whether they were just the typical lore of the gods common to all early civilizations of that epoch, ranging from Valkyries in the Nordic countries, to the Druid tree-worshipping religion in Central Europe, to the Egyptian pantheon of gods, to the Babylonian pantheon, to the Hindu pantheon in India, and many, many other earlier religions and fertility cults that were completely customary among mankind in those times. But of course, the other religions didn't have the seven-day week.

The Caliphate

The term 'the Caliphate' is becoming more widely heard among Western peoples. It refers to a supranational pan-Islamic government ruled by one man. This man would be the leader of the community of Islam, the successor to the prophet of God, the representative of Allah on earth, and this man would rule over more than one and a half billion Muslims (roughly five times the population of the USA). And he would be a man, never a woman. His dominion would stretch from Morocco to Pakistan and then even include the country of Indonesia in Oceania, as well as part of the Philippines, Malaysia, Thailand and Brunei. In fact, he would be the spiritual leader of all Muslims, even those living in India, Europe or the USA. Muslims everywhere would owe their allegiance to this one man and his pronouncements would carry more weight than the laws and criminal codes in effect in the countries where the Muslims may be living. This man would single-handedly control about one-third of the current exportation of the world's petroleum and about 60% of the planet's proven oil reserves. The power of this man would be almost irresistible by Western military might. No government or earthly army would dare to attack a nation as widespread and as populous as the Caliphate. No Western president or prime minister would dare to not maintain cordial relations with this man. *He* would determine what the price of a barrel of petroleum would be, not the markets.

And this man would be an Islamic fundamentalist. He would pursue, without pity, the advancement of the interests of the religion of Islam. He would not care about the well-being of his people nor would he advance the cause of liberty and freedom of self-expression. His mission would be a divine mission, inspired by Allah. His pronouncements would not lead to an increase in the standard of living of his people, to the rise of consumerism among his subjects, to the turning away from Muslim laws. The code of sharia would be imposed by him to the extent that it would be tolerated by the peoples. Adulterers and those who copulated outside of the official marriage would be stoned to death. Those who merely engaged in kissing or fondling outside of official marriage would be arrested, imprisoned briefly and fined. If fondling involved undressing, then a penalty of cane strikes could be imposed as well.

All art produced in this vast region would not depict humans or animals. Any representation of the human figure would be prohibited. Human figures in medical textbooks, anatomical charts, instruction manuals, could be censored by the government. Sex education would be prohibited. Women could be prohibited from having any education, even from learning to read or write. Women in this huge area would be required to cover their hair when in public and to wear one-piece robes that covered their bodies from head to toe. They would be prohibited from speaking to men.

And the frontiers of the Caliphate would not be stable. At first, the khalifah would use his power to lead his people to a more perfect understanding of Islam, to a more complete adoration of the one god Allah, to prepare themselves to live a blameless life that would allow them to enter the eternal paradise upon their death. Then the khalifah would seek to spread the perfect vision, the communion with Allah, the teaching of the Qur'an to the peoples on the frontiers of the Caliphate. Muslim preachers, imams, and men inspired by faith would cross the nation's borders to spread out into the surrounding countries. These holy men would preach the word of Allah to the heathen societies that bordered the Caliphate. They would seek to convert the faithless to the one true religion, the worship of the one god, Allah.

If the teachings were accepted, then peace would prevail on the Caliphate's frontiers. If not, then Muslims everywhere must obey the holy call of the khalifah and take up arms in holy war, Jihad, to bring the word of the one true god to those who refuse to hear. For they too must be saved. They too must be given the opportunity to escape the eternal pain of a fire that never dies, to accept Allah into their daily lives, to commune with the one true god. They too must form part of the Islamic community, the Caliphate.

Such a Caliphate did exist. It began a long time ago in the year 10 of the Hijra, almost 1,400 years ago. In those days people were different to today. They had limited opportunities compared to modern peoples. They had to rely on faith to organize the dealings among individuals. The governments had to rely on force to impose their will among the citizens. The khalifah reigned, not by the will of the people, as there were no popular elections, but rather by providence and divine inspiration. It became hereditary. Allah wanted the son of the previous khalifah to succeed him upon his death. At times, the line of succession was broken, when a new dynasty was imposed by another family line to whom Allah had given a stronger military following. Assassinations frequently occurred in the line of succession.

But the system worked and it worked for a long time. In fact it worked until shortly after my father was born. The Caliphate existed until the Christian year of 1924. That year the Turkish state broke with a 600-year history and abolished their claim to the Caliphate. After the Ottoman Turk Empire had been defeated by the Allied Forces in World War I, the reconstituted Turkish nation decided to end the institution of the Caliphate, which, after all, had been militarily defeated by the Western armies. But the dream didn't die there. Many Muslims today still remember the might that was wielded by the khalifah, the glory that his court enjoyed, the power of the unity of hundreds of millions of Muslims.

That dream lives on, in chats among Arab intellectuals in men-only cafes throughout the Middle East, in international political organizations, many of which are outlawed in both Europe and the Arab countries, and in Friday prayer meeting sermons by devout imams. After all, as Europe seeks to develop one constitution for what now are twenty-five different countries, as the Anglo-Saxon nations continue to wage war as one state when any of them are threatened, and as South American nations join together in trading blocks, the Arab peoples know that their region will fall behind in terms of economic and military significance if they too don't join into larger population blocks. The fragmented Arab leadership has little influence compared to the dominant position the Caliph would enjoy. Their fragmentation allows Western powers to dictate economic conditions to them, to attack individual nations and overcome the small, ineffectual armies, and to impose political decisions on the weakened national governments. None of this was permitted by the Muslim nation until the defeat of the Caliphate in World War I.

What choice do the Arab countries have but to try to re-institute the Caliphate? Should they be faced with huge population blocks, such as the European Union, that was never united before, when the Arabs themselves were one nation until a mere eighty years ago? Should the Arabs accept the break-up of their political unity imposed upon them by the victorious English and French armies? There were no such countries as Iraq and Jordan, Lebanon or Saudi Arabia until the 1930s and 1940s, when the occupying forces of France and the UK relented under world pressure and abandoned the Arab lands. At this time arbitrary lines were drawn on maps by European cartographers, which delineated the borders between these new nations that before had been one continuous state for countless generations. What did these lines in the sand really mean to the wandering Bedouins who needed to cross the area in search of water and scrub?

Al Qaeda's main goal is to unite the Muslims in a supranational state through waging continuous, unrelenting war in as many simultaneous fronts as possible. The overwhelming pressures that will result from the simultaneous wars against many powerful enemies, such as the USA, the UK, Russia, Israel and any other nations that Al Qaeda can provoke into attacking Muslim nations, will serve to awaken within the Muslims an international sense of identity, to unify the Muslims into one people, and to galvanize the Muslims into fighting for their survival, independence and power. It will also teach the foreign powers how dangerous the Muslim fighters can be when they wage war and foster a fear among the infidels of the future armed forces of the awaited Caliphate.

Petroleum is to be the main weapon in this attempt to revive the Caliphate. Many of Al Qaeda's attacks are now directed at increasing the cost of petroleum to the consumers. Strangling the petroleum supply is to be the pitiless weapon used by Muslim fundamentalists to bring the West to its knees. This will serve several purposes:

1) The unrelenting increase in the price of petroleum will demonstrate to the Western peoples and their governments the weakness of the military might of their armed forces, as their supposedly overwhelming use of deadly force fails to even

secure a reliable supply of essential petroleum at a price that their economies can afford. This will discourage the use of force by Western nations and cause them to sue for peace on any terms.

2) Political tensions will increase dramatically inside Western nations as the price of petroleum climbs to unexpected levels and the Western economies grind to a halt. As transportation, electricity production, and the manufacturing of goods quickly becomes much more expensive, Western citizens will rebel against their own governments, which have failed to provide them with a standard of living to which they have become accustomed. Civil unrest, rioting, looting could easily break out in the USA and other Western nations if the economy collapses. This will lead to internal conflict and could seriously weaken the USA's ability to wage war against the Caliphate. A fragmented, rebellious population facing a great increase in the crime rate, a sharp downturn in their standard of living, and increased repression from their own police forces will be far easier to distract and discourage from the waging of warfare against the newly reborn Caliphate.

3) Should the strangulation of the oil supply be highly effective, the USA's actual ability to wage war may be affected, as the government faces choices between supplying fuel to its armed forces or averting an economic collapse and electricity black-outs in major cities and industrial plants.

4) The incredible increase in the price of petroleum benefits the Arab and Muslim nations enormously, where 60% of the world's oil supplies are located. The incalculable transfer of wealth that is taking place at an accelerating rate between the wealthy West and the currently impoverished Arab nations is beginning to take on historic proportions. The Western nations have placed themselves in a situation where they will pay practically any price for a commodity that is controlled by their sworn enemies. The Caliphate will be reborn wealthy as well as powerful.

The emir of Dubai, now one of the wealthiest men on earth, recently said, 'My grandfather rode a camel. My father drove a jeep. I drive a

Rolls Royce. My son drives a jeep. But my grandson, he will ride a camel.'

What does the West expect the Arabs to do when all their petroleum has been sold to the world's consumer at a price that the world economy can afford? When all the oil is gone, should the Arabs revert to goat-herding? Should they forget about the wealth that they are accumulating now and the prestige and political influence that they have developed? Should they revert to being second-class citizens as they were for centuries under the European colonizers and the Ottoman Turk occupying forces? The only other resource that exists in the Arab lands is sand. There is a lot of sand in many places of the world. Sand is not an exportable commodity, nor does it make for a pleasant land to live in.

Or is it more likely that the Arab peoples will unite in an effort to sell their only commodity, their only source of wealth, for a price so high that the income acquired from the sale will propel the Arabs as a whole into an economic and political situation that will place them among the wealthier of the world's peoples, not among the poorest as they rank now? The fact is, the Arabs need to sell the petroleum that remains in their land for a price that will bring them wealth that will last for centuries. They must trade the extraction of petroleum for new economies that depend on other factors, such as tourism, manufacturing, service industries, research and development, and also nuclear energy. For if they only acquired currency from other nations in exchange for petroleum, the Arabs, as they have already seen, will find that the money accumulated in their coffers – to the point where they could buy ridiculously large or crucial portions of the USA or the UK – would become unusable through sanctions imposed upon them by those same nations. The US dollars given to the Arabs can only be used by the Arabs in international circulation. The dollars must be used by the Arabs to purchase things that are circulating in the world economy outside the borders of the USA. The dollars are not redeemable for title deeds and control over essential properties and industries crucial to the economic security of the USA.

Yet the foreign powers, such as the US and British oil companies, were until recently in control of the Arabs' only source of wealth, the petroleum deposits. It was this inexpensive control, this advantageous economic relation, that caused petroleum to become the essential commodity that it is today. At the beginning of the Petroleum Age there were other sources of combustion available. Nearly all motors and engines are manufactured today to burn petroleum derivatives. Even though the end of the petroleum deposits on planet earth are within sight, industry, consumers and national governments nearly all refuse to initiate the necessary research and development, the retooling, the production and manufacturing of alternative sources of fuel. Why? Because as long as it is economically less expensive to pay the suppliers of petroleum the price that they want than to undertake a worldwide effort to retool factories to build new engines fuelled by alternative fuels and to construct new systems of re-supply of these engines, then it doesn't make economic sense to undertake the expense involved in this massive retooling effort.

As a matter of inertia people generally refuse to change anything that is working OK for them for something new and untested. The general outlook of the population seems to be, 'Let us use up the last of the petroleum until it is nearly gone and then we will convert to another fuel.' The main suppliers of petroleum, the Arabs, have a different perspective on this issue. They might think, 'What do these people think, that they will take our only resource, pay us a pittance, and then treat us as they did before the petroleum was discovered?' Al Qaeda also enjoys support because of this outlook shared by many Arabs. Al Qaeda is not just an extremist branch of a radical ideology. It actually represents what many Muslims and Arabs believe in. The continued misjudgment of this actuality on the part of Western administrations is one of the leading causes of military and policy setbacks in the West's efforts to impose itself militarily over the Islamic world.

The USA is now beginning to turn more to the use of ethanol to fuel automobiles. In Brazil ethanol is also widely used and readily available at service stations. In Egypt natural gas fuels the majority of taxis and many private vehicles. In Europe, however, an alternative energy vehicle is practically unheard of and the supply of natural gas or ethanol is mostly non-existent for use in vehicles. In the USA the sales of the available hybrid automobiles are lagging behind expectations. The consumers don't seem to want to take a chance on these newfangled vehicles that haven't been proved out yet. The consumers don't want to give up that acceleration and power that gasoline vehicles can deliver. Perhaps the Caliphate will provide the incentive needed by the average consumer to reconsider his use of the earth's resources.

Islamic Societies Today

Islamic nations today vary widely and there is not one stereotype that can be applied to all of them. There are however different general regions where characteristics are similar, even though the individual nations within the regions differ. An Islamic nation is defined as a nation that officially adopts Islamic law as part of its legal framework and where the vast majority of the population are Muslims.

In many large, poor Islamic nations a Western visitor will be struck by several characteristics that will seem unusual. One is that the average driver shows a near total disregard for traffic laws, ignoring red traffic lights, squeezing five automobiles into a three-lane road, narrowly missing other vehicles and pedestrians, etc. Many drivers prefer to drive with the traffic lane line under the center of the automobile, perhaps to better guide them to their destinations. Drivers honk their horns every few seconds as a protest at the continuous near-accidents caused by others, to warn pedestrians to run for it, and at anything that dares to be on the road. In fact, nearly all Arab drivers would immediately be arrested in Western nations for driving to endanger and other offences. Their constant horn honking seems to be a reflection of the general attitude held by them, something like, 'Outta my way, you crumb! I'm on my way to get mine!'

This lack of respect for others is reflected in other aspects of their societies. For example, when a Western tourist pays for anything with currency larger than the price agreed, many of the recipients of the currency will argue with the tourist in order to keep the change. Some will become almost violent, hoping to frighten the tourist into leaving his change. Most of the able-bodied men are employed as police, private guards or armed forces. With an average salary of less than $90 per month, these men produce nothing for years and are limited to standing around with machine guns, intimidating the population hopefully into curbing some of their more primitive passions. It is common in most Arab capital cities for a soldier or policeman armed with an assault rifle to be stationed every thirty feet or so. Therefore, the majority of the men of productive age are not contributing to the economy but rather are employed in intimidating the population into accepting poverty.

In all television programs, movies and billboard advertising, women are featured wearing Western clothes and living Western lifestyles. Yet in most countries, nearly all women wear Arab-style clothes and veil their hair. Many actually veil their face according to their tribal custom, some showing only their eyes through a narrow slit. In the oppressive heat, women completely cover themselves from head to toe in several layers of clothing, even wearing gloves. The eye slit makes it difficult for them to see the ground and accurately judge where they tread. Even though these Arab women may be in close daily contact with women from other countries such as Europeans, Asians, Africans, who dress in modern, loose-fitting, revealing clothes, most of the Arab women continue to cover themselves completely and at least veil their hair. Is it that the sight of hair drives men wild?

The Gods are still worshipped in the Arab countries and throughout most of the rest of the planet. In the Arab countries, in Japan, all of Europe and the Americas the vast majority of advertising posters and billboards that have women on them feature an attractive, tall, blonde, blue- or green-eyed woman, even though hardly any may actually live in that area or are native to the region. People everywhere admire the Gods aspect and think that it is superior to other looks. Billions of women everywhere dye their hair blonde or blondish. Hardly any natural blondes dye their hair brown or black. A white-skinned, golden-haired beauty with eyes that reflect the color of the sky or the forest lords over nearly all advertising campaigns. A short, dark-skinned, brown-eyed, compactly shaped human may actually have superior genes to the Gods' genes, as far as surviving better in hot, sunny climates and not being nearly as susceptible to skin cancer as the Gods and their related peoples are. However, featuring such a genetically superior woman on an advertising campaign does not bode well for the sales prospects of the advertised product nearly anywhere on the planet.

Morocco

Beginning in the westernmost reaches of the Islamic sphere is situated the area known as the Maghreb. Morocco, Western Sahara and Algeria make up this region, where the people speak a dialect of Arabic and it is quite difficult for the true Arabs and these peoples to understand each other. This region was under the dominion of the Germanic BerBer tribes (*BarBar* in German), prior to the Islamic conquest by a Syrian dynasty, the Umayyads. Pure BerBers today still remain isolated from the general population in many remote towns and villages and are distinguishable by frequently having blue or green eyes and light-colored hair. 99.1% of the population of more than 33,000,000 is Arab BerBer, and 98% is Muslim. They speak a dialect of Arabic, called Maghrebi, but also the language BerBer, and many speak French, which is an official government language used on documents. This is due to France (as well as Spain) having colonized great parts of Morocco.

The literacy rate is only 51%. Many children aged between seven and fifteen are put to work as servants in private homes. Unemployment is near 20% in urban areas. 40% of the labor force is employed in agriculture. 19% of the population is below the poverty line. An average salary is only $125 per month. A great number of Moroccans attempt a dangerous ocean crossing in smugglers' boats, trying to enter Spain without papers, a voyage which frequently ends in tragedy.

The infant death rate at birth is 40 per 1,000, in comparison with the US's IDRAB of only 6.5 per 1,000. Morocco is, however, a young population and a rapidly growing one as well. Population growth is more than one-third faster than the US's. The average age of a Moroccan is only 24, whereas the US citizen's average age is 36.5. This means that there will be more Moroccans in the near future and the already extreme pressures currently inducing Moroccans to migrate to Europe to attempt to earn a living will increase, as the Moroccan economy is unable to deliver necessary services or even sufficient food to a burgeoning population.

Some 80% of Moroccan towns and villages are without electricity. Morocco depends nearly 100% on imported coal to fire its electricity plants. There are some wind farms operational now. However, due to a coal tax, the cost of electricity in Morocco is actually higher than in

European Spain or Portugal, where the average wage is ten times higher. Morocco has very small discovered reserves of petroleum or natural gas. The government is therefore attempting to attract foreign investment in wind farms and bio mass-fuelled electricity generating plants.

There are some 3,500,000 Internet users, about one in ten of the population. The wealthiest 10% of the population consumes about 31% of the national domestic product. Morocco is ruled by King Mohamed VI, son of the last king. However in the 1990s, a type of senate and congress have been instituted. The representatives, unlike the US chambers, are elected by local councils, labor syndicates and professional organizations, not by the population at large. There are exactly thirty women representatives elected from the National List of Women, in the lower chamber of 325 seats. Women do have the right to vote or to present themselves for office. Since only 51% of the population can even read, the government thinks it wise to not allow them to vote. In reality, what would these people know about selecting a government? They could be easily manipulated by un-scrupulous politicians. In fact, when the king has to visit a disaster area, such as after an earthquake, the army must take the zone first, as the people are unpredictable and extremely hard to intimidate. There are, however, more than ten major political parties with seats in the senate and congress, far more than the Republican and Democrat parties that dominate USA's democracy.

Almost 44% of Moroccan roads are unpaved, and many of the paved areas are in a terrible state of disrepair. There is an intermedi-ate risk of contracting an infectious disease in Morocco. Morocco's main exports consist of leather goods, textiles, produce, fertilizers and transistors. The textile and transistor factories are the only modern manufacturing industries in the country. Northern Morocco is an important producer of hashish and near-daily smuggling runs by boat are attempted into nearby Spain or Portugal. Hashish provides an important source of income for the Northern Moroccan population.

Western Sahara

This is one of the most arid lands on the planet, where rain is practi-cally unknown. The few plants that survive in this Colorado-sized piece of land mostly depend on collecting the dew as their source of moisture. For many months of the year, the air can be obscured by dust and sandstorms or heavy fog. The natives take to covering their bodies with ankle-length robes called dish-dashes, which protect them from sun exposure and the dust. They also frequently resort to covering their faces with light scarves, which filter the dust from the air they breathe. There are only about 275,000 humans living there (whereas in Colorado there are about 4,500,000) and they mostly depend on oases to grow some fruits and vegetables. Herding goats, as well as sheep and camels, is also a popular occupation.

There are only seven major towns in the entire country. Phosphate mines operate in some regions. The fishing resources in the long Atlantic coastline are very under-utilized due to the remoteness of the area and the difficulty in accessing the uninhabited coastline. There are only 2,000 telephones in the entire country (and no cell phones). There are no television stations and no Internet access.

There is, however, a low-level war between the native BerBer Arab population and the Moroccan BerBer Arab peoples that invaded the country in the 1970s and attempted to impose Moroccan rule. The armed conflict has no solution in sight and has been going on for thirty years.

The long Atlantic coastline is punished by strong continuous winds. Studies have calculated that the best use for this area would be to build enormous wind farms that would be capable of generating sufficient electricity to power the entire European Union. This electricity could be delivered to central Europe by an electric power line similar in length to the power line that now delivers the electricity supply to New York City from its Lake Michigan power plant. But to date, nothing much has been done along these lines.

Algeria

Algeria is also a Syrian Arab mixed BerBer population, that was also ruled by France for more than a century. France fought a war for more than ten years to maintain its dominion over Algeria but was expelled in 1962. Algeria is a far richer country than the other two BerBer nations that occupy this part of Africa, as it has the fourteenth largest oil reserves on earth and is also the second largest natural gas exporting nation.

Some 60% of the government's revenue comes from petroleum exports. 97% of the entire nation's exports are petroleum and natural gas products. However, this oil wealth has largely not trickled down to the population. Unemployment remains at 22.5% and some one-fourth of the population is living below the poverty line, more dire statistics than neighboring Morocco, which has no petroleum resources and income. Average salaries are about $190 monthly. As in Morocco, the wealthiest 10% of the population consume some 27% of the national domestic product, as compared to the USA where the wealthiest 10% consume 30.5%. Wait a minute. If this is so, it means that the Algerian elite have more consideration for their fellow citizens than the US elite...

Algerians, as in Morocco, also support more than ten major political parties, whereas the USA only has two. The Algerians have also adopted a senate and congress system and the representatives are popularly elected. Women are allowed to vote. However, the Algerian president was placed in power in 1999 by the secular army, as a result of the army winning a vicious civil war against the Muslim fundamentalists. This civil war lasted between 1992 and 1998 and caused more than 100,000 to be killed and more than 500,000 refugees. There is ongoing guerrilla warfare these days, with the occasional massacre of villagers by Islamic fundamentalist armed groups. In fact, the average citizen has to be careful in his everyday life, as attempting to deviate publicly from Islamic norms can attract threats from Islamic fundamentalists. Algerian homosexuals, for example, live in an underground scene, fearing attacks by Islamic fundamentalists.

Also, Algeria is home to more than 100,000 refugees from Western Sahara, who are based near their country's border, and who use the porous frontier to launch attacks against the Moroccan occupiers. In fact, Morocco is undertaking the construction of a very long security wall (similar to the one being built by the Israelis) to try to prevent the exiled Saharawis from entering their ex-nation.

Also, ethnic BerBers who remain isolated in the mountainous regions frequently agitate for autonomy, many times with the force of arms. There are also problems with large gangs of armed bandits who roam the desert regions attacking and looting entire towns in southern Algeria.

Arab BerBers make up 99% of the population and profess Islam (of the Sunni branch). The population is also young, at an average age of 25. The population is growing about 25% faster than the USA's population, in spite of a high infant mortality rate of 30 deaths per 1,000 births.

Whereas nearly 80% of males can read and write, only 61% of females are literate. There are only 850,000 Internet users.

Algeria remains a troubled and dangerous land with several ongoing internal armed conflicts. Islamic fundamentalists are everywhere, although their army was defeated and disbanded by the secular army in 1998. Algeria has the experience of fighting a serious war against France for more than ten years in the 1950s and again a destructive civil war, thirty years later, that lasted for six years.

Tunisia

This smallish nation, about the size of the state of Georgia in the USA, has a population of some 10,000,000 people, 98% of whom are Arab. The BerBer peoples did not settle in this area and are limited to the three aforementioned countries and Libya. Tunisia is the site of ancient Carthage, the best-known Lebanese (Phoenician) colony, which rivaled Rome in power for many decades, until Rome succeeded in destroying Carthage. Tunisia is today one of the best run and most well-off of the Arab countries. It has a thriving tourist industry, offering several major yacht marinas. Women's rights are unmatched in any other Arab country. Three decades ago the poverty rate was 33% but has been reduced by government social programs and micro credits by the Development Bank to just 7%. The USA's poverty rate is 12%.

Since Tunisia obtained independence from France in 1956 there have been only two presidents. The first ruled for thirty-one years and the current one has also been continuously re-elected (with more than 98% of the votes) for nineteen years. There is a senate and a congress, a percentage of whose representatives are popularly elected. There are six major political parties. The Islamic fundamentalist party is outlawed. There have been some bombings of a synagogue and other Jewish targets, however Tunisia is mostly a peaceful place doing its best to attract tourism.

The population average age is only eight years younger than the USA, and the population growth rate is about the same as the USA. There are, however, 24 deaths per 1,000 live births. The unemployment rate is 13.5%. 83% of males are literate but only 65% of females. The average income is about $220 per month, about the same as the Czech Republic a few years ago.

Tunisia produces petroleum and natural gas in an almost sufficient quantity for its own consumption. Gasoline is extremely cheap to buy in Tunisia. About 9% of the population uses the Internet.

Overall, it's a nice place to visit and one of the more prosperous, trouble-free and socially stable of the Arab nations.

Libya

Perhaps most famous for its head of state, Muammar Qadhafi (for whose name there are more than eighty different spellings in English), Libya has wielded far more political influence in the world than far larger nations. With a population of only 5,900,000, 97% of whom are Arab BerBer and Muslim, Libya has, in the thirty-seven years that Qadhafi has led the nation, launched attacks against its neighboring countries Algeria, Niger and Chad. It even threatened a war with Egypt, a country with ten times its population. It has also engaged in international terrorist acts and served as a training camp and operational base for Irish Republican Army terrorists and all sorts of Arab terrorist groups.

Libya became independent from its colonial master, Italy, in 1951. Qadhafi, a colonel in the army, rose to power in 1969 and looks set to either die in office or pass the leadership on to his family. Qadhafi espouses an anti-Marxist, anti-capitalist alternative political system that he expected, for some decades, would be an alternative to both systems and that would be embraced by peoples everywhere. In reality, he and his immediate family have amassed a huge fortune by diverting the income of the state into his personal coffers. Libya allows no political parties. 95% of the export earnings result from the sale of petroleum, the level of income of which would give the country one of the highest GDP per capita in Africa. However, the unemployment rate is over 30%. 90% of the land is desert and Libya must import 75% of the food it consumes. The literacy rate among males is high, 92.4%, but among females is only 72%. There are only 200,000 Internet users.

Libya has a young population, with an average age of only 23 years. The death at birth rate is high, with 24 deaths per 1,000 live births. The population is growing rapidly, at 2.5 times the growth rate of the US population.

Since Libya was ostracized from the international community by the sanctions imposed by the United Nations between 1992 and 1999 technological and commercial development were greatly slowed. During those years trade with the outside world was severely limited and no commercial flights were allowed in the country, so that one had to fly to Tunisia and then drive some fifteen hours to Tripoli. Since Qadhafi made arrangements to pay off the families who lost members in the various terrorist attacks carried out by his secret services, all nations have lifted their commercial restrictions against Libya, most recently the USA. Now there are more than 100 American oil company executives lodged in hotels in Tripoli, waiting for several months for their opportunity to have an audience with Qadhafi.

Egypt

A millenary civilization with more than 5,000 years of antiquity, Egypt is today the most populous of the Arab nations with some 79,000,000 people, 98% of whom are Egyptian. There are about 1% BerBer, Nubian, Bedouin and 1% European. 90% profess the Muslim faith and about 9% cling to the early Christian faith, called Coptic Christianity, which predated the Arab invasion. Another 1% are of more modern Christian faiths.

Egypt is a poor country with the average income only $120 per month. Unemployment is about 10%, and 20% of the population is below the poverty line. It is, however, self-sufficient in oil and gas production and actually produces some 135,000 barrels per day more than its needs. The government continues subsidizing the basic necessities for many of its citizens.

Egypt has a young population with an average age of only 24 years. The population growth rate is about 75% higher than the USA. The death at birth rate is 31 per 1,000 live births, a reflection on the lack of available good medical care. About 68% of men can read and write but only 47% of women. There are only 5,000,000 Internet users.

The government is safely in the hands of Hosni Mubarak since 1981. Mubarak, in late 2005, had to face the first popular election in the history of the Egyptian republic, which he won with an 88.6% vote favoring his re-election. He then had the losing opposition candidate imprisoned for a five-year sentence. The previous presidents were appointed by the people's assembly, which is a 454-seat assembly elected by popular elections. There is only one major political party in Egypt, and three very small ones. However, 112 of the 454 seats are in the hands of independents. The Muslim Brotherhood is illegal but active and expanding its base.

Egypt made peace with Israel in 1979 and has withdrawn its troops from a confrontation line on its easternmost border with Sudan. It is trying to develop its considerable tourist attractions, which include the Red Sea beach and diving facilities, and of course the many pyramids, ancient temples, ruins and archaeological sites throughout the ancient kingdom. However, several bloody terrorist attacks in the recent past have caused harm to its thriving tourist industry.

Sudan

The northern region of Sudan is inhabited by Arabs and Negro Muslims, whereas the southern region is inhabited by Negro tribes mostly following animistic religions. This cohabitation has led to fairly continuous warfare since Sudan achieved independence from the UK in 1956. Two prolonged civil wars have caused more than 2,000,000 deaths, as well as severe famines. Islamic-oriented military regimes have governed the nation since independence. The taking of Negro youths and children as slaves by the Muslim troops has been widespread. One tribe holds an annual sale of its women, which is widely attended by wealthy men from all over the world. This tribe has more Rolls Royces and Mercedes per capita then any other area of Africa.

Sudan is the largest country in Africa, although much of the land is desert. It is about one-quarter of the size of the USA. There are some 41,250,000 people living there, about 52% Black, 39% Arab, and 6% Beja. Mostly concentrated in the northern region, 70% profess the Sunni Muslim religion, whereas in the southern fourth of the country are concentrated the 25% of the population that follow animistic creeds and about 5% Christian. It is a very young population with an average age of only 18 years. The life expectancy is only 59 years. There is one of the highest death rates per live birth, which is 61 deaths per 1,000 births. The risk of contracting infectious diseases in Sudan is very high. Even so, the population growth rate is 2.55%, or some 2.5 times the growth rate of the USA.

The main languages in Sudan are Arabic and Nubian. The male literacy rate is 71%, but for females it is only 50%. There are only 1,140,000 Internet users. There is a 2.3% AIDS infection rate, as compared to the USA of 0.6%. Unemployment is 18.7% and the poverty rate is over 40% of the population. Sudan also has a high inflation rate currently of 11% annually. Sudan is however an oil-exporting nation, producing some 275,000 barrels per day more than it consumes. There are also substantial natural gas reserves that are currently unexploited. The average wage is only $54 per month, one of the lowest in the world.

Sudan has had a military president since 1993. There have been four different constitutions since 1973, which have each been suspended by military coups. Islamic law, *sharia*, is compulsory in the northern area, along with English common law. The south has its own constitution since December of 2005 and has been granted six years of autonomy. The region of Darfur has suffered more than 200,000 killed in the most recent conflict, which has been going on since 2003. The United Nations is in the process of placing troops in the area to separate the warring factions in the now abated civil war. However, Al Qaeda has recently called for Muslim radicals to move to the region to evict the newly arriving UN troops.

Sudan has had large influxes of refugees from neighboring Ethiopia and Chad. There are also some 6,000,000 internal refugees that have fled the civil wars, some 15% of the population. Sudan was one of the strong bases of Al Qaeda and was the headquarters for Osama Bin Laden for several years. There were training camps for Islamic terrorists in Sudan, however in 1996 the Sudanese government, under pressure from the Saudi government, decided to cooperate with the USA and international authority by offering to turn Bin Laden over to the US government. However, Osama Bin Laden was allowed to leave the country, and then moved to Afghanistan.

Jordan

Jordan achieved independence in 1946 from the UK, which had made Jordan a colony after the Allies defeated the previous colonial masters, the Ottoman Turk Empire in World War I. Jordan was ruled by King Hussein for forty-six years and now his son, King Abduhlah, has succeeded to the throne in 1999. Parliamentary and municipal elections were held for the first time in 2003. Only the congress is elected by the voters. The equivalent of the senate is appointed by the king. In the congress six seats are reserved for women. In the 2003 election some 89.6% of the representatives elected were not affiliated with any political party. Islamic law and French codes of law form the basis for Jordan's legal codes.

Jordan is a small nation with a population of about 5,900,000. There is a 91% literacy rate, one of the highest among the Arab nations. 98% of the population are Arabs but only 92% profess the Sunni brand of Islam, whereas 6% are Coptic or other early Christian sects. It is a very young population with the average age being only 23 years. The population is growing at about 2.5 times the rate of the USA. There are 17 deaths per 1,000 live births, about three times the death rate in the USA.

It is a poor country that does not produce oil and must import all its petroleum consumption, about 60,000 barrels per day. There is about 30% unemployment and 30% of the population is below the poverty line. The average income is only about $130 per month. There are about 600,000 Internet users.

Of the population of 5,900,000, some 1,830,000 are Palestinian refugees. Some of these refugees have participated in armed groups that have fought against Israel. Some Palestinians attempted to take over Jordan with an armed attack against the Jordanian government in 1970, which resulted in a two-year-long civil war that ended with the Jordanian forces successfully evicting the Palestinian Liberation Organization. Relations have been strained for many decades between the Jordanians and the 31% of the population that are Palestinian refugees. Jordan and Iraq were joined as one nation for some time and share a common lineage. The uncle of the current king of Jordan, Prince Hassan, would be the successor to the throne of Iraq, should Iraq reinstate a monarchy.

Saudi Arabia

A large country, about one-fifth of the size of the USA, Saudi Arabia's land is mostly uninhabited sandy desert with frequent sand and dust storms. Beneath the desert is 25% of the planet's proven oil reserves. Saudi Arabia is the number one exporter of petroleum in the world. 75% of the government's budget revenues comes from oil and 90% of the nation's export earnings. 45% of GDP comes from oil. The private sector accounts for only 40% of GDP. The government's 2005 budget shows a $54,000,000,000 surplus. In comparison, the USA runs a $347,000,000,000 government budget deficit. The Saudi 2006 budget surplus should be much higher due to the increased value of oil. The 2005 trade surplus was some $120,000,000,000. Where does this money go?

Saudi Arabia has pledged economic aid funding to Afghanistan, Iraq, Pakistan, Lebanon and Palestine totaling about $2,000,000,000. The average salary is high for the large Arab countries, being about $350 per month. More than 5,600,000 of the 27,000,000 people living in Saudi Arabia are low-paid foreign workers. Some 35% of the population between 15 and 64 years of age are foreign workers. Estimates of the unemployment rate range between 13% and 25% and only males are counted, as women may not be spoken to except by their families. 85% of the males are literate but only 71% of the females. Only 30% of the roads are paved. There are only some 2,500,000 Internet users.

Saudi has a very young population with an average age of only 21.5 years. The growth rate is more than twice that of the USA. The life expectancy is 75 years. There are 13 deaths per 1,000 live births. 90% of the population are Arabs and some 10% are African and Asian. 100% profess the Muslim faith, by law. There are some 240,000 Palestinian refugees.

Even the local mayors and town councils were appointed by the king until 2005, when the first elections were held for half the seats in the local town councils. The other half remain appointed by the king. Also one-third of the congress was elected for the first time in 2005. Maybe that's where the surplus income of the nation has been going. Only males over 21 years of age can vote. Recently Saudi Arabia has been suffering several terrorist attacks. Al Qaeda and other home-grown political organizations have vowed to overthrow the Saud monarchy and institute a more perfect form of Islamic governance. Saudi Arabia is now ruled by a strict form of sharia law. Even so, for the Saudi-based Wahabi sect of Islam, the government is permissive and has deviated from a strict interpretation of Muhammad's teachings, and must therefore be overthrown.

Syria

This nation which figures prominently in the Old Testament as a frequent invader of the Jews' lands, often allying itself with one of the Jewish kingdoms against the other, also launched under Islam many centuries later the great Umayyad dynasty of Arab invaders that conquered all of North Africa and the Iberian Peninsula. In more recent times, Syria was part of the Ottoman Turk Empire until the end of World War I, at which time it became a possession of France until achieving independence in 1946. Since independence, Syria has been ruled by the al Assad family, the previous president having been succeeded by his son who was also popularly elected (something like the USA currently). However, the current president had to fight a small one-day war against his uncle, who claimed to be the popularly elected president, but upon finding his forces outgunned by his nephew's troops the uncle was forced to flee the country. Very recently Syria agreed to end its decades-long partial occupation of neighboring Lebanon and withdrew its troops. Syria, however, remains listed as a potential enemy of the USA, due to its defiance of US dominance in the area and its alliance with Iran.

Syria is mostly desert or semi-arid and suffers from dust and sandstorms. It is, however, an oil-producing nation, exporting some 285,000 barrels per day. It is also self-sufficient in natural gas production. There are some 19,000,000 people of which 90% are Arabs, the remaining 10% being Kurds and Armenians. 74% profess the Sunni branch of Islam, other Muslim creeds account for 16% of the population, and about 10% follow Coptic and other original Christian sects. There are small Jewish communities still in the same cities where Peter the Apostle attempted to convert the resident Jews to the cult of the Nazarene by founding churches there to compete with the established synagogues. Syria is a very young nation, with the median age being only 20.7 years. The lifespan is low, having only a 70-year life expectancy. The population is growing almost 2.5 times as fast as the USA. The deaths per live birth are only 4.81 per 1,000, lower than the USA's rate of 6.5 per 1,000, probably a reflection of the good practice of Syria's socialized medicine. Al Assad's government tolerates several communist and socialist political parties. The literacy rate among men is 89.7%, but among women, only 64%. Women, however, are allowed to vote and even enlist in the armed services. The average salary is only about $100 per month. The unemployment rate is over 12%, and 20% of the population are under the poverty line.

The Syrian judicial code is based on the Ottoman Turk laws and the French Napoleonic Code. The Brothers of Islam are outlawed and were in fact victims of a major massacre of some 20,000 of their men, women and children a few decades ago, carried out by the Syrian armed forces under the leadership of the uncle of the current president when the Brotherhood attempted one of their frequent uprisings. There is a popularly elected congress consisting of 250 seats, however the Syrian constitution guarantees that at least half of the seats will be occupied by the al Assads' Ba'ath party. There are about 432,000 Palestinian refugees living in Syria, as well as 15,000 Iraqi refugees. As a result of Israel having invaded the Golan Heights, some 170,000 Syrians were displaced and have been refugees since 1967.

Iraq

This ancient land, cradle of civilization that hosted one of the earliest city-states, Babylon, was also known as Mesopotamia, the fertile crescent, and Assyria in biblical times. Encompassing the fertile land between the Tigris and Euphrates rivers, Iraq is nevertheless mostly desert. Some years spring brings serious flooding with the melting of the snows in the mountainous border regions. Iraq obtained independence from the UK in 1932, after it had been liberated from the Ottoman Turk Empire in World War I. Iraq has been ruled by a series of strong men since 1958, the latest being Saddam Hussein, who was, of course, ousted and imprisoned by USA forces in the current war. The Iraqi economy is currently in a shambles as the nation is teetering on the verge of civil war.

The population of some 27,000,000 people is 77% Arab, about 18% Kurdish, and some 5% Assyrian, Turkmen. 97% profess the Muslim faith, being comprised of 60% who follow the Shia sect and 37% who follow the Sunni sect. Some 3% are Christian. The literacy rate is among the lowest in the Muslim countries, being only 55.9% among the males and an incredible 24.4% among females. It is a very young population with an average age of only 19.7 years. There are 48 deaths per 1,000 live births, one of the higher rates on earth, reflecting the effect of the economic sanctions imposed on Iraq by the United Nations. The average lifespan is only 69 years. Even so the population is growing at a rate about 2.5 times that of the USA.

The economy and the government's budget are mostly dependent on the exportation of petroleum. In spite of continued sabotage of oil pipelines on the part of the insurgents, Iraq continues to be able to export about 1,420,000 barrels per day, about the same level as when the oil for food program was in effect. Iraq is self-sufficient in the production of natural gas. There is a 25% to 30% unemployment rate and 40% of the population is below the poverty line. Iraq is also suffering a 40% annual inflation rate. Some $33,000,000,000 has been pledged to help Iraq reconstruct its economy and war-damaged infrastructure. However, due to the continuous attacks of the insurgency and the apparent near-civil war state of the nation, very little progress is actually being made in the reconstruction effort. There are more than 1,000,000 internal refugees, fleeing from sectarian violence. Iraq has also housed some 23,000 Palestinian refugees since the Israeli wars, and recently most of them have fled Iraq for safer havens, and although thousands of them massed on the Jordanian border, they were not allowed to enter Jordan. Syria finally gave them sanctuary.

Certainly other developments of note will take place in Iraq after the writing of this chapter, as the situation there is very unstable and progressing from crisis to crisis.

Kuwait

It is a small nation but very wealthy due to its vast petroleum and natural gas reserves, without which the dry desert country and the intense heat would make Kuwait a very inhospitable place to live. Sandstorms occasionally plague the inhabitants, as well as sudden, fierce, damaging cloudbursts during the winter. Today Kuwait has a population of some 2,400,000, more than half of whom are foreign workers who have chosen to migrate there for employment opportunities. These immigrants comprise more than 80% of the active work force. Whereas the average Kuwaiti enjoys an average annual income of some $22,000, foreign workers can earn a bit more than in the surrounding Arab countries, about $150 monthly.

Kuwait is almost totally dependent on food imports because, except for a fishing industry, hardly any food can be grown there. 75% of the potable water is also either imported or distilled from seawater. Petroleum accounts for 98% of export revenues as well as 80% of government income. 10% of the planet's proven oil reserves belong to Kuwait.

The population is youngish, averaging 26 years. The deaths at birth are less than 10 per 1,000, reflecting the availability of good prenatal care and medical facilities. Some 85% of the population are Muslims, of which 70% are Sunni and 30% Shia. Christians, Hindus and Parsi make up the remaining 15% of the population. There is a 83% literacy rate. There are some 600,000 Internet users.

Kuwait is ruled by emirs, which are similar to absolute monarchs. The first elections for a fifty-seat national assembly were organized in the 1960s but women will be voting for the first time in the upcoming elections in 2006. Islamists currently hold 21 of the 50 seats, whereas the emir's supporters only won fourteen seats. Political parties are illegal. Because of the fear of the political influence of the majority of foreigners, only those who have been citizens for at least twenty years are permitted to vote. Citizens enjoy a cradle-to-grave social welfare system and pay no taxes of any kind.

Bahrain

Another tiny country on the Persian Gulf, comprised of one larger island and several small ones, Bahrain shares with the other Gulf nations the oppressive climate as well as the oil riches. Bahrain is mostly arid desert suffering periodic droughts and dust storms, with very hot, humid summers, but mild winters. However, Bahrain's oil wealth is not as extensive as its neighbors' and oil reserves are already running short.

Some 60% of Bahrain's exports are petroleum and petroleum by-products, as Bahrain has invested heavily in refining plants so as to serve as a refining and reshipping facility for the other countries in the region. Also, 60% of the government's income is derived from petroleum. However, Bahrain is the recipient of economic foreign aid, as both Kuwait and the United Arab Emirates have been donating some $50,000,000 per year to Bahrain since 1992.

Of the small population of some 700,000 people, some 37% are foreigners, attracted by the lure of possible employment. However, the unemployment rate is high at about 15%. The average income is some $20,500 per year. Of course this is factoring in the income of the emir and his family, which accounts for a large percentage of the GDP earnings. As in the surrounding countries, the foreign workers earn about $120 per month. 81% are Muslim, with Christians accounting for about 9% of the population. There is a 90% literacy rate. The deaths per 1,000 live births stand at about 17.

The emir in 2002 changed his status to that of king and the first elections were held for a national assembly. The congress has 80 seats, of which 40 were elected directly and 40 were appointed by the king. Some religious, Islamic and leftist groups are politically active, but political parties are outlawed.

Qatar

The current emir overthrew his father in 1995 in a bloodless coup, as the father was siphoning off such large amounts of money for so many years from the government coffers that the nation's economy was not progressing. Petroleum and natural gas accounts for 85% of export earnings and 70% of government revenues. Qatar has the third largest proven natural gas reserves on the planet and is expected to be the number one liquefied natural gas exporter by 2007. At the current export level the oil reserves will last about twenty-three years more.

Qatar is a peninsula of flat, barren desert covered with loose sand and gravel. Qatar mostly depends on desalination plants to supply its fresh water necessities. The climate is very hot and suffers from an oppressive humidity during the summer months.

There are some 885,000 people, who are about 60% foreigners

attracted by the lure of possible employment. Some 18% are Indian, 18% are Pakistani, 10% are Iranian, and other nationalities account for 14%. Only 40% are Arab. 95% profess the Muslim faith. The literacy rate is 89%. The average age is mature at 32, similar to the US at 36.5. The death at birth ratio is almost three times that of the US, at 18 deaths per 1,000 live births.

The first elections were held in 2003 for nineteen seats on the municipal councils. The current emir plans to allow national elections in 2007 to constitute a national assembly, which would serve in an advisory capacity. The citizens earn about 80% of the income of the more prosperous European Union countries and enjoy one of the world's fastest growing and highest per capita incomes of the planet, assuming the new emir doesn't divert as much money for his own use as his father did.

United Arab Emirates

The UAE are comprised of the union of seven tribes that occupy the horn of the Arabian Peninsula. These tribes were subject to their emirs, who decided to join together for mutual benefit in 1971. The association remains somewhat loose, as each emir retains independent control over his traditional land areas. The land is flat, barren, coastal desert that disappears under the soup-warm Persian Gulf. Inland, the desert turns into rolling sand dunes which give way to mountains on the eastern border with Saudi Arabia. The area is subject to frequent sand and dust storms and oppressive heat and humidity in summer, with temperatures reaching 55 degrees centigrade (more than 130 degrees Fahrenheit), making it one of the hottest places on earth. The UAE depends on desalination plants for fresh water.

The Emirate of Dubai, in particular, has become the richest in the area, where the construction of what is slated to become the tallest building in the world is underway, as well as several artificial island formations offshore where the likes of Rod Stewart and David Beckham and wife are to take up residence. There are more than fifty residential skyscrapers under construction in Dubai, ranging from 55 floors to 210 floors (nearly twice the height of the defunct World Trade towers in New York). Dubai also has the world's most luxurious hotel, where diners frequently arrive at the 1,000-foot-high (300 meters) revolving restaurant by landing their private helicopter in the high-rise helipad. There is also the world's third largest shopping mall, featuring an indoor 400-meter-long snow ski and toboggan tracks. Even seventy years ago, the only permanent construction in Dubai was the sheik's walled compound at the mouth of the Dubai Creek, which was surrounded by the people's huts made of dried palm tree branches, and the major occurrence from that era was when the local coffee house, also entirely made from branches and sticks, caught fire and the people rushed to throw sand on the flames. Only thirty years ago oil and gas deposits were discovered and the area quickly changed from one of the most impoverished to now having a high standard of living. At the present levels of production the oil and gas reserves should last more than 100 years. Since 1971 the Abu Dhabi Fund for Development has donated about $5.2 billion in aid to fifty-six different countries.

Now, 2,600,000 people live in the UAE, with more than 150 nationalities represented. Only 19% are national citizens, with Arabs and Iranians accounting for some 23% of the total population, Indians about 40%, and Filipinos, Malaysians, Chinese, Westerners and Africans are also present throughout. Even though all these different cultures are prevalent in the UAE, and the citizen's income per capita is on a par with leading European Union nations, and all the advertising on television or billboards features women in Western or modern dress, the local women are among the most severely dressed in the world, covering themselves completely in long black robes, wearing black gloves and veiling their faces in black so that only the eyes show through a slit.

Even though some areas are among the most advanced on earth, overall the literacy rate is only 78% and there are 19 deaths per 1,000 live births, about three times the USA's death rate. Indian workers are now staging frequent large strikes demanding an improvement in their working conditions, as they are sometimes crowded twenty into one room in the foreign workers' sleeping quarters and are paid about $165 per month for building all the skyscrapers of the future UAE, working in 120°F heat. There is one construction site, Dubai Marina, where some 35,000 Indian workers are toiling.

The seven UAE emirs themselves vote for the president and vice-president of the nation, and the president also appoints the judges for the legal system. The first direct elections were announced for early 2006 but have not yet taken place. A national council is to be constituted in which 20 of the 40 seats will be allotted by elections. The other twenty seats will be appointed by the emirs. The council will have the power to review legislation only, not to change it. The emir of Dubai is currently building himself the largest, most expensive yacht ever known to mankind.

Oman

Oman (the only nation that begins with 'O' in English) occupies the tip of the Arabian Peninsula and the very tip of the horn in an enclave separated from Oman by the UAE territory. It also is dry desert, albeit with a summer monsoon in the far south. Rugged mountains dominate the terrain in the north and south. There are large dust and sandstorms in the interior and also periodic droughts.

About 3,100,000 people live in this land, of whom 580,000 are foreigners attracted by job prospects. The average Omani salary is about $1,000 per month, but the foreigners earn much less. There is a 15% unemployment rate. The average age of the population is very young at only 19 years. There are 19 deaths per 1,000 live births, about three times the rate of the USA. There are about 245,000 Internet users. The literacy rate is about 76%.

Oman has its own sect of Islam, called Ibadhi, to which belong some 75% of the population. The remainder are Sunni, Shia or Hindu (the many Indian foreign workers).

Oman exports some 720,000 barrels of petroleum per day as well as 7,500 cubic meters of natural gas, which constitute the main source of export revenue and government income. Oman has been independent since 1650 when it expelled the occupying forces of the Portuguese Empire, although it maintains even today an allied posture with the United Kingdom. Elections were held in 2003 for the 83-seat lower chamber of the national assembly, which has limited powers to propose legislation. The current sultan overthrew his father in 1970 and has ruled ever since.

Yemen

Yemen (the only nation that begins with a 'Y' in English) is the poorest nation in the Arab world. The average income of its 21,500,000 residents is only $70 per month. The median age is only 16.6 years, one of the youngest on earth. The population growth rate of 3.46% is 3.5 times the growth rate of the USA. The life expectancy is low at 62 years and there are 60 deaths per 1,000 live births, about ten times the rate of the USA. There are some Afro-Arab, South Asians and Europeans living in this mostly desert land, where the population is concentrated along the narrow coastal plains. Further inland flat-topped hills give way to rugged mountains and then towards the Saudi Arabian frontier there lies one of the harshest deserts on earth. There are sandstorms and dust storms in summer. The population is predominantly Muslim but there are small numbers of Jews, Christians and Hindus.

The literacy rate is 70% among males but only 30% among females. The people mostly devote themselves to agriculture and herding. 45% live below the poverty line and the unemployment rate is some 35%. Only 1% of the population uses the Internet. Yemen exports 370,000 barrels of petroleum per day, which constitutes the main source of export earnings and government income.

Yemen was unified in 1990, when North Yemen, which had been liberated from the Ottoman Empire at the end of World War I in 1918, joined with South Yemen, which had become independent from Britain in 1967. However, the South had developed a Marxist government and much friction was caused among the peoples by the attempt to impose Marxist doctrine on them. There was a secessionist movement in 1994, which was put down by armed forces. The current president was elected in 1999 for a seven-year term with 96.3% of the popular vote. The lower house, consisting of 300 seats, is also elected by popular vote. There are more than twelve political parties represented in the lower house. The government is struggling to control excessive spending and rampant corruption. Large-scale riots broke out in 2005 over a reduction in fuel subsidies.

Iran

Iran was known as Persia until 1935 and is the remains of the very long-lasting Persian Empire. The Shia branch of Islam is, in fact, the remains of the Persian Empire, which has resisted extinction since the time that it was conquered by Alexander the Great and his Macedonian troops. Iran became an Islamic republic in 1979 when the US-backed shah was overthrown and, after his death, his family moved to Massachusetts. Conservative clerical forces established a political system with ultimate authority vested in a religious scholar. Smoldering resentment over the US government's backing of the previous authoritarian regime led to the USA embassy in Tehran being seized by Islamist revolutionaries in 1979 and its personnel being held hostage for fifteen months during Jimmy Carter's presidency (an avowed born-again Christian). Iraq attacked Iran during the prolonged hostage crisis, with the backing of the USA, and the US navy engaged in attacks on the small, ineffectual Iranian navy during the eight-year-long war. A US navy ship destroyed an Iranian civil Boeing 747 airliner that was taking off from the civilian airport in Tehran, killing hundreds of Iranian passengers aboard. This atrocity was retaliated on within a few months with the bombing of a Pan American Airways Boeing 747 while in flight between London and New York over Lockerbie, Scotland. Some 270 people were killed in this bombing, of which 180 were Americans. Iran has continued to sponsor several terrorist groups, mostly active in Lebanon and Palestine. The USA has maintained some economic sanctions and export controls on trade with Iran to punish Iran for its anti-US stance.

A reformist government had been elected in the late 1990s, but its attempt to implement liberalizing reforms were suppressed by clerical hardliners who have reversed the reforms and in mid-2005 succeeded in backing the election of an arch-conservative to the post of president of the republic. The new government is actively backing the development of nuclear energy and seems committed to making Iran a nuclear-armed nation, goals which have given rise to great alarm among the USA and European nations.

Iran is a large country, slightly larger than Alaska, and is mostly arid or semi-arid, with a rugged mountainous rim. It suffers from periodic droughts, as well as flooding. Dust storms, sandstorms and large, damaging earthquakes are frequent. Some 69,000,000 people live there, of which 51% are Persian and only 3% are Arab. The remainder are peoples that have mixed in this great central plain lying between Asia, Europe and Arabia, such as Azeri, Kurds and Turkmen. 89% profess the Shia branch of Islam and some 9% are Sunni (the Arab branch of Islam). There still remain very early Christian sects as well as Zoroastrian, Jewish and Bahai sects. The median age is 25 and the population growth rate is 1.1%, only slightly higher than the USA. The death at birth rate though is about 40 deaths per 1,000 live births, more than six times higher than the USA. The literacy rate is about 79%. About 10% of the population uses the Internet, some 7,500,000 people.

Most economic activity is controlled by the government. The private sector consists mostly of small-scale workshops, farming and services. Iran exports some 2,500,000 barrels of petroleum per day and is one of the world's top producers. The income derived from petroleum exporting accounts for 80% of export revenue. Iran has, however, been the recipient of economic foreign aid in recent years, as 40% of the population is below the poverty line. The unemployment rate is acceptable at 11% and, for those who have work, the monthly income, at $260 per month, is twice as high as the larger Arab countries. Iran is currently experiencing a 16% annual inflation rate. Iran is a major transshipment area for Afghani and South-east Asian heroin into Europe and the Iranian government maintains treatment programs for its more than 2,000,000 heroin users.

The current ultra-conservative president, elected in mid-2005 with a 62% popular vote, has embarked on a course of fomenting confrontation with the USA and resisting the pincer action that US armed forces have mounted in the surrounding countries. The liberal candidate had acquired 36% of the popular vote but suffered electoral losses as his supporters have been gradually intimidated by the Islamic hardliners into abstaining from political activities or even voting. The Islamic Consultative Assembly, a 290-seat unicameral congress, was last elected by popular vote in 2004, when the conservative Islamists won 190 seats and the reformers and independents managed only 93 seats. The USA and Iran have not reestablished embassies or diplomatic relations since the US embassy hostage crisis in 1979.

All males, upon reaching 18 years of age, are subject to military service of one and a half years, and sixteen-year-olds may volunteer for the armed services. During the Iran–Iraq war, males as young as nine years were recruited and fought against the Iraq forces. Successive suicide waves of youthful volunteers stormed through Iraqi minefields and into the concentrated firepower of well entrenched Iraqi troops, a tactic which caused much loss of life to the Iranian troops with no positive effect on the outcome of the battles. There are some 1,000,000 Afghan refugees living in Iran as well as 100,000 Iraqi refugees.

In Iran, Christians may carry up to two liters of alcohol in their vehicles, but Muslims are subject to jail and fines if the frequent police controls detect any alcohol in their vehicles. The national identification card specifies the religion of the bearer. As in the surrounding countries, the punishment for a Muslim who converts to Christianity can be death. For a Christian who converts to Islam and then back again to Christianity the proscribed punishment is impalement, having a sharpened stake driven up the anus a sufficient distance to support the weight of the body, which is to be held aloft for several days.

Afghanistan

Afghanistan was founded in 1747 (some thirty years before the USA in 1776) by a tribal leader who managed to unite the majority Pashtun tribes, who still comprise a 42% majority of today's population. Occupied at various times by British and then Soviet forces, the Afghans inflicted heavy losses on the occupying troops, eventually driving them from their lands. Currently nominally pacified by government and former Northern Alliance troops, some of whom also served either the former communist government or the opposition mujahedin, a recent series of attacks on government and coalition troops seems to indicate that the defeated Taliban are regrouping.

Afghanistan is a large country, about the size of Texas. It is mostly arid and semi-arid and suffers through cold winters with snow and subfreezing temperatures and hot summers. It is mostly comprised of rugged mountains. Although 12% of the land is arable, the country's natural resources are vastly underutilized. Most of the population suffers from severe shortages of potable water, housing and electricity. There are 31,000,000 citizens, of whom some 4,000,000 have fled the country as a result of the nearly continuous warfare. In the past few years some 2,300,000 have been persuaded to return and resettled. The Afghans are not Arabs, but are of mostly White European lineage, mixed with Mongol genetics.

In spite of the US invasion and over eight billion dollars pledged in economic aid by international donors since the fall of the Taliban regime in 2001, Afghanistan remains one of the poorest countries on earth and highly dependent on foreign aid. Medical care is rudimentary. The average life expectancy is only 43 years, one of the lowest on earth. There is a high risk of contracting a number of infectious diseases. About 1.6 babies of each 10 born die at birth, one of the highest death rates on earth. Even so, the population is increasing at a 2.67% growth rate, more than two and a half times faster than the USA.

It is a very young population, with an average age of 17.6 years. Some 80% profess the Sunni branch of Islam and some 19% follow the Shia branch. 53% fall below the poverty line and there is 40% unemployment, as well as an annual rate of inflation of 16%. The average monthly wage is only $60, one of the lowest on earth. Only one in 1,250 people use the Internet. Only one in 620 has a fixed telephone line. One in 50 has a mobile telephone. There are some 250,000 people who are internal refugees, fleeing drought or political instability. The literacy rate among males is 51%, but among females it is only 21%, again one of the lowest on earth. Most women are obligated to wear the burkha, which is one of the most oppressive items of clothing imaginable. The burkha covers the women from head to toe, even veiling their eyes and obstructing their ability to see. Women have been beaten in public for refusing to wear the burkha. Some have had their painted fingernails torn out.

Expanding poppy cultivation and a growing opium trade account for one-third of the gross national product. Hashish is also a large cash crop. Afghanistan is the world's largest producer of opium, a now much maligned and misused medicinal drug. 80 to 90% of the heroin consumed in Europe comes from Afghan opium. Many narcotics-processing laboratories throughout the country provide revenues for various armed groups.

The US has successfully installed a democratic government for the past five years and the people now enjoy a bicameral national assembly, some of whose members are directly elected by the people.

Pakistan

When British India was liberated by Mahatma Gandhi's peaceful revolution in 1947, the largely Muslim state of Pakistan and mostly Hindu India became politically separated. India and Pakistan have fought three major wars since then. In the course of the last war in 1971, East Pakistan became a separate nation, Bangladesh. In response to Indian nuclear weapons testing, Pakistan developed and tested its own nuclear weapons in 1998. The world held its breath until tensions between India and Pakistan eased in mutual talks since 2002. In 2004 the two nations instituted a ceasefire in the disputed and heavily fortified border region of Kashmir.

Pakistan is mostly hot, dry desert, with arctic climate in the northern mountainous region, which contains some of the highest peaks in the world, such as K2. One-fourth of the land is arable but vastly underutilized. The majority of the population has no access to potable water. As in Afghanistan the population is descended from mostly White Aryan types, in Pakistan's case mixed with Indian genetics. There are 166,000,000 people living there with one in three falling below the poverty line. Although the official unemployment rate is only 6.6%, underemployment is widespread. The average monthly wage is $75. Many workers migrate to the rich Arab Gulf states seeking employment opportunities. The use of child labor is widespread. Typical Pakistani exports are textiles, leather goods, sports goods, carpets and rugs. Pakistan imports some 300,000 barrels of petroleum per day, but is self-sufficient in the production of natural gas. Some 2.4 billion dollars in economic aid have been granted to Pakistan in the past two years by international organizations, mostly as a reward for cooperating in the war on terror.

The population is young, with an average age of 19.8 years. The life expectancy is low at only 63 years. There is a high risk of contracting an infectious disease. There are 70 deaths per 1,000 live births, more than ten times the USA's rate. Even so, the population is growing at more than twice the rate of the USA. 97% are Muslim, with 77% following the Sunni sect and 20% the Shia. The literacy rate among males is 61.7% but among females is only 35.2%. There are less than 10,000,000 fixed line or mobile telephones, or one per 16 people. Only one in 22 use the Internet.

Suffrage is universal at the age of 18. The bicameral parliament is constituted by the 100-seat senate elected by provincial congresses and the 342-seat national assembly directly elected by the people. Sixty of the latter's seats are reserved for women and ten for non-Muslims. The military, however, remains the most important political force, with the current president being the former military chief of staff, who took over the government in a relatively bloodless coup in 1999. Sixteen-year-olds may volunteer for military duty. The first female air force pilots have recently begun service.

Some 2,500,000 Afghan refugees have been repatriated but 1,000,000 still remain inside Pakistan. The border with Afghanistan is porous and uncontrollable, although the government has sent troops to the remote border regions in an attempt to control cross-border terrorist and narcotics-smuggling activities. Pakistan both grows poppies and serves as the principal transshipment point for Afghan opium. There are some 3,000,000 internally displaced persons inside Pakistan, fleeing adverse economic conditions and political instability.

Where Can They Go From Here?

So, as we have seen, the Islamic nations, although diversified, do share some similar characteristics.

1) The terrific oppression, unparalleled anywhere else on earth, of female citizens.

2) The complete lack of any democratic government as far as the Arabic Islamic nations are concerned.

3) The very low level of average annual income per citizen among the more populous nations.

4) The lack of high technology industries, precision-manufacturing plants, research and development centers, which prevents them from receiving benefits from the international value-added economy. All Islamic nations are basically suppliers of raw materials and low-value manufacturing to the world economy.

5) Islamic nations in general have very repressive laws regarding sex. Prostitution in several Arab countries is punishable by death. Homosexuality is punishable by death. It is a shame for an unmarried woman to speak to a man and in many Arab countries, is seldom done. No images of humans or animals are permitted in painting or sculpture (since the artist might produce scenes of fornication). The marriage ritual requires a wait of several months after the ceremony before the couple can engage in copulation or even kissing. The divorce laws are heavily biased towards the husband. Sex education is completely non-existent and is prohibited. In some countries the female's clitoris is removed to prevent women from enjoying sex.

However, although legal in all Arab countries, in practice very few women are willing to be a second, third or fourth wife. Nearly all marriages are limited to one wife these days, with the occasional exceptions, since men are legally allowed to marry four women, but only with the consent of the number one wife.

6) Only a few nations have a tradition of suicide attacks, or vicious attacks on innocent civilians. All Islamic countries have these traditions. Only Japan, some regions of India, and the Tamil Tigers (Indians who moved to Ceylon) in Sri Lanka have similar traditions.

7) The Middle Eastern Islamic nations have probably the cruelest legal codes on earth, where the respect for human life is practically non-existent. For thievery, the punishment is the cutting off of one hand. If there was more than one offence the offender may also lose a foot. Writing a check without funds is a serious crime resulting in imprisonment. Taking a loan and not paying it back also results in imprisonment, so mortgages are extremely rare. The banks only deal in business loans. In some areas of some countries, adultery can result in the offender being publicly stoned to death. In Saudi Arabia, having the odor of alcohol on one's breath is punishable by six months in a hellhole prison and thirty to fifty cane strikes. Trafficking in prohibited drugs, unless you are in the family of the president, can be punishable by death. Of course, more serious crimes such as murder, treason, armed robbery, assault with injuries, are punishable by death.

One would think that with such a tough penal system these countries would be relatively crime free. Not so. The value of human life or the value of the property of a human is very low. Although not as dangerous as the USA or most of the rest of the countries in the Americas, an obvious Westerner would not be advised to venture alone in the less touristy areas of any Islamic country, with few exceptions.

So beginning from these facts, what could realistically be expected to be the immediate future of these peoples? The USA and the UK have elaborated a plan to break the back of the fundamentalist Islamic movement. Counting as pro-West the North African nations, Morocco, Algeria, Tunisia, Egypt, and now Libya, has recommended that Arabs and others should not attack the US and its interests as this is no longer profitable or conducive to the results desired, and, discounting the backward and mostly black Islamic countries (south of these countries) as irrelevant, the US and the UK have taken military positions on both flanks of the most dangerous Islamic country, Iran. By occupying Iraq and Afghanistan, Iran is truly menaced with a possible military punishment.

Further east, Pakistan (at least the government) is pro-West. In the Middle East itself, the US and the UK have troops positioned in Saudi Arabia, Qatar, Oman, the Emirates and Kuwait. Jordan and Israel are pro-West. Only Syria is considered at this time as a possible enemy, but a weak one. The rich Gulf countries, Qatar, the Emirates and Bahrain, are pro-West. Only Yemen and Oman are very dangerous countries, but very weak military powers. So by occupying Iraq and Afghanistan, the US and the UK are making a bold move to implement democracy in the Arab countries, an experiment that has never been tried. Should democracy take hold, then the pseudo-democratic system in Iran might turn to the West's favor and put into power a liberal pro-West government, as a large percentage of the people are actually against the repression forced upon them by the conservative mullah hierarchy that has ruled the country by the Islamic code since the return of the Ayatollah Khomeini in the mid-1970s. Should this happen, other nations in the region may eventually overthrow their presidents for life or their absolute monarchs and institute some form of democratic government. So Iran, now, is the big target for the penetration of Western ideals and the USA and UK must keep up the pressure on the Iranian government, while at the same time sustaining the fragile, new-born democracies on both Iran's frontiers, Afghanistan and Iraq.

Should the plan succeed, the US could look forward to a hegemonic region, where fledgling democracies allow their citizens to vote for their favorite political parties, whilst the natural economic drives of the natives, newly liberated by the lifting of governmental and bureaucratic oppression, would then surge forward, causing the region to enjoy a flourishing of development, the construction of factories and the creation of service industries, thus resulting in an increase in the income of the average citizen. The happy, free citizens would then dedicate themselves to capitalist commerce and would no longer support the terrorists among them, thus the entire region would cease to be a threat to the US and the American way of life. Another enormous section of the planet would have been converted to capitalism, adding to the triumphal march of the American way after its recent victory over the communist world.

But is democracy apt for the Arabic peoples? What will be the result of this experiment? Are the Arabic peoples prepared educationally, economically, emotionally to completely change their perception of the purpose of their life on earth from one of serving the precepts of Muhammad, the prophet of Allah, to one of seeking material advantage and accumulating electric appliances? What are the USA and the UK offering to the billion followers of Islam that could attract them more than the paradise of cool water, fruits and endless copulation that awaits them for eternity? The acquisition of a refrigerator hardly compares with eternal bliss, especially if it is punishable by the continuous burning pain of one's skin being consumed by eternal fire. The Arabic peoples are not just afraid of tanks and machine guns. They are afraid of eternal punishment that will continue on after the Americans have blown them to bits and can no longer make them suffer. That's when Muhammad's Allah will take over and really make them sorry that they didn't continue with the lifestyle that has served them for 1,400 years. What do the Americans have to threaten with or offer to the Arabic peoples that compares to this?

Just the opening of a stock market, at which company shares can be traded among speculators that have nothing to do with the operation of the companies, where future values of commodities can be gambled with by professional mark-up men who never take delivery of the commodities, purchasing only with the intent of marking up the cost of the commodity to the actual users. Perhaps an eventual increase in the availability of electric appliances and automobiles. But very likely that possible increase in the availability of consumer goods will, as in the communist nations now turning to capitalism, benefit only the few who find themselves in the upper middle classes for many decades. If, in a nation such as Egypt, where an excellent wage is $120 per month (lower than Mexico), there appeared more appliances, unless the population began to draw a much larger wage, which could only result from engaging in manufacturing jobs, then the vast majority of the people wouldn't be able to buy anything. The upper classes already have far more than their Western counterparts. After all, the Arabic lifestyle is the originator of the definition of luxury. Do people dream of living like a pasha or a sultan, or like an American millionaire? The millionaire is humble in comparison. So this possible increase in appliances some fifteen to thirty years from now does not convince the vast majority of the population living on subsistence wages. In any event, the USA has not even considered how these electrical appliances are going to be delivered into the Arab countries, because the US may not be taking into account the Lebanese mafia.

In the Arab satellite television field, advertising is controlled by powerful Lebanese advertising agencies. If a manufacturer or exporter is not paying one of the Lebanese advertising agencies, then his goods frequently become damaged at the ports of entry. This is due to the ancient kingdom of Tyre. For the past 3,000 years, the cities of Tyre and Sidon (now Lebanon) developed colonies of their citizens all around the North African coast, Carthage being the most powerful and famous colony. These colonies were the ports of entry for all marine traffic, as the ancient Lebanese controlled the maritime routes to North Africa through their fleets of ships well up into the apex of the Roman Empire. These expatriate descendants of Lebanon are still there, manning their posts at the ports of entry, working as shipping managers, stevedores, customs officials. Though the network of the Lebanese advertising agencies, word comes to them that, let's say, General Electric is not paying. Suddenly all kinds of problems develop with the entry of GE televisions, toasters, whatever, into the Arab ports. Damage to the cargo increases, deliveries get lost, paperwork is not in order at customs. So how are these electrical appliances the USA wants to sell to the Arab peoples going to get to them? And even if they did, how will a family earning $120 per month be able to pay GE the tremendous price they need in order to make it worthwhile to ship their products to the Arabic peoples?

Of course, the popularity of television does make the average Arab family endure any severe hardships in order to be able to afford one, but not many can afford a satellite receiver, so they mostly watch the official government ground-based free-to-air television transmissions, which are pure propaganda with a dose of Arabic music concerts, endless hours of transmissions of people lining up to kiss the king's hand or similar, black-and-white movies, and political talk shows. Ground-based private television stations are mostly not allowed in the Arab world and only a few government-funded television satellite stations operate under the guise of being quasi-independent.

So is this introduction of appliances and automobiles really going to work to conquer the hearts and minds of the Arab peoples? Certainly no sane person in government in the USA or UK is considering that Christianity will suddenly make headway in the region. Maybe Bushie will, being a born-again Christian... having been saved from alcoholism by TV preacher Pat Robertson... but surely wiser heads will prevail. After all, everyone knows about the efforts made by the crusaders for hundreds of years. And the fact that Islam arose well into the heyday of Christianity in Europe and Christianity was then and has always been well known to Arabs and they've never shown any interest in it, and the actual teachings of Islam are designed to allow Muslims to take advantage, enslave, or at least develop an advantageous commercial relation with the hapless Christians.

In fact, one of the Arab satellite television transmissions is a Bible-Belt, Christian fundamentalist transmission that has been going for several years... in English. As maybe a tiny percentage of the Arab audience actually understands English, it is doubtful if Bible-thumping TV preachers shouting, 'The Lohd Jeezus, the Lohd Jeezus! Repent ye sinners!' has made any converts in the years it's been on. There is a higher chance of the Arabs converting to Judaism than to Bible-Belt TV preacher worship.

But other efforts have been made by the US government to conquer the Arabs though television. The US congress has funded an Arabic television news station (in Arabic!) called Al Hurra. The setup costs were $75,000,000. The fact that everyone knows that it's based in Langley, Virginia, the headquarters of the CIA, sort of let the potential audience deduce that it would take a pro-US slant on the news reporting and be a source of disinformation. So the audience levels are a real disaster, as the Arabs have not been keen to find out what the CIA has to say to them and as the Arabs who earn enough to be able to afford a satellite receiver are above average in intelligence as well as income, the programming has fallen on deaf ears. Another effort was made by the US with Iraq TV, the ground-based free-to-air Iraq government television transmission. However, the insurgents targeted the roving reporters, news directors, producers for assassination and blew up many of the transmission antennas, so Iraq TV was quickly reduced to studio-based transmission in a heavily defended compound, as many of its personnel have been killed.

But there is another option for conversion and security: the military option. By occupying the areas with ground troops, the USA and the UK hope to kill the hardcore fundamentalists and physically intimidate the Arab populations. But since the US has lost twenty times more soldiers since the war was declared won by Bushie, it seems the pacification program has not been going according to plan. In fact the Arabs have a saying, 'Sure, with 200 tanks you can go all the way to the center of Baghdad. But the problem is, how do you get them out?' So the true test as to whether ground forces can have an enduring positive effect on the hearts and minds of the 20,000,000-strong Iraqi population, or at least vanquish the long-time ruling Ba'ath party and Sunni minority, is yet to be played out on the world stage. But now Bushie is threatening military action against more radicalized Iran, in order to keep the new fundamentalist government from acquiring nuclear weapons. Probably a good thing, remembering the tens of thousands of Iranian youths who performed suicide and hopeless charges against Iraqi lines during the Iran–Iraq war. One would conjecture that the Iranian mullahs who rule the nation would not hesitate to detonate a nuclear bomb at the first opportunity, and considering their past economic, logistic and military support of various terrorist groups that have performed kidnappings, airline hijackings, indiscriminate civilian terror bombings, etc., one could expect that a nuclear option in the hands of the mullahs would quickly have dire consequences for the Great Satan and its allies. Although with 66,000,000 people (roughly one-fourth the population of the US), Iran would prove a prohibitively tougher nut to crack than Iraq or Afghanistan as far as occupation.

So the introduction of appliances and automobiles seems like a viable option. If properly advertised through the Lebanese advertising agencies, the USA might find that the irresistible urge of having more time off from household chores and easier travel would have such a powerful effect on the psyches of the Arab people that they would opt for a bit of paradise here on earth, rather than take a chance on an eternal paradise that none have ever seen. The desire for appliances can be easily instilled by advertising, needs can be created and then filled, even planned obsolescence can be introduced to increase profits. This is truly one of the weak points of Islamic fundamentalism, which offers no appliances. After all, the basic reason for the success of the Jewish, Christian and Islamic religions is the offer of a day of rest every six days. If appliances give one more rest and less work, they are certain to triumph over any other consideration for the vast majority of Arabs.

The problem remains that not many Arabs can afford appliances or automobiles. Surely the Western manufacturers are not going to give their products to the Arabs to convince them to convert to capitalism? After all, the whole point of the existence of the manufacturers is to achieve an advantageous economic relation with their customers. So the income of hundreds of millions of Muslims must be increased so that they can be converted to capitalism. The only few possibilities of achieving this feat seem to be in either, a) increasing the productivity of hundreds of millions of Arabs through education, training, investing in advanced manufacturing plants in their countries; or, b) the Western consumer paying more for the raw materials supplied to the West from their lands (as the export of manufactured objects from the Arab countries to the West is insignificant). The first option is very unlikely, to say the least. Never before has the West attempted to improve the manufacturing capacity of hundreds of millions of poor ignorant people, who hardly do any manufacturing now, although the European Union is making a valiant effort in attempting to absorb the poorer nations of Eastern Europe. Besides the sheer magnitude of the task, obstacles present themselves in the lack of Arab speakers that would be needed for such an ambitious and enormous program of education. Also the closed-minded, backward-thinking attitude of nearly all Arabs would prevent the West from even being permitted to address the Arab population in any capacity, much less as teachers. Arabs are not like the Japanese businessmen of recent times, eager to share their management techniques with the West. Rather, the Arabs think that they already know everything and since their religion came 650 years after Christ, there is nothing that an ignorant Christian could teach them.

The West launching an investment program in Arab countries in order to build advanced precision manufacturing plants would face many problems. One is that few Western companies would risk any capital in building plants in countries where all the previous Western company investments have been nationalized and the Western companies kicked out with little or no compensation. Also in these countries, the crooked way is the only way, and the costs of obtaining permissions from myriad petty officials and bureaucrats that stand ready to block any acquisition of land, importing of machinery, hiring of workers, entry visas for foreign specialists, export licenses, energy hook-ups and so on, is so vast and difficult to calculate that no sane company would consider any unprotected investment. Protection comes from the physical presence of the country's armed forces, which is the only thing that would convince the would-be grafters. Also, the risk of terrorist attacks is extremely high, and those people are not convinced even by the presence of the armed forces. Also the untrained, unskilled labor available would require an enormous, patient, painstaking training program that could take some time to bear fruit.

In fact, the Western investor might be surprised by some of the local customs, such as for example a newly hired delivery driver sucking the gasoline from the petrol tank and selling it, or even removing parts from the engine and selling them, then claiming that the vehicle broke down, instead of finishing his first day on the job. And the fact remains that the national policy of all Arab countries is nationalization of foreign investment at the first opportunity and throwing out the foreign investor under the force of arms if need be. So an education program is absurd, training would be useless without the existence of advanced machinery, and investment in any capacity is strictly for madmen or CIA and US, UK government-infiltrated or associated enormous businesses such as the major oil exploration and international construction companies, that have some hope of intimidating the Arab governments through the threat of attack from the US and UK armed forces. So the hope of improving the acquisition capacity of hundreds of millions of Arabs through these means is really non-existent, at least in the lifetimes of those alive today. So the appliances the USA hopes to sell to the Arab masses are more likely to produce a backlash of envy and disillusion when the Arabs continue to be unable to afford any of them and that bit of paradise remains just out of their grasp.

The second option, that the Western consumer would be willing or able to pay more for the basic exports from the Arab countries, which are petroleum or natural gas, also seems very unlikely. The increase in benefits produced by an increase in sales price does not filter down to a great number of people. In Saudi Arabia, for example, or Kuwait, the great part of the profits derived from the sale of the nation's resources remain in the hands of a few hundred people. Witness in Iraq that Saddam Hussein built some of the most ostentatious, humongous palaces ever known to mankind, many of which he seldom had time to even set foot in so that they remained empty for decades, while the people of Iraq did not have access to basic, essential medicine. This is the situation with all governments in Arab countries. The people are willing to sacrifice their comforts, even their very lives, so that their rulers may expose to the world riches and wealth beyond compare. In any event, the majority of the Arab countries' populations do not have many oil reserves, so that the Western consumers' contribution to the development of the oil-rich nations would actually do more to ruin the non-oil-producing countries' economies, as their oil-producing neighbors would be certain to charge them the same price per barrel as the Western consumer was willing to pay. Even if the increase in income due to the Western consumer being willing to pay a much higher price for petroleum did in any way filter down past the ruler's household to the population of the producing countries, their neighbors, the non-producing countries, would certainly not be cut in to the benefits acquired by the already rich producing countries, and would actually suffer an economic crisis perhaps worse than that which would arise in the West due to the oil price shock and the increased cost of transporting goods, raw materials and people, as well as the increased cost of generating electricity though fossil-fuel fired plants.

So really there is no price that the Western consumer could pay for petroleum that would raise the standard of living among the vast majority of the Arab population. Rather, as we can see now, the continuous oil price escalation will only serve to further enrich the Saud family and will drive them to new conspicuous consumption and spending excesses; will benefit the new radical Iranian government and give them funds to equip their armed services with more destructive weapons; will benefit Muammar Qadhafi and he will probably use the funds to invest in core European enterprises such as banks, media companies and football teams; will benefit the Kuwait royal family and they will probably pass on some of the benefits to the citizens and probably use some of the money to fund the opening of more mosques in Europe, as they have been continuously doing for several decades; will benefit the royal family of Qatar, which may use some of this windfall to continue to fund the money-losing Al Jazeera satellite television network with their virulent anti-American, anti-West 24-hour news coverage; will benefit the sheiks of Dubai and they will probably continue to buy major international businesses and bribe current and past US presidents to lobby for them; and ironically Iraq, the country that most needs the funds, will not benefit so much as their current oil production is fairly reduced by sabotage by the insurgents.

So neither the option of manufacturing plant investment by Western companies or of simply attempting to pump more money into the Arab countries' economies by paying more for their production of raw materials, has really any chance of succeeding in improving the standard of living of the vast majority of the Arab population and allowing them therefore to purchase all those appliances that the USA would like to sell them to lure them from their radical fundamentalism.

But what about democracy? Obviously nearly everyone cares a lot more about electric appliances than they do about their form of government. In all Arab countries that do not have kings, the supposedly popularly elected president always wins the elections with more than a 99% victory margin (except in Iran, which is not an Arab country), and is in effect elected president until he passes the post on to his son or is assassinated by some other popularly elected president. This has not bothered the Arab populations and very few zealots have risen up intent on delivering the nations into the hands of a democratically elected government. Rather, the anti-government uprisings have been in the opposite direction without exception, intent on delivering the nation into the hands of despotic rulers that followed a stricter Islamic fundamentalist code.

The reason is that democracy and Islam are not compatible. One can't follow Islam and be democratic at the same time. One can't order women to cover their bodies, chastise them in public for allowing a wisp of their hair to poke out from underneath their veil and also give them the right to vote. One can't prohibit the drinking of alcohol under the penalty of fifty canings, imprison people who fall behind on their mortgage payments, cut off the hands of petty thieves and give the population the right to make the laws. One can't kill prostitutes and homosexuals and also give them the liberty of free association. And certainly one can't order those who analyze or criticize Islam to be assassinated and give the people freedom of speech.

So what is this democracy that the USA seeks to implement in the Arab world? Is it really a complete change in the lifestyle of hundreds of millions of people? Is it a sudden break with traditions of thousands of years? Are the people going to be psychologically able to accept such a radical new world, where what yesterday was a crime punishable not only by death here on earth but also by the revenge of Allah, who would burn the transgressor's skin and make it re-grow again to be burned anew, now today becomes a commonplace occurrence protected by the police?

And don't the Arabs have democracy now? At least a form of democracy that suits their psychological makeup? After all, unlike the priests and prelates of the Roman Catholic Church, who are appointed from above by the Catholic hierarchy, the Muslim imams are pretty much self-appointed, although in practice the formal mosques are funded by governments. But there is no established hierarchy in Islam. Anyone can become an imam as long as he draws an audience to his preaching, much like the TV preachers in the US. There is no Pope in Islam, although the king of Saudi Arabia, King

Abduhlah, is the official Keeper of the Holy Mosques and Defender of the Faith, but he does not actually do any of the preaching. No particular desire has been demonstrated by any Arabic nation to implement democratic elections. Rather, much blood has been shed in attempts to implement fiercer, more stringent controls over the masses. In any event, as the Arabs say, the US says it wants to give freedom to the Arabic peoples, but is forcing freedom on them at the point of a gun.

So is this US-elaborated plan, this democracy thing, this free market capitalist system going to be accepted by the Arabs? Or is it a Bushie solution like the genetically altered tree that is going to absorb all the excess CO_2 and return the atmosphere to its prior state? If one puts a moderate pashtun in nominal charge of Afghanistan, such as President Karzai, does this do away with the oppression of women, cause the warlords to surrender their private armies, allow an increase in manufacturing, food production and service industries? Afghanistan is a tough nut to crack. The country has rejected the armies of the British Empire and the Soviet forces. They didn't do it by winning the battles from the start. At first they were occupied, but over time the Afghanis chopped away at the occupying forces until it became too expensive to maintain a presence there, and then the Afghanis went back to their way of life. The fact remains that the production of opium is the main export of Afghanistan and the US leads the world in prohibiting the world's peoples from consuming this drug, which for millennia was not only legal but was actually considered as God's gift to mankind and was in popular use as recently as forty years ago in the form of laudanum that your mother may have applied on your chest or given you to drink when you had a cold as a child. In fact, opium was the best medicine available to mankind for thousands of years.

So what made it suddenly into an abominable substance whose possession is punishable by up to twenty years in prison? Anything more than the intent of Western-based synthetic drug manufacturers to replace the drugs grown in other nations with their own version? Is this part of the democracy that the US hopes to implement in Afghanistan? Do they hope to market Valium there instead of opium? It seems, if anything, that poppy production has increased since the occupation and should the US try to interfere with this production, the consequences for the US troops on the ground that the Afghans can get their hands on could be dire.

So will the world really see this democracy panacea take root among Muslims and bring about the peaceful election of representative politicians, the outbreak of capitalist entrepreneurs among the newly inspired population, the gradual increase in the income of the average worker, the building of manufacturing plants, the increase in production, the development of service industries? Will these freed up, industrious Arabs then turn to consumerism and away from Allah and eternity? Will there follow an outbreak of personal liberties, women freed from the heavy yoke of millenary oppression, people allowed to criticize Muhammad and Islam without being immediately killed by the mob, homosexuals allowed to marry instead of being hanged?

This could happen if the repression was imposed from the top, from the apex of a pyramid of power. But this is not the case in the Arab countries. It is not King Abduhlah or the presidents for life of the Arab nations that oppress the people. In fact, in nearly every case, the rulers are actually a moderating influence or are in an outright war with Islamic fundamentalism. If one removes the current rulers, then far more radical Islamic powers will occupy the leadership. The impetus for Islamic fundamentalism is located at all levels of the pyramid of power. It is an unidentifiable enemy. One never knows when teenage British citizens are suddenly going to be enveloped in Islamic teachings and decide that they must blow up a few hundred of their fellow Britons during the morning rush hour, or singer Cat Stevens or others such as Cassius Clay will suddenly decide to convert to Islam and preach to their public the benefits of conversion. The problem remains that the implementation of democracy and capitalism is a battle of ideals, of thoughts inside people's minds, and almost anyone is susceptible to be converted from one band to the other at any time.

On one side we have Islam, which proclaims that one must submit to Allah, the all-powerful eternal God, so that one must always think that God is watching what one does and thinks. What's God's take on this, am I doing what God wants me to do? Am I thinking what God wants me to think? How does one know what God wants one to do? Well, the five times daily meditation sessions repeating the words taught by Muhammad certainly help to concentrate one's mind on the proper attitude in the presence of God. The weekly prayer meeting on Friday gives the Muslim an opportunity to hear the preaching of a learned imam that dedicates his life to studying the Qur'an and counseling parishioners in the ways of God. And of course the readings of the original writings of the prophet Muhammad, the last prophet, gives one an opportunity to absorb the rules for living, although the vast majority of them were designed for a far more cruel world of swords and daggers, rather than today's world of supersonic bullets and explosives. So the Muslim takes whatever information about what God wants him to do that he chooses and cobbles it together into some code of conduct that suits him.

But some of the things that God wants are clear to all Muslims. The daily prayer, the weekly prayer meeting and the fasting during the month of Ramadan. The giving to charity, although hardly any Muslim does that these days (as the God of capitalism has made serious inroads into Muslims' faith) and the trip to Makkah to throw stones at the meteorite (probably sent by Allah as a sign to mankind). And of course the killing of anyone who speaks against Muhammad, Islam or Allah, or, if not practical due to the circumstances, the outright refusal to hear the words of anyone who blasphemes. Also the oppression of women and the dealing harshly with criminals, prostitutes, drinkers or homosexuals, all of which are codified in the Qur'an. If one does all these things then one can expect an eternity of drinking cool underground water, eating desert fruits and copulating with lots of nice, manageable women. If one doesn't, then the worst pain imaginable by man, the eternal burning of the skin. This is the set of ideas that can at any time attach itself to the mind of anyone and cause him to convert to Islam. These are the precepts that keep the pressure on within the pyramid of power, so that those who would break away always have to be on the lookout for their neighbors, who might see their opportunity to achieve a reward from Allah by impeding one from digressing from the teachings of Muhammad. So the system itself functions because of a set of concepts which are highly influential to the minds of men, not because of any particular individual's position within the system.

On the other side we have democratic capitalism. Democracy or capitalism doesn't know much about any invisible God. Democracy teaches that every person in the age of reason, over eighteen years old, should be allowed to occasionally elect by majority vote a representative to govern over them and ordain their lives and relations. These elected officials should be accountable to the public and replaceable for misconduct while in office. Their power should be limited by laws interpreted by an independent judicial body. This is pretty much what Islam has now. The imams are allowed to preach to the congregations by the parishioners. A bad preacher does not draw an audience and soon disappears. The imam's conduct is regulated by a set of laws contained in the Qur'an and these laws are interpreted by other imams and the people in general, so that if an imam violates these laws the people themselves chastise him. The imam is always accountable to the parishioners and can be replaced at any time. So this democratic ideal is nothing new to Islam. So it really brings nothing new for Muslims to think about. The only difference is that the sets of laws that rule Muslims' lives are different to the laws that rule the West. So what the USA really wants is to change the laws by which the Arabs live. What the USA really wants is to prevent the Arabs from following the laws of the Qur'an and to replace them with the laws originated in the Magna Carta developed in the UK in the early 1200s, that have evolved into legal codes, quite different but sharing some similarities, in effect in parts of Europe and the United States and other Anglo-Saxon ruled nations.

In reality the Magna Carta failed to convince even the neighboring countries, such as France, whose penal code is based on Napoleonic law, or Germany, Italy or Spain, each with a different heritage and quite different laws. But the US hopes that its brand of democracy and rule of law is going to convince a huge race of people whose point of view in comparison to the USA is similar to aliens from another planet. Because the USA knows that it's right and they're wrong. And how do they know that? Because the USA has more refrigerators and electric toasters (which is true) and because the USA can kick their ass (which we don't know yet for certain).

The main advantage the USA has, the preponderance of electric appliances, has been brought about by free market capitalism. The exporting of this pseudo-democracy to the Islamic nations will not be of the slightest interest to the tribal-minded natives, unless it is somehow linked to electric appliances and automobiles. So what does capitalism have to offer Muslims? Only a tiny minority of Arabs live in tents these days (although Qadhafi and some super-rich Saudi princes prefer to spend a lot of their time in tents), where the accumulation of material goods is difficult and the supply of electricity is limited to batteries or portable generators. So electric appliances and a higher standard of living have a great attraction to Arabs.

The ideals of free market capitalism are as follows:

1) An individual or company should be able to buy an article for a certain price, and then sell it to someone else for a higher price, thus making a profit. This can be a result of having acquired the article at a bargain price, or marketing the article to a customer with a lot of convincing hype for a high price, or of having borne the costs of transportation and distribution of the article, or of having retained the article for some time until the demand for it increased. Sometimes cheating is involved, but it's not necessarily punishable by law. Well, the Arabs pretty much created this concept. For probably the past 10,000 years the Arabs have acted as a conduit for goods (beginning with stone-age flints and cutting edges) between the continents of Africa, Europe, Asia and India. Their camel caravans were the only means of transport in the desert areas of this land bridge between the continents. The Arabs are experts at buying and selling. Just visit any souk (bazaar) and you will immediately fall victim to capitalism in its purest form. In fact, one would have to say that the Arabs invented the concept of buying and selling for a profit. Nothing new there to conquer their hearts and minds.

2) The investor or capitalist, once he has acquired a surplus of money through this profit-making of buying and selling, should be allowed to simply put his money to work by convincing groups of people to do as he says and build him a factory, machinery, and other means of production, in exchange for (these days) paper with some colored printing on it. Then people will work with this machinery inside the

building (that now belongs to the capitalist under penalty of law and enforceable by armed employees of the state, called police) and produce goods (which also belong to the capitalist) in exchange for more pieces of colored paper. This is where the Arab world falls down; the machinery revolution has had a difficult time penetrating Arab culture. A lot of work is still done by hand, by artisans. Many shoes and slippers, lamps, tables, teapots are made by artisans.

However, Arabs have no problem in joining together to collaborate under some capitalist as a sheik, a sultan, an emir, a king, or a plain businessman soon finds plenty of labor available. The quality of the labor is where a deficiency manifests itself when compared to the industrialized nations. So Arabs don't need the idea of capital investment, which they probably also invented. As the caravan transport more often than not required the boss of the caravan, the head capitalist, and all the other merchants funding the trip, to arrive at the Gulf of Persia and pay for and acquire the goods that had been transported there on sailing ships. Then the caravans would transport the goods to the Mediterranean Sea, where they would be sold, at a profit, to a different group of merchants who would load the goods onto ships to distribute in Europe and Africa. So nothing new there either. The Arabs won't be excited by the idea of the capitalist and capital investment. They don't need the idea as they developed the system thousands of years ago. What they need is the machinery and the training.

The capitalist, instead of investing his accumulated pieces of colored paper in means of production, may put his money to work by depositing (lending) the money in a bank or directly to an end user (borrower). The end user then goes about exchanging the colored paper with people who are willing to work for him or give him goods in exchange for the colored paper. But the capitalist is taking a risk that the end user won't give him his colored bits of paper back, because the borrower will lose them or just plain keep them. So to compensate for this risk, the capitalist demands a profit on the loan, or a rate of interest applied over a certain time period. This allows the capitalist to do absolutely nothing in life of any use to anyone, except make decisions as to whom he shall lend his colored paper, and thereby support that person or company's efforts in their business.

This is the apex of every capitalist's dream. To be the decision maker who doesn't have to work, doesn't have to produce anything, to be the one who just has free time to live as well as he wants and acquire material goods. If the Judeo Christian Islamic religions have success because they give a day of rest every six days to their followers, then having the freedom of having nearly all days of rest and infrequent days of decision making and contract signing is certainly quite similar to a paradise right here on earth. However this practice, known as usury, was prohibited in the Bible and throughout Europe until the Age of Enlightenment. Until the Rothschild family developed and demonstrated the usefulness of being able to transport money from one country to another without actually taking the money with you (a service for which they had to charge fees), the charging of fees for allowing someone the use of one's money was both a sin and a crime. However, the Qur'an mentions this concept as well. It allows Muslims to charge non-Muslims interest, but prohibits it on loans among Muslims. So this idea is also nothing new – nothing to win the hearts and minds of the Arabs with there; again, a concept that was codified at least 1,350 years ago among Arabs. In fact, Arab banks were functioning internationally and outside their empire, doing this very function of crediting money to depositors at the end of their commercial journeys, thus facilitating commerce, at least since the year 800, 900 years before the Rothschilds applied the concept in Europe. The Rothschilds, of course, were Jews related to the Middle East.

3) Another fundamental capitalist concept is that the free market is usually the best determinant of the value of goods and services. In other words, if people are willing to pay $100 for a gallon of gasoline, then the government shouldn't interfere to

keep the price at a lower level. However, in the US, wage and price controls were imposed by the Nixon administration, and in many cities throughout the US, rent control maintains the cost of renting some apartments at absurdly low levels. Again, nothing new there. Arabs have had laws about rent control, have lifted laws about rent control, and have followed the free market gyrations for millennia, and one can be certain that they are selling their petroleum at the highest price the market will bear. Nothing new there either.

Surely the USA doesn't pretend to export its pseudo-democratic governmental system as an example to other nations? The only country in the western hemisphere (other than Haiti) to sit the son of an ex-president in the presidency, a land where senators and congressmen serve for twenty, thirty years, elections where nearly always less than half the eligible electorate bother to vote (presumably because the majority would have preferred to vote for none of the candidates), the democracy of the USA may fool some of its own citizens, but overseas its political system has been eclipsed by more representative forms of government for decades. If the US couldn't fool the 10,000,000 Cuban people 90 miles away into trying their democracy, how can they expect to convince hundreds of millions of Arabs that have a far more radical point of view than the Cubans could even imagine?

In any event, Arabs don't want a complex multiparty government. The lack of a strong central authority will only open up inter-tribal, or inter-religious faction warfare. The opening up of opportunities for political power delegated to a multitude, instead of one man, will dramatically increase corruption among the totally corrupt bureaucracy. The only thing that keeps the corruption in check now is the fear the average bureaucrat has of being caught and punished by the top man. If power is delegated to many, then the bureaucrats and officials will jostle to make each their own little kingdom where they can squeeze the public for even more bribes. The Arabs have dealt with democracy thousands of years ago. They were Hellenized by the Greek culture long before the Roman Empire was a gleam in the eyes of a she-wolf. Greek city-states flourished in Egypt, Turkey, Cyprus, Syria and Lebanon. Their multi-millenary experience with letting everyone have a say in running the government was negative, as it led to warfare, fractious wrangling and divided effort. They look for one strong man at the apex of a power pyramid. It's also less expensive to furnish the one man and his family with the luxuries of good living than to have to supply a large number of less powerful minor officials. The rugged individualism that arose in the USA, as newly arrived settlers faced vast expanses of empty fertile land, has no place in a land where there are cities such as Jericho, that are 8,000 years old. All that was going to be said and done about dividing up the land and its resources was hashed out thousands of years ago.

So the USA really has no new ideas, no invading thoughts, no virus-like replicating concepts that could be introduced into the minds of some of the Arabs in order to convert them to capitalism and cause them to influence other Arabs, and get a huge ball rolling, and motivate them to start producing and consuming, and start electing free governments and start investing in factories, and maybe have more consumer goods available, and raise their standards of living, and become educated, and light up a thousand points of light as beacons shining in their societies to help the poor and disadvantaged.

The Arabs invented capitalism 10,000 years ago, they have a more democratic system in their religion than the Roman Catholic Church, and what they need is machinery and training and education, but their society won't allow a foreigner to invest in it safely, or even to visit as a tourist at times.

So the Muslims have concepts that can invade the minds of Western man, namely endless copulating with manageable women in paradise, and the West has no idea that could influence the minds of Arabs. Nothing that they haven't been doing for thousands of years or are doing now to a further limit than the Western wealthy. For example, Dubai has the only six-star hotel on the planet.

So when an invading culture has no new ideas that can convert the subjected peoples to their way of life, then it must attack the ideas of the subjected peoples and take them away from, 1) their educational system; 2) their media; and, 3) their places of meeting.

Doubtless some of these ideas are offensive to Western and Christian morals, beginning with the basic concept of Islam, the use of violence to achieve one's goals. But do the Christians have any concept that effectively refutes the validity of using violence against other people to convince them to do what one orders them to do? After all if it works, and it is what Yahweh did to his followers for thousands of years, who is to say that Muslims shouldn't practice this method? But in any event, as long as the US and the UK have set about to convert the Arab world to a more peaceful, less terrorist-supportive stance and way of life, they should make an effective effort that has a chance to achieve the results desired. The consequences of total failure, such as being forced out of Iraq and then Afghanistan in a military campaign waged by the insurgent Muslim fundamentalists, would very likely have disastrous consequences for the status and military standing of the US and UK. And this is a distinct possibility. Afghanistan alone forced out the British Empire at the height of its power, as well as the USSR armies at the height of their power. The US has attacked Iraq simultaneously, one of the most powerful ancient empires that held sway over the Middle East for centuries and is threatening Iran, the ancient Persian Empire that dominated vast tracks of the planet until Alexander the Great's invasion. The risk of total failure is higher than the invasion of Vietnam. The US could be facing a combined population among the three nations of over 100,000,000 people, as well as a continuous stream of fanatic foreign fighters. The blow to US prestige, should it be forced to flee, could also lead to severe economic consequences for its citizens.

But the US has, however, a huge reserve of allies against Islamic fundamentalism. And that ally is Arab women. Although powerless now, not even permitted to drive an automobile or open a bank account in Saudi Arabia, the Arab women are on a campaign for political and economic power that is similar to a struggle between, well, men and women. Arab women are tough, and have racial pride as well as Arab men, but they place their interests on a higher plane these days than they did in the recent past, or at any other time before. The insurgence of Arab women seeking equality with men is a real threat to Islamic fundamentalism. Islam and the Arab countries would be a totally different system and world if women had full equality in jobs, in political power, in matters of sex and marriage. And many of them want this equality and are quietly rebelling and carrying out actions to bring about this emancipation. The last generation was the last one where many men enjoyed the practice of plural marriage. The women have practically put a stop to that in current times. In all North African countries, the veiling of the woman has practically ceased with this generation. In Tunisia, for example, the older women who still carry on wearing the veil, often grasp the ends of it between their teeth, rather than tying it underneath the chin, as if to express the anger and rebellion at feeling obligated to carry on with this custom. The wide availability of rifles and handguns has allowed some women to kill their husbands in Afghanistan and elsewhere, and this really was the root cause of women's emancipation in the West. When the overbearing hubby realized that his docile wife could easily end his life with the squeeze of a finger he had to think about giving some rights to the little woman (or about not giving her a good beating to show her who is the boss). In Iran, women have stood up and protested over their right to wear make-up and attractive clothing. In Saudi Arabia, women have protested to be given the right to drive. In Morocco very recently, the divorce laws that allowed a man to divorce his wife by going to the mosque and saying to the imam 'I divorce thee' three times and thus avoid any further financial obligation to his wife or her children, have been abolished, and replaced with more Western-style laws. So women are on the rise, and by their sheer numbers and impact on the husbands' quality of life – as no man wants to live with a wife that makes his life a living hell every time he goes home – the Arab women could also have a decisive impact on winning this war of ideologies. Also, women are the ones who most want the electrical appliances that the USA wants to sell to the Arab countries. And, as we have seen, the USA has no invading idea, no superior culture and no moral concept with which to motivate the Muslims into accepting American superiority.

The Arabs, seeing the weakness of American society and political systems, do not even give credit to the USA's stated intention of bringing a free, democratic society to the invaded countries. The Arabs see it simply as a power play to gain influence in the area and a grab for petroleum at a cheap cost – just as all the countless invasions of myriad empires that have invaded the area over the last 5,000 years. However, it is by influencing women that the US could most easily undermine the Muslim world. Another option is to subliminally attack the very basic ideas and mental mechanisms of Islam with propaganda. The purely military occupation solution will soon prove to be too costly to be maintained and the only lasting impact the US will have on the Muslim world, once it is forced to run with its tail between its legs, is to leave the impression of the victory of Islam and increase the power of the Islamic fundamentalists, which will lead to foreseeable showdowns with the US and further isolation of the Arab world.

The Best Defense, Offense?

So why should the West put up with being attacked by terrorists? Is it necessary for the average person in the First World to live in fear of being blown up in the commute to work on the train, or of crashing while flying on an airline, or even of having a nuclear device explode in their city?

For many decades during the Cold War it was necessary to live in constant fear of being vaporized by nuclear bombs. In fact, the US government frequently bought this expectation to the minds of all Americans through the emergency early warning system drills, when all radio and television emissions in the USA would be taken over by the federal government to emit their one-minute beep. All school-children in the country would be herded into the hallways where they would huddle in the corners, sitting on the floor with their head between their legs in the safety position that would give them the best protection from a twenty-megaton blast five miles away. People would hustle into nuclear bomb shelters in preparation to survive what would certainly be the end of civilization, maybe even mankind. 'This has been a test of the emergency early warning system. Had this been a real emergency... etc., etc.' (Wasn't the announcer the same guy that did the introduction to the *Outer Limits* TV show?)

But everyone knew that if it had been a real emergency, everyone had to run – run for the countryside, run for the hills, anywhere away from the target centers. Don't bother to take the car because there would surely be a traffic jam of biblical proportions. The president of the USA, one man with his finger on a red button, could cause hundreds of millions of people to start running for their lives (leave the children behind, they'll only slow you down and you can make new ones, maybe). The good old days, what nostalgia.

And when there was increased tension with the USSR over some international incident, the frequency of the tests of the emergency early warning system would increase, sometimes to several times per week. Prepare the people to survive a possible apocalyptical rain of nuclear warheads, between three and five per city, enough to blow the very surface of the earth clean away, leaving huge craters, miles across, which the ocean would rush into, in the case of coastal cities. Tough to run away on foot from something like that. But you had to try, to see how far you could run in the twenty-minute time period that the early warning system gave you before the first bomb would detonate. Maybe try to get behind a hill or something.

So the government of the USA has lost the attention of the people. It can no longer concentrate their minds, focus their efforts on a common reality that held the attention of the masses for so many decades. Without a common enemy the masses turn to what interests them the most. And that of course is to having days off from work, acquiring electric appliances to do their work for them, and trying to live like successful capitalists that no longer have to work because they only invest their money. Their money works for them and other people are the ones that have to work in order to be able to pay back the money that I (the capitalist) invested in them (the workers), plus the interest that I charge for having taken the risk of letting them touch my money.

And so the common enemy of the Islamic terrorist really helps to focus the First World peoples and mold them into a more compliant mass. The exceptional measures needed to detect possible terrorists allow the governments to implement laws and police procedures that would, under normal non-war circumstances, cause an uprising of the masses in the defense of individual freedoms that they had become accustomed to. People can put up with terrible hardships, but when authority tries to take anything away that they already have then people feel cheated and try to resist. So the recently enacted laws in anti-terrorist countries such as the USA, UK and Spain, designed to detect and report to the government the movement of money that could be used to buy explosives, quantities as small as $10,000 are accepted by the population without a whimper. Most people probably weren't going to buy explosives. Maybe they just wanted to avoid some government taxes or just didn't want the government to know that they had $10,000, but in the current climate of war against terrorism the population feels that they have no choice but to submit to tighter government control, loss of privacy and personal freedoms, and increased government oversight of their finances.

The motto of the defunct USSR secret services, the KGB, was 'The key to offense is defense'. They realized that their political system was weak and could cause many of their own people to become traitors to the cause. They needed to control all the information that even their own trusted officials received; they controlled any contact with foreigners who might give their people a new reality (even through a few minutes' chat), and prevented their own people from leaving the country under penalty of death for trying. The US society, likewise, has to make certain that in this war against Islamic fundamentalism, the home ground is adequately defended. The chances that millions of Muslim troops are going to land on American soil and occupy the nation are non-existent. However, past immigration from Islamic areas certainly has allowed considerable numbers of fundamentalists to enter and settle inside the US borders. Some of these Muslims may constitute a fifth column, perpetrating devastating attacks inside the USA. Doubtless some terrorist cells are inside the USA today.

An altogether different problem is the clash of ideology. After all, the war is not about the physical differences between the Arabs, Indonesians, etc., and the American peoples. Al Qaeda terrorists attacked the USA not because they don't like how the Americans look or because they hoped to loot the goods of the USA to benefit their own people, or because they hoped to take over the land and force the Americans to work for them – the usual reasons for war. The USA was attacked with the intent of winning an ideological war. The USA was suddenly and very visibly hit by a propaganda slogan, a marketing campaign, a merchandising effort to sell an ideology to people.

When the Japanese bombed Pearl Harbor they achieved two things. One was the destruction of the US Pacific fleet, which would effectively delay US efforts to attack Japanese forces, and the other was the sending of a propaganda message to the US government and its people. The message was, 'Look how dangerous and effective our armed forces are. Perhaps your nation should consider not trying to militarily push our armed forces from the lands that we have conquered and occupied.' This message clearly had the opposite effect that the Japanese High Command hoped for, as the Americans, incensed at the sneak attack, then devoted more energy to attacking the Japanese than they would have if the Japanese had chosen a soft defense of negotiation and concession and had forced the USA to declare war on them.

A similar situation arose with the September 11, 2001, terrorism attacks. The US population, angry at the sneak attacks, supported the US president in invading two nations far away from the Americas and only in late 2005 began to run out of angry energy to motivate the vast effort at occupying these nations, Iraq and Afghanistan, and suppressing the resistance.

So the initial ideological attack of the Al Qaeda terrorists had the opposite effect of their intended one. Perhaps they hoped that there would be an uprising of Muslim fundamentalists, and that further attacks would take place throughout the Islamic world on US forces, embassies and interests. Surely they expected to roll back Westernizing influences in the Arab world. Instead the US has occupied their principal training bases and positioned itself to break the spine of the Arab world's anti-USA power centers. The USA now tells the governments of Afghanistan and Iraq that their governments are to be secular, not to be denominated as Islamic republics.

But Islam is not like Japan. There is no Hiroshima or Nagasaki to bomb, no homeland to invade. Islam is a state of mind and traditions, based only in the beliefs of a billion people, in the following of a code of conduct founded on violent conquest, not peaceful resistance like Christianity. To defeat Islam, the US must destroy an invisible world of angels and Satan, of Jinn (Jeenies, which are written about in the Qur'an), of a paradise of copulation, a hell of burning fire, an all-powerful God, The killing of a few thousand Iraqis, or tens of thousands, or even hundreds of thousands will only serve to strengthen Islam. The US belief in the power of science is a far more effective weapon against Islam than tanks and bombs.

So what was the propaganda slogan that the Al Qaeda terrorists hoped to get publicized in the world media? By attacking the Pentagon, the control center for US armed forces, they rightfully expected to show to the world, and the Muslims in particular, the symbolic vulnerability of the USA's mighty armed forces, when attacked by a few true believers armed only with ingenuity and faith in Allah (remember Muhammad's two miracles?). And by attacking the World Trade Center and shutting down the New York Stock Exchange located on nearby Wall Street, they hoped to get all peoples to think about what their system of beliefs are and what it would lead them to when faced with the Day of Judgment and the eternal world after death. And it certainly had that effect.

The US economic recession that had started in November of 2000, when Bush and his brother Jeb used political power to impede the Democratic Party candidate from taking office as president of the United States in a popular election that Al Gore had probably won, immediately ballooned in the aftermath of the September 2001 attacks into a sudden major lack of confidence on the part of consumers and businessmen in the viability of the US's capitalist system. This lack of credibility quickly spread to Europe and other nations and became an economic crisis. The central banks reacted by lowering the interest rates to the lowest level since the Great Depression, in order to let the borrowers and consumers know that the money was worth hardly anything. What was important was that people continue to consume and produce, continue to have faith in other Americans exchanging their products and labor with each other. The money could be borrowed practically with the promise of paying it back and a little bit on top to keep the banks in business and their millions of employees working. So although the Al Qaeda strike had the opposite effect of intimidating the US's armed forces, the main message of the terrorists was, 'What is going to be the outcome of people's wheeling and dealing, making profits, speculating, taking advantage, cheating each other, when death comes, as it surely will, and you have to face an all-powerful God that has been watching what you have been doing all your life?'

And, 'Have you thought about eternity today?'

Muslims think about eternity five times every day.

So the American public was taken aback and paused in their consuming and buying, awed, not just by these messages, but also by another basic concept of Islam: 'I am willing to die in order to kill you.'

Hardly anyone in the USA is willing to die in order to kill others. Occasionally the unbalanced sniper may start picking off total strangers with a long-range rifle, or unhinged schoolchildren may live out their immature fantasies by butchering their classmates and teachers, but when faced with an entire community of people who profess their wish to die in attempting to kill them, the American consumers stood back emotionally for a time from their get-ahead world and considered these propaganda slogans. But soon the low interest rates had their effect. The average American wasn't going to buy these new ideological products so cleverly advertised. Although the merchandising was highly effective, very cleverly presented, and certainly an attention-getter, the invisible world, the all-powerful God that never does anything that can be clearly identified, the life after death for eternity while we can all see the cadavers decomposing, just couldn't compete with getting some really good electric appliances right here on earth and enjoying the life people are certain exists.

Why should Americans take a chance on what might turn out to be a complete load of rubbish, whose origins in the minds of mankind can be traced back through time, obviously developing from even more primitive concepts, when everyone can touch an automobile or a flat-screen plasma TV? Although, true, bank accounts and stock shares certainly require a great degree of faith on the part of many people to allow them to exist.

And so the American economy has recovered, pulled back from the brink of collapse by the very institution and businesses (the Federal Reserve Bank and private banks) that were both a sin and a crime punishable by law a few hundred years ago. And so it seems that sin is recovering its dominion over the minds of Americans as they reject the thought of how they should behave if there really was an eternity to face and an absolute good and evil of some type that would be enforced by an all-powerful God evolved from Yahweh, God of the Armies, imposed by the God tribes in Europe and the Arabs in North Africa, the Middle East and the Far East areas near their ancient trading colonies.

So the American psyche is collectively recuperating its confidence in the pillars of American capitalist thought. What are those pillars?

That all men and women are to be treated equally under the law, except for the president of the United States, who has immunity while in office, and in practice for life, as well as accredited foreign diplomats who can only be expelled from US territory for committing crimes, rather than imprisoned.

That people may claim a legal title to land and any construction upon it, as well as movable goods whether titled or untitled, and the police forces of the state will enforce this right to the individual's private property, even to the point of killing another individual who refuses obstinately to respect this right.

That people have the right to cast a vote in occasional elections to elect the overseers of the governmental bureaucracy, or to present themselves as candidates for such elections as long as they have not been convicted of a felony, are affiliated with the Democratic or Republican parties, and are not known transgressors of social, moral or economic mores that are generally in effect among the electorate (with rare exceptions).

That people have the right to commit most crimes, and if they are not accused for the period of seven years following the detection of the crime (the seven-year jubilee from the Bible) then they can no longer be accused. If, however, they are accused and caught they have a right to be defended by a lawyer, to not incriminate themselves or their spouse, and to trial by a jury or their peers. Recently they've also acquired the right to spend the rest of their lives in prison if they are convicted of a third crime (one of them with violence) or if they possess a small amount of distilled cocaine (but only if they are black).

People have the right to borrow money from individuals, banks and other entities and if they don't pay it back it is not punishable by the penal system (as long as they have made a truthful loan application to a bank, or they could be accused of bank fraud). Not paying back a loan to a bank or individual in Arab countries is a serious crime punishable by imprisonment.

That people have the right to own guns, pursue happiness, worship freely, and move about inside the USA (external travel requiring a passport has become somewhat difficult under the Patriot Act).

That people have the right to assemble in groups and speak their mind. Unless they threaten to kill the president of the USA, which is a federal offence punishable by up to five years in prison, or incite racial or religious hatred, or conspire to commit a crime. However, speaking one's mind on radio or television transmissions requires a federal license and one may not cuss (name sex organs or some bodily functions explicitly). This is not the case in Spain, for example, nor is nudity considered illegal.

That the individual is an important part of the nation, that personal effort can be central to one's success, and that anyone can, even though starting with nothing, achieve a very high status in American society and realize one's dreams.

These, then, are the ideas that form the pillars of American society, the very foundation of the legal relations among those who live within the boundaries of the US frontiers. There is no other country on earth where they apply. These basic rights are derived from the English common-law system. Only in the United Kingdom and other Anglo-Saxon ruled nations are similar laws and expectations in effect. In fact, the English once ruled and occupied both militarily and through settlement the greatest empire the planet has ever known, extending throughout North America, great parts of Southern Africa, India, Burma, Singapore, Australia, New Zealand, etc. The English attempted to impose this legal system, this framework of mores and morals, on the subjugated peoples. They attempted to educate the subjected peoples for decades, even hundreds of years. In fact the entire Arab Middle East was for some decades under the control of the British. It was Great Britain that gave independence to Saudi Arabia, Iraq and Jordan, a benevolence that especially the Saud family much appreciates still today.

However, the legal system that the US is attempting to impose on Iraq, although shopped throughout the region and great parts of the planet for decades with meticulous, continuing effort on the part of the British, didn't find widespread acceptance. In some countries it simply disappeared completely, or was replaced by a cruel imitation where presidents for life continuously win elections with more than 99% approval rating. In others, such as Singapore, a very small nation of people who chose to migrate there, it took root. In India some of its precepts continue today, although in a highly modified version adapted to local conditions. In all the Arab countries it just evaporated as a mirage in the desert heat. None of its precepts had the slightest effect on the region under dominion of the ruling British liberators.

Yet the USA expects to implement this socio-political system within a few years, as they are in a hurry to get back home. The US wants these silly Arabs to take their freedom, organize their elections and get on with producing and consuming like 'normal' people, as the US has got its own business back home to attend to.

But 'the key to offense is defense'. The USA is certainly offending a great number of Arabs. Has the USA provided for an adequate defense of its homeland? The measures taken through vigilance, police controls, monetary controls, although harsh, realistically cannot be expected to provide complete security against further terrorist attacks. A few determined, well-prepared terrorists will always have a great tactical advantage over all the police and military efforts of the US forces. The advantage to strike when least expected at unprotected targets in a land as vast as the USA cannot realistically be compensated for. As Al Qaeda demonstrated in London, terrorist cells could blow up crowded commuter trains pretty much every week if they wanted to. The only advantage the defense forces have is that the terrorists fit into a particular typecasting. For them to be willing to act in the name of Islam, they must have been exposed to Islamic teachings. Very few well-off non-minority members would be liable to be recruited for suicide bombing missions. The London bombers, however, were not the typical Middle Eastern types. They were British, Pakistani youths, even Jamaican. So we see that Islam presents an ideological danger to the West not just through its traditional areas or dogmatic influence, but also through influencing black and mixed-race people. So the precepts of Islam have some potential to infiltrate American and Western societies. And since these precepts are so devastating, even a very small number of converts can pose a real danger to the safety of large numbers of people.

The American dogma – the basic worth of the individual, the sanctity of human life, the rights to liberty, freedom of worship, self-expression to be enjoyed by all – are in decided contrast to the Islamic dogma – the value of life on earth is nothing compared to the Islamic paradise that will last for eternity, the individual will enter this paradise if he dies while trying to convert the faithless to Islam, personal freedom is better sacrificed in the service of Allah, freedom of worship is to be limited so as not to contaminate the faithful, self-expression in the form of criticism of Allah, Islam, the prophet Muhammad, or even its more respected imams or mullahs is to be punished by death.

So we can deduce that the American dogma has an intrinsic advantage over the Islamic dogma, which, if properly exploited could eventually lead to the destruction of Islam as a set of reference for human thought. That advantage is that the American set of precepts is based on the existence of the individual, and everyone can see that the individual, themselves, exists. The desire to satisfy yourself and make yourself happy here on earth while you are alive is very much noticeable in the vast majority of people and difficult for the individual to suppress.

Islamic thought, on the other hand, is based upon the existence of an invisible world, really a copulating paradise, to which the faithful believer will accede upon dying. In no Islamic writings has anyone ever presented any statement of having personally acceded to this copulating paradise. No one has ever been there and come back to tell humanity about it. So a billion people alive today (and billions who have already died) have set their life goal to be one of acceding a copulating, fruit-eating, cool water-drinking paradise that no one has ever claimed to have been in. There is just no proof that this paradise exists! There is not even a single writer of even doubtful credentials who says that he has been there!

But people continue to ordain their everyday lives in order to be allowed to enter this paradise when they die. The copulating paradise is a very powerful attraction among people and should not be taken lightly among sexually repressed Anglo-Saxon puritans. This paradise has some following among certain kinds of people in the US and does have the potential to convert large numbers of people to Islam within the USA. In fact, if there was easily seen proof that this paradise existed, one would venture to guess that the conversion rate to Islam would immediately become overwhelming. But there isn't any proof now, nor has anyone ever claimed that there was. This is truly a weak point of Islam. The very basis of the entire religion and system of thought, namely an eternal paradise and burning hell, could just be an evolution of ancient Babylonian religions cobbled together by primitive tribes, changed and merged with other primitive religions into an effective crowd-control set of dogma that was imposed by the force of arms and used to facilitate the conquerors' control over the defeated peoples. It could actually just be a self-perpetuating set of dogma that has successfully convinced many people to spread its teachings because it appeals to certain basic human desires.

Just like a computer virus convinces Microsoft software to email the virus to its list of email contacts and then infects those other computers, Islam mostly appeals to the males' natural and frequent testosterone releases. Primitive Amazonian Indians, still living in near isolation from other peoples, when approached by an expedition of researchers and scientists, recently became familiar with the expedition party and confided to them that when the men have free time from their chores of hunting and defending the small tribe, they relax by thinking about their women. Before the invention of television, radio, books, men would spend their free time thinking about women, food and drink. Men are subject to a small release of testosterone, the male sex hormone, into their bloodstreams every few minutes. Women, on the other hand, experience a comparatively massive release of hormones only one time per month, which brings on their pre-menstrual irritability, increased sex urges, aggressiveness, swelling and finally the hemorrhaging of menstrual blood. Men are therefore naturally inclined to think about copulating with women every few minutes, as the testosterone activates their sex drive. When a man is busy, working or even watching an interesting program on TV, the man may not notice the testosterone effect, but when a man's mind is idle, not concentrating on anything, the powerful urge brought on by the testosterone suddenly coursing through the bloodstream causes the average healthy man to desire sex.

Islam was designed by Muhammad to appeal to the strongest natural desires of the Arabs – sex, sweet food and cool water – and conversely to frighten them with the greatest pain known to man, the total burning in a fire that never dies. If the West could prove to the

Arabs that these concepts are false, that there is no such hell or paradise, then the entire religion of Islam would fall apart and the terrorists would have no motivation to commit suicide bombings.

The other option is to make life on earth so satisfying to everyone that the dreamed-of paradise conditions are approached right here in real life and few would want to take the chance on leaving this earth any earlier than they had to, in order to ascertain if better conditions really existed in this invisible, unproven world. And this, incredibly, is the option that Bush and the US government have chosen in their effort to conquer the hearts and minds of the Arabic peoples. The official policy of the US government is to forcibly institute a new set of concepts in Iraq among the population that will somehow lead to an improved standard of living and paradise-like (at least USA's concept of paradise) conditions eventually arising among the masses. This earthly paradise is expected to develop within the next year as the USA would like to pull its military forces back home. The major obstacle in implementing this legal and ideological reform has recently shown itself to be the introduction of majority rules, representative government – in other words the much-vaunted democracy of the US. This concept, above all, is to be the justification for all wars and invasions undertaken by the USA, to free the peoples from the oppression of dictatorial rulers and minority aggression. To give the invaded peoples the freedom to elect their own rulers by a majority vote.

Right off, it turns out that the Shiites comprise 60% of the population of Iraq and voted for a Shiite government. The Shiite-elected officials wanted the nation of Iraq to be an Islamic republic. The US occupying officials said no. Iraq is going to have to leave its Islamic history behind and completely change its code of laws to laws more akin to US laws. The democracy with majority rules, after all, is not apt for Iraq. Immediately, the moral reason justifying the invasion, the basis of the USA's hope for the empowerment of the Iraqi people, the panacea that was going to solve all the problems of the Iraqi peoples and, once introduced successfully into the area, that was going to spread like a virus and conquer the hearts and minds of the peoples in the surrounding countries eventually converting the entire region into modern, prosperous, pro-West commercial partners, an exemplary democratic government, turns out not to be appropriate for Iraq after all.

The fledgling democracy must be tampered with and resembles more a temporary compromise between tribal factions, which may be all it is ever going to resemble. It seems the innate enthusiasm among the natives to adopt the American way of life and American laws has not yet taken full root. So the realistic possibilities of the USA being capable of motivating the Iraqis into instituting a copy of the USA's own legal code and way of life are miniscule and the expectation that the basic standard of living among Arabs would improve dramatically as a result of emulating the USA's economy are unlikely. So the US really has a low probability of bringing about this paradise on earth that will cause the Arab people to turn away from Islamic fundamentalism. A much more likely outcome will be that the US troops will head for home soon, as a result of pressure from pacifists within the US and growing frustration among the US population in general at the lack of progress in bringing democracy to the Iraqi people. Once the troops are gone, depending on the circumstances in which the troops abandon Iraq, the Islamic fundamentalist movement could find itself even more powerful than it was before the Iraqi invasion, which could result in new terrorist attacks in the USA.

The previously mentioned option of taking away the basic precepts from the Arab mind that the US disagrees with, therefore, remains as a viable option. However, Muhammad had foreseen this ideological attack 1,350 years ago. The genius of Muhammad was that, unlike Jesus Christ, he devised a system of thought that appealed to man and therefore propagated itself quickly, as well as coming equipped with a set of self-defense mechanisms that made its destruction very difficult. Jesus Christ's system, from what can be devised by the scant writings of purported actual eyewitnesses and participants in the teaching activities of Jesus Christ, seems to be this – 1) the taboos on unmarried men and women being in each other's company and camping and traveling together were lifted for his followers; 2) the property of any of his early followers was to be sold and the earnings to be turned over to the apostles in order to sustain the early Christian groups economically; 3) the laying on of hands and faith healing of illnesses and the expelling of demons was the main activity, although after the original twelve apostles died, this healing ability ceased to exist; 4) Jesus Christ preached that people should love each other, practice peaceful submissive co-existence, honor their parents, obey the commandments, and if they did, when they died they would be raised up to Jesus Christ's father in heaven, and if not they would be punished with being placed in an oven where they would be cooked and burned; and, 5) he also convinced his apostles that the people alive then would see the end of the world.

Not much to offer mankind there, really. Jesus Christ refused non-Jews entry into his religion, the prohibition on private property certainly only appealed to poor people who, if joining a Christian group, would benefit by being able to live without working from the sales of property of newly converted members who were relatively wealthy, probably convinced of the upcoming end of the world and fearful of being placed in an oven should they not obey and donate their property to the church leaders. The expelling of demons only worked in the lands where there were demons, not even working in Jesus Christ's home town as the people there had no faith in him and presumably weren't fooled by his shenanigans. When Christianity spread to Egypt, Turkey, Greece and Rome there weren't any demons there to expel as the people had never heard of them, so that practice quickly died out in one generation. The only enduring contributions of Jesus Christ's teachings were that people should love each other and lead submissive peaceful lives, obey general rules for co-existence, and not be concerned about hoarding wealth in this life, as a very hot burning oven waited those who transgressed, for eternity. The early churches' mixing of men and women apparently led to a lot of fornication as Paul sought to impose his anti-sex views on the early Christian followers in his repeated admonitions through his epistles preserved in the New Testament of the Holy Bible. Early going for Christianity was therefore difficult as it really was not a very appealing religion. It was a negative religion relying on the upcoming end of the world, an eternal punishment of burning ovens, to convince its followers to give their property to the leaders of the Christian communities. Other than that, its appeal lay only in the prospect of a peaceful life on earth in a brotherhood of man, a prospect that has never been realized.

Muhammad's religion, on the other hand, was very well thought out. The main precept was designed to take advantage of a fundamental weakness in the then rapidly expanding and official religion of Christianity. Muhammad taught his followers to physically attack other peoples and subjugate them into slavery or into allowing their land to be occupied and paying tribute. The surrounding nations in those days were overwhelmingly Coptic Christian. In a world full of meek, obedient Christians this was a winning strategy. But Muhammad had to convince his followers to obey him and fight for a common cause. So he borrowed the Christian hell, which didn't and doesn't exist in Judaism, elaborated on it, making it more horrible, and frightened his would-be followers with it. He recognized the truly central winning teaching of Christianity as this invisible burning hell. When you can actually convince people that, even after they die, Allah is going to make them suffer excruciating pain for eternity unless they obey you now, then the followers are easy to motivate. Muhammad also borrowed the Christian paradise, expanded upon it, made it much more vivid to the minds of men, made it exactly what men in those times daydreamed of, and gave it to his followers as a reward for obeying him. He elaborated a quite powerful mental virus capable of easily invading men's minds through the constant testosterone discharges, through everyone's fear of death and uncertainty of what happens to one then, and through people's fear of the excruciating pain of burning. This fear of burning is much greater in a world where fire is used for daily cooking and heating. As First World peoples have invented antiseptic means of doing these things, their contact with fire has been practically eliminated and their fear of it has been much reduced. But if you think back you may remember the moment when someone first warned you as a child not to touch that pretty flame. Fear of fire is one of the most important lessons all children learn.

This virus was capable of replicating itself as it dominated the minds of those whom it infected and caused many of them to preach the virus to other people they came into contact with. But Muhammad also prepared an anti-virus to preserve the minds of his followers from being contaminated by any other argument but his. This, as in Christianity up to the 1600s, was the edict that any convinced follower had to kill anyone who tried to convince him that his religious ideas were wrong. So Muhammad's well-thought-out system has remained impervious to ideological attack for 1,350 years.

Another advantage that Islam has over Christianity is that Muhammad's teachings have been preserved in the original form, in their original language, for 1,350 years. Christ's teachings, on the other hand, preserved in the Holy Bible, are a mish-mash of sometimes opposing traditions, conflicting interpretations by dozens of authors, the majority of which have not been selected to form part of the Holy Bible, and the only thing one can be certain of is that not one word of the Holy Bible has been written by Jesus Christ or dictated by him to the authors. Also, every word has been translated through several languages, and of course details, facts, ideas, even basic concepts are usually lost in translations, especially of ancient dead languages.

So Islam proves itself to be, to an impartial observer, a far more effective and well-thought-out religion than Christianity, and well prepared to resist attacks from even a reasonable modern ideology such as the American way. In fact, Muhammad's precepts have the USA war strategists stymied as they are afraid to face Muhammad's teachings and fight them head on. One problem is that when the teachings have convinced followers of the existence of an invisible world, even though there is no proof or experience of the existence of this invisible world, there is equally no way to prove that this world doesn't exist. The only way, really, is to remove it from the minds of people. Also, as this world was fashioned from the Christian tradition that pre-dominates in the West, any ideological attack upon it is an attack upon one's own mental world. The pragmatic reason, though, is Muhammad's anti-virus. The US strategists are afraid of the consequences of large numbers of incensed followers of Muhammad triggered into action by Muhammad's orders to kill all those who speak out against Islam, by appearing to be propelling a concerted effort to blaspheme against Islam.

So, as the reader can deduce, the USA really has very little possibility of making any inroads against Islamic fundamentalism. A ground-based military occupation, in the face of intensive guerrilla resistance, will soon be phased out. The intent of bringing Anglo-

Saxon democracy to Iraq or Afghanistan didn't have any influence under the British Empire and is the only bet on the table for the US. Should it lose, the consequences could be highly negative. The only option that would do away with the Islamic fundamentalism problem, selling science and deductive thought to the Arabs so as to replace dogma of faith, is unacceptable to the US strategists as they fear a backlash of suicide warriors intent on carrying out Muhammad's instructions of killing the blasphemers. So Muhammad's Islam remains a great and resistant set of concepts, showing surprising resilience in today's modern world and continuing to expand faster than any other religion on the planet, and it is already the largest most powerful religion on earth, or ever known to mankind. Is the USA susceptible to Islamic expansion?

Certainly discontented minorities within the USA have already, decades ago, adopted Islam as a means of uniting its members and combating oppression by the USA's government and the white majority. The Black Muslims is an organization that has been going strongly for many decades. Jamaican Rastafarians also practice a cult that is anti-white domination, a cult that features smoking marijuana as a religious ritual and chanting 'Killum the Popum'. Two Jamaicans have so far been arrested for attempting suicide bombings as part of Al Qaeda attacks on a US-bound airliner and in a London Tube train. The number of mosques in the USA in 1900 was probably zero. In 2000, a hundred years later, it is over 2,000, not counting the Black Muslims' meeting halls. So we see that a number of Arabic, Pakistani and Indonesian Muslims have migrated to the US and many of them are spreading the system of thought, increasing the number of converts.

Some white people have been converted, most noticeably Cat Stevens, who recently stated that he was amazed that, after practicing Islam for three decades, he had found that Muhammad ordered the killing of those who criticized Islam and Muhammad. How ignorant does a person have to be to practice a religion for three decades without knowing what its basic precepts are? This enlightenment did not dissuade Yusuf from continuing to practice Islam, even agreeing that if Muhammad said so, then it must be right to kill those who criticize Islam. Does this mean that we can expect Yusuf to kill someone who criticizes Muhammad in his presence? Or would some of that right-of-free-speech indoctrination that he received in his past life as Cat Stevens overcome Muhammad's anti-virus trigger?

In reality, Islam's penetration of the average white American male could become a possibility, except for the power of women. American women are generally the most adamantly opposed to Islamic precepts. Even among the rebellious American teenagers who have adopted rap or hip-hop as the music of choice to demonstrate their anger against their parents' control, Islam cannot take hold, as the girls won't have it. This is another structural weakness of Islam. It was designed to penetrate the minds of men. This was effective in the time of Muhammad, when men dominated women, but Muhammad didn't foresee the change in the power balance between men and women. In today's First World, women offer the first line of defense against Islam. Women also offer one of the best lines of attack against Islam in the Muslim world.

So does the US have any real concerns about a possible invasion of Islamic ideology? Perhaps it should. Immigrants from Muslim countries certainly represent the best source of recruitment for possible terrorist cells. Also Black Muslims may be easily convinced to take action against US interests, if they feel that it would benefit them, or if they feel discontent due to lack of economic opportunity or discrimination. Jamaicans have demonstrated their willingness to attack US and British civilians in terror bombings. However, the US remains intent on allowing freedom of worship and expression, one of the basic precepts of the American way. In the UK, however, the Blair government is taking steps to detain or expel Islamic fundamentalist preachers who advocate taking action against non-believers. The US remains in the Islam-lite attitude, preferring to believe that any religion similar to Christianity must be basically good and good for the people to follow. Better for the Arabs to worship God in their own way than to not worship God at all. US officials, though, should realize that Islamic teachings are the same everywhere, and not subject to interpretation. The degree to which a convert decides to accept these teachings is the only variable.

The US plan of ideological defense is really non-existent. The government officials are so certain of the manifest superiority of the ideology of the American way over primitive Islam that no efforts are made to combat Islamic ideology. The US combated and nearly prohibited communist ideology. The current strategy is simply to absorb Muslims with the expectation that they will be converted to the American way by merely being in contact with Americans who believe in it. Likewise, this is also the offensive ideological strategy. The US government expects that simply by sending US soldiers to Islamic countries to physically remove the oppressive leaders that dominate the population, and by allowing contact between the soldiers and the people as well as between the US-appointed representatives and the new government leaders to instruct the new leaders on how to implement the American way, the American ideals will propagate themselves throughout the population, as the Arab people will see first-hand just how beneficial and superior the American concepts are to their old Islamic ones and will themselves become the standard bearers and agents for change within the Arab world. Although these expectations may prove to be overly optimistic, there are real possibilities for at least limited success along the lines that US strategists envision.

The US-devised strategy of surrounding Iran with troops, locating bases in Kuwait, Qatar and Saudi Arabia so as to influence the supply and price of petroleum, and rolling back Syrian influence in Lebanon, has a chance of accomplishing its goals, as long as there is not an Islamic fundamentalist uprising among the Arab populations. This, of course, is what Al Qaeda was betting on when they launched their offensive against the USA. A concerted effort on the part of the population to evict the US troops from their soil would be unstoppable. Such an effort is underway in Iraq and should it succeed, could serve as an inspiration for other nations. Already the number of attacks against US troops in supposedly pacified Afghanistan has increased manifold in late 2005 and 2006. The US should make all efforts to win the hearts and minds of the population and discourage it from attacking the US soldiers. If the ideological battle is lost to Al Qaeda, then the ground war will be as well.

To win the ideological battle, the US hopes to free up the business restrictions imposed by governmental bureaucracy in Iraq, thus eventually allowing the creation of some type of well-to-do middle class who, imbued in the American way, would serve as an example to the masses and would agitate to imbed the American way into the framework of Iraqi life. This strategy may have worked in Germany and Japan after World War II, but only because it was supported by a massive economic and reconstruction aid program (called the Marshall Plan), which put the surviving population to work rebuilding their constructions and their infrastructure. The US hopes that the improvements in Iraq's infrastructure will come about as a result of the operations of the free market, as countries interested in purchasing petroleum from Iraq will invest in reconstruction and modernization, knowing that they will be paid from the income derived by Iraq from the sale of oil.

The other prong of the strategy, the influence of the broadcast airwaves, rests on the US-owned Al Hurra all-news Arabic satellite TV broadcaster funded by the US congress, which broadcasts from Langley, Virginia, and Iraq ground-based free-to-air Iraq TV. The nature of these propaganda efforts is limited to 'the US is nice, we're here to help you', etc. Also the US has intimidated and reached agreement with Saudi-owned Al Arabya all-news satellite TV broadcaster, which has changed its slant from rabid anti-Americanism to support for the US mission in Iraq. Al Jazeera remains anti-US occupation and ANN (Arab News Network) owned by Rifaat Al Asad, uncle of Syria's president Basher Al Assad, also is certainly not helping the US to win the hearts and minds of its audience even though it is based in London. Rifaat also owns some 40% of Astra satellite, which carries the majority of European satellite transmissions to Europe, in German, English, Dutch, French and Italian. So the Arabs are aware of the importance of owning the means by which to reach the masses. The US effort to penetrate the Arab satellite TV transmissions is actually inferior to the Arab effort to buy means with which to penetrate the Europeans' TV satellite transmissions to Europe.

Al Qaeda's basic goal was not to defeat the US armed forces with maybe 25,000 trained guerrillas. Rather, it was to draw the US into a ground occupation of some Arab country that would provoke an uprising among the Arab peoples, who would then successfully evict the US forces and then, enjoying the support and prestige gained by this victory over the faithless invader, to consolidate Islamic fundamentalism's hold on power in as many Muslim countries as possible. The US is merely to be used as a catalyst in carrying out this strategy for long-term growth and eventual ascension to power. And this is exactly how the situation is playing itself out. The Arabs have had experience with foreign invaders before. They eventually evicted the European crusaders who successfully seemed to have conquered the Middle East every time the Europeans marched their troops there. As time went on, the situation became untenable for the European occupiers. The Mongol hordes also invaded Turkey and the Middle East and conquered the entire region, but eventually were absorbed by the Arab population and were converted to Islam, becoming the Ottoman Turks who eventually founded the Turkish Empire and conquered Istanbul and great parts of south-eastern Europe for Islam.

So Al Qaeda leaders had elaborated a long-term strategy, based on historical experience. They are not seeking short-term rewards, such as power for themselves. They are carrying out a long-term plan designed to at first lose territory, draw in a common enemy that will unite the Arabs in the effort to evict the faithless invader, and once that relatively simple task is accomplished, the Islamic fundamentalists will once again enjoy a surge of control, a resurgence in Islamic power and a further expansion of Islam. Islam has only lost territory in the Iberian Peninsula in its 1,350-year history. It now dominates some thirty nations and has large populations in some ten more. The USA is just the great enemy selected by Al Qaeda to galvanize the Arabic peoples into a united effort at holy war, jihad, to create a fertile ground for Al Qaeda and other Islamic fundamentalists to sow the seeds of Islamic domination of Arabs' and other peoples' minds, morals, governments and realities. The US has been played and has obligingly stepped into the role of the invading blasphemer, probably not even realizing that it was helping Al Qaeda to achieve its goals and forge a stronger Islamic fundamentalist resurgence, that it may once again have to face in decades, maybe even centuries. For Islam does not conquer by force or arms alone. It also conquers by invading the minds of men with its ideology.

Does the USA have a realistic chance of extricating itself from this conflict without strengthening Islamic fundamentalism? Does the US have a chance of conquering Islam with materialism, technology, representative government? The US's chances of success would certainly be aided by an effective ideological attack, maybe even an ideological defense on the home front. Communist ideology was battled with barrages of propaganda, prohibition of diffusing communist thought, outlawing convening groups to discuss communist ideals. Islam is immune to these methods at this time under current US legal norms. There are a number of malcontents within the US citizenry to whom Islam has some appeal. An Islamic victory in the Middle East will embolden these individuals and a victorious Islam will seem as a bright beacon shining in the darkness of American materialism to attract new converts. The US strategists seem to consider Islam itself as some innocuous, beneficial system of thought that is suitable to primitive peoples. The reality is that it is actually a work of genius, a self-propagating group of precepts that is resistant to any logical or physical attack and which appeals to men's basic desires.

For example, a Muslim man may marry a woman of any religion but a Muslim woman must convert a foreign man to Islam before the marriage ceremony. When Muslims marry outside their faith it causes an expansion of Islam. The Muslim man will presumably dominate the foreign woman and the mixed children will be reared as Muslims by the dominant father. The Muslim woman will have converted her future husband before marriage, so that the desire of a man for a woman is used to expand Islam. The current Al Qaeda strategy also is not to be taken lightly. The US has been suckered into playing a role designed to strengthen Islamic fundamentalism. Whether the US was defeated in the process or temporarily victorious was irrelevant to the central true goals of the plan. The plan is about creating a fertile ground for the expansion and strengthening of Islam, not defeating the US military. The USSR also fell apart as a direct result of being defeated in Afghanistan by Islamic fundamentalists. A similar withdrawal from Iraq, which should be taking place by 2008, will boost Islam's credibility as an effective, victorious system of beliefs. As the situation is now, never has the world seen such a great number of Muslims convinced that committing suicide bombings is an effective means of achieving their personal goals. If the US used a cleverer strategy, the long-term battle of ideologies could be won in the next few years or decades.

As we have seen, Islam has developed some structural flaws that have arisen as a result of changes in the situation of mankind over the last hundred years. The main flaw is that the copulating paradise where the lucky man copulates continuously with as many wives as he wants, never really appealed to women that much. This was not a problem in the times when men dominated women, but in the last 100 years, as easy-to-hide, fire-and-load handguns became generally available in the industrialized areas, women achieved emancipation for the first time in the history of mankind. Women obtained real political power and near equality in some areas, and this way of thought has spread among women into the Islamic countries. Muslim women have effectively put an end to polygamy, that was common in Islamic countries at the beginning of the 1900s. For a man to attract several wives these days, he must be outstandingly wealthy, not just well off as before, and in some countries even that will not suffice. Women in many Islamic countries have shed the veil, and opt instead for attractive, Western-style clothes. Women are forcing changes in the divorce laws which left them without any maintenance or child support payments.

The Western ideals have also developed an advantage with the successful distribution of material goods among its followers. Islam can be seen in many ways, and one of them is as an ascetic religion, rejecting material goods. Another is as a bountiful religion, allowing the accumulation of a harem of wives, incredible wealth, even castrated human servants bred just for service. But as the pleasurable rewards of Islam, as far as the masses are concerned, are reserved for the invisible paradise after death, the industrial revolution in the West and the economic system derived thereof has made the Western lifestyle very attractive to many people. The undeniable existence of the individual, coupled with a political economic system's real ability to satisfy the needs and desires of the individual, is a very powerful antidote to one of Islam's strong points, namely that the invisible world, being unprovable, likewise cannot be disproved. The individual obviously is and the things he wants also obviously are, especially if he can get them. The invisible world is strictly an exercise in faith, resulting from peer pressure and childhood indoctrination.

Science, however, remains as the strongest argument in the ideo-logical arsenal of the industrialized nations. Another structural flaw in Islam that has developed over the last 150 years is the unforeseen advances achieved by scientific thought and methods. Muhammad did not provide for an ideological antidote to scientific success, which also caused the fabrication of handguns that allowed equality for women. So science is the most powerful belief system today that can overcome Islamic thought. Science appeals to everyone, both men and women, and especially to youth. Even the suicide bomber would prefer to use a nuclear bomb than a homemade, ineffective explosive. The dedicated terrorist prefers attacking with a Kalashnikov instead of a dagger. So the Islamic fundamentalists are already convinced of the superiority of scientific thought. They reject modern advances and the supplying of modern appliances to the masses because it corrupts them and turns them away from traditional Islamic prac-tices, but in the field of armament they want the latest scientific equipment.

So Islamic thought has shown great structural cracks in its very foundations. One is the desire for personal satisfaction right here on earth, as the god of capitalism has invaded Muslims' minds and prevented them from giving charity in accordance with Muham-mad's teachings. Another is the recognition that the god of science may be superior to the power of Muhammad's Allah, and provides effective means to achieve success here on earth. Yet another is the rising to power of women in Islam's ranks, many of whom reject the invisible copulating paradise, as it never really interested them that much. The remaining strong points of Islam are, however, formida-ble: the invisible world that cannot be disproved and the edict to kill anyone who speaks out against Islam or Muhammad.

The US could take advantage of these weak points in Islamic thought that have developed and also launch attacks against the strong points. Ordinary people, who feel that they have a personal stake in the success or failure of the US invasions into the heart of Islamic territory, can also take actions that will help the US achieve its goals of safety in the homeland and ideological domination overseas. The advantageous commercial relation that the US consumer wishes to maintain with the suppliers of petroleum will be greatly influenced by the outcome of this ideological warfare and the US invasions.

One action that almost anyone can take is to join the local mosque. Locate the place where Muslims meet and convert to their religion. Then you can join them in their weekly Friday prayer meeting. By taking one hour out from your free time, the average American or UK citizen can greatly influence the future of Islamic penetration in their country. Conversion is easy. You must simply take off your shoes before you enter the mosque, approach the imam and tell him that you wish to convert to Islam. He will probably give you some material to read, perhaps even a free copy of the Qur'an in English. You must then attend the Friday prayer meeting for at least a month, taking care to stand up and prostrate yourself (shoeless of course) at the same time as the other faithful around you. After a month or so you can approach the imam and ask for an appointment to perform your conversion ritual. At the ritual you must simply say, '*Ashadu anala y la ha y la la. Wa hanen Mohammeden rasulo Allah*,' which means that you accept Allah as the only God and Muhammad as his prophet. You will then select your new Arabic name. Muhammad is good, or any other name you desire. Soon after, the imam will give you a certificate written in Arabic with your new name, which states that you are an official member of the Muslim faith (you must provide government-issued identification to obtain this certificate). With this certificate you can obtain a visa from the Saudi Arabian consulates for entry into Saudi Arabia, as well as access to any mosque and its services, libraries, reunions, etc. Islam is a simple faith with simple rituals. The Qur'an repeats the same statements or types of statements hundreds of times. It was a simple religion designed to convince simple people in simpler times.

Once you have joined your local Muslim community, there are many things you can do to help the USA or UK governmental efforts. You may detect some possible radical cells that could take actions against your interests in the future and you may wish to report your suspicions to police agencies. You may wish to speak out against what you feel are offensive precepts in Islam that should be changed. The very presence of large numbers of new converts who are obviously non-Arabs would have an intimidating effect on the more radical activities of the mosques.

The US and UK governments, however, could take forceful action to both undermine radical Islamic concepts and also implement the democratic ideals that are its stated goals and principal reasons for invading the Arab countries. The language barrier prevents most people from effectively communicating with Muslims in their home country. However, the Internet is slowly expanding throughout the Arab world. A number of Arabic language chat rooms have existed for years. A government-funded project to pay Arabic speakers to join these chat rooms and continuously try to modernize Arab ideas through winning the hearts and minds of the millions of Arabs who chat in them would cost very little money and would have some impact on disseminating more progressive ideas among the Arab population. The setting up of well-publicized chat rooms, forums, websites aimed at Arabic women would be particularly effective. Arabic women are very receptive to Western ideals, as we have seen, and represent the best line of attack against Islamic fundamentalism. A converted housewife will have a tremendous impact on her family and her husband's belief systems. A housewife, newly awakened to the injustices that she is suffering as compared to a Western woman, will become as an ideological missile aimed directly at one of the structural defects of Islam in the modern world. Her impact in making her husband's life miserable will go a long way to convincing Arab men that more modern thought systems than Islam must prevail. Websites aimed at Arab youth, exposing the benefits of science, analyzing the latest consumer electronic gadgets, advancing democratic and self-fulfillment ideals, would be one of the most influential means to undermine radical Islamic fundamentalist thought among the Arab youth. Islam could be portrayed as a sort of superstition and set of antiquated customs to the Arab youth. Many of them are already inclined to think that way. A little push in ideology when one is young can have a lasting effect on one's thinking.

The guerrillas and terrorists use the Internet as their main source of propaganda. The West should do so as well. Also, many Arab governments and organizations fund Islamic madrasses (Qur'anic schools) throughout the planet. In these schools, young people receive the indoctrination that prepares the next generation to carry on the Islamic fundamentalist strategy. In these schools are prepared many suicide bombers, terrorists, martyrs, Islamic activists. The Internet effort on the part of Western governments could be seen as the Western thought schools that would help the Arab population in understanding what the Western precepts are and how they have developed.

More costly would be the setting up of an entertainment-focused Arabic satellite TV broadcast. Al Hurra, with its all-news programming, is a government propaganda effort that is falling largely on deaf ears. The acquisition of existing semi-commercial Arab satellite TV stations or the funding of a new one in a surreptitious manner, so as not to suffer the skepticism that would arise among the Arab audience, could, if properly funded, allow the US to acquire a large daily audience of up to 50,000,000 Arabs. Programming aimed at contravening the basic stable datum of Islamic thought could be beamed through this TV station, or several stations, especially directed at younger audiences.

The well-known Islamic ritual of traveling to Makkah to, among other customs, throw small stones at a building housing a meteorite, is in these days of modern astronomy another weak point of Islam. The Saudi government has prohibited the chemical or scientific analysis of this rock, rightfully fearing a great reduction in the credulity of the faithful should it become known that it is a meteorite. A religion based on meteorite worship, as the story goes that the devil threw this fiery rock at the land, can easily be held up to ridicule by modern science. Therefore, programming seeking to educate the Arab public about the solar system, space travel, meteorites, examining other known meteorites, etc., would serve to undermine the Muslims' faith in Islam. In time this great tradition could be made an object of ridicule, especially among younger Arabs.

Using a satellite transmission, the US could also beam access to the Internet to vast rural, underdeveloped areas of the Arab world, thus bypassing the very slow pace of installation of Internet access in the Arab countries. The cost of these satellite transmissions is only about $500,000 per year, as it can readily be purchased from the existing commercial Arab satellite ventures, NILESAT, ARAB SAT, or the HOT BIRD SATS, which also cover the area from Morocco to Pakistan. Private enterprises may find it profitable to launch such stations, as major Western companies are paying for advertising their products on the Arab satellite transmissions.

The advertising of appliances and products itself is a very useful tool to undermine Islam. As advertising penetrates the awareness of the masses and they find themselves unable to purchase the highly desirable products that they can see on their television screens, accompanying programs showing Arabic peoples practicing Western lifestyles and possessing these appliances could induct into the Arabs' minds the idea that by emulating the Western lifestyles they would gain access to the appliances. Properly designed and produced television shows could convince many Arabs that Western products are essential to their happiness and that these products would become easily acquirable if only they adopt Western ideals and imitate Western lifestyles. Women are particularly susceptible to product and appliance advertising, and the younger generation particularly apt to imitate Western lifestyles.

Of course, television broadcasts by the West to the Arabs are also very useful in undermining any particular government with which the USA disagrees. By broadcasting information about scandals or impropriety on the part of Islamic leaders, the people can be induced to rise up and overthrow their government. For example, a broadcast in Farsi to the Iranian people could prove decisive in tipping the political balance in favor of the West, and causing the liberal Iranians to obtain control of the government. A few million dollars invested in television and Internet broadcasting in Farsi now could well avoid a nuclear confrontation later on. In any event, it is better to bombard a people with ideas than to fire bullets and rockets at them, at least from the Christian viewpoint.

Education could also be transmitted through an Arabic television broadcast. Arabs are very interested in educating themselves and their level of basic skills could be raised through television viewing, thus preparing them to acquire more specialized skills useful in gainful employment in hopefully newly installed productive industries.

The US could also broadcast programs designed to inform the Arabs of the US nuclear capability and the consequences of an all-out nuclear bombardment. Properly designed programs that would bring vivid images and detailed information into millions of Arab and

Persian homes about the effects of a US-launched nuclear attack, would serve to bring awe and respect of the US military into the audience. Just the graphic depiction of the outcome of an extermination attack would serve as a great deterrent to Arab illusions of overcoming the US in armed conflict. Well-informed Muslim populations would be far more pliable and less aggressive as a result of seeing such programs. The Soviet Union withstood the mutual assured destruction stand-off for some decades, but they had weaponry of a similar caliber with which to hit back at the USA. The current actual military situation is so overwhelmingly tipped in favor of the USA that merely bringing this reality into the forefront of the Islamic world's attention could lessen the popular support for terrorist attacks upon and confrontation with the USA.

Also, programs glorifying life and showing the sadness, destruction and misery left behind by suicide bombers could de-sanctify to some extent the suicide bombers as role models. Programs that would effectively show the true nature of suicide bombs could cause the audience to look upon the perpetrators, not as martyrs in a holy cause, but rather as misguided fools who willfully diffuse their body parts into gelatinous material barely recognizable as human flesh. Also, programs that would question the notion of paradises and hells, that would expose the many concepts of God and gods that are now common throughout the world, and that would educate the Arab audience about the many radically different viewpoints that are common among people in other countries as well as the varying lifestyles in different regions, would be helpful in broadening the horizons of the Arab audience and in allowing them to accept other ways of life.

Also, broadcasting programs of an erotic nature, especially late at night, could lead to changes in the official moral codes of Arabic countries and its laws regarding sex. The increased information about sex and the awakening of sexual desire within the audience could lead to a breakdown of the extremely repressive moral code prevalent in Muslim countries and therefore open the door for women to increase their power over men and make it easier for women to achieve more equal treatment with men. The copulating paradise is particularly attractive to men when sex here on earth is prohibited. By increasing sexual tensions within Arabic countries, Arabic societies would come under internal pressures and social and political changes would more easily take place.

The remaining strong points of Islam, namely the existence of an invisible world loosely based on the Christian invisible world, presents a real ideological problem. The nominally Christian West is reluctant to attack its own concepts and traditions. Also, entering into arguments about invisible unprovable worlds is inconclusive and unproductive. Nothing can be demonstrated either way. Can anyone prove that Jinn don't exist, or that there aren't any leprechauns in Ireland?

Further, the edict of Muhammad to his followers to kill anyone who attempts to dissuade them from the existence of this invisible world, precludes a Muslim from engaging in such an argument, and at the very least, to initiate such an argument is highly offensive to most Muslims. As Salman Rushdie demonstrated by having to live in hiding for fifteen years after writing a book making unpalatable allegations about Muhammad, and as Theo Van Gogh, the Dutch movie producer who was recently assassinated in Holland by a true believer for having produced a film that did not show Islam in the light that Muslims would like, or as the Muhammad newspaper cartoon riots demonstrate, the truth is one never knows when a Muslim is going to go off and attempt to kill someone who doesn't agree with Muhammad's vision, or is simply commuting on a train or bus. Muslim fundamentalists are likely to strike out for myriad reasons: to eliminate modernizing influences in their population centers; to evict non-Muslim troops from their land; to increase the influence of Muhammad's thought system; to right some perceived wrong; to impose their code of conduct on others; to force non-believers to convert to Islam; and certainly to prevent blaspheming.

To debunk a set of concepts in the mind of a human will lead to a search for a new set of concepts to replace them. The basic foundations of Western thought – 1) that the individual knows he is real (I think, therefore I am) and can achieve personal satisfaction and happiness right here on earth; 2) that science has allowed mankind to produce myriad products undreamed of 200 years ago and in the future may provide for all of mankind's needs and wants; 3) that the individual is happier when allowed the greatest possible measure of freedom and self-expression; and, 4) that the weak, the disadvantaged, the poor, the sick should enjoy some measure of protection and support from the state – are a set of concepts that are very new to mankind, only existing as a viable conjoined system of thought for about 150 years. The future of this set of concepts is, at best, uncertain. Changing conditions on the planet could, at any time, prove the fallacy of some of these basic premises and undermine Western reality. Islam's set of precepts have functioned well for 1,350 years.

Printed in the United Kingdom
by Lightning Source UK Ltd.
120112UK00001B/14